JILL ALWAYS BEGINS HER STORY OF THE ACCIDENT THIS WAY . . .

"It was a beautiful morning and the snow was like velvet . . ." And when asked how she feels now about skiing, she answers after a silent moment, "When I'm alone with myself and its absolutely quiet, I can feel what it's like, skiing. I can still remember the runs—every slalom course, every downhill—and in my mind I can still feel where I want to prejump and where I'll have to check. I know I could still ski . . . if I could ski."

THESE ARE THE WORDS OF A CHAMPION REMEMBERING A TIME OF GLORY.

But, Jill Kinmont has become a new kind of champion since that tragic accident, and in many ways, her achievements are more exhilarating than her skiing victories.

She has climbed

THE OTHER SIDE OF THE MOUNTAIN

ALSO BY
E. G. VALENS

The Other Side of the Mountain: Part 2

PUBLISHED BY
WARNER BOOKS

THE
OTHER SIDE
OF THE
MOUNTAIN

(Originally: *A Long Way Up*)

E. G. Valens

WARNER BOOKS

A Warner Communications Company

Library of Congress Catalog Card Number: 65-20443

ISBN 0-446-82935-8

This Warner Books Edition is published by
arrangement with Harper & Row, Publishers, Inc.

Warner Books, Inc., 75 Rockefeller Plaza, New York, N.Y. 10019

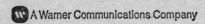 A Warner Communications Company

Printed in the United States of America

Not associated with Warner Press, Inc. of Anderson, Indiana

First Printing: April, 1975

Reissued: December, 1977

45   44   43   42

Author's Note

Public concern about Jill Kinmont's nearly fatal ski accident began at the moment it occurred, high on the shoulder of Rustler Mountain where more than a hundred and fifty spectators had gathered at the most dangerous drop-off on the racecourse. It was the last weekend in January, 1955, and Jill was competing in the annual Snow Cup giant slalom in the mountains east of Salt Lake City. Sunday morning she was the most glamorous young skier in America, as well as the fastest and the most publicized —at eighteen, a leading candidate for the U.S. Olympic team. Sunday afternoon she was a quadriplegic with a broken neck, paralyzed from the shoulders down.

Jill's early months in Salt Lake and Los Angeles hospitals were followed in the nation's press, but for almost a decade she was pretty much forgotten. In 1964, *Life* magazine sent reporter Janet Mason and photographer Burk Uzzle to Seattle to find out what had happened to this girl whose life had been focused entirely on the world of competitive skiing. An intensive, three-week interview led to a 14-page article in *Life*, which was later reprinted in the U.S. Information Service's foreign-language magazine, *America*.

Public response to the article was extensive and it included a suggestion by Harper & Row that Jill's life to date be chronicled in full detail. Miss Mason asked if I would be willing to write such a book. She contributed her own research and interview material, with *Life*'s permission and blessing. She and I then spent another three weeks with Jill and her family, questioning and probing without let-up for ten or twelve hours a day. We had at first planned to work as co-authors, but she had to return to *Life*, and the task of researching and writing was proving to be far more extensive than we had anticipated. Miss Mason graciously withdrew as co-author but continued to contribute criticism and suggestions as the material—and eventually the manuscript—grew in bulk.

Meanwhile, Burk Uzzle was so impressed by Jill's spirit and humor and leathery fortitude that he returned to Seattle on his own time to shoot more photographs for this book. He then put together, with Miss Mason's help, the 16-page photographic essay included here. All but the first eight photographs are his own.

The wealth of detail in the book and whatever subtleties of insight may have survived the translation into print are the direct result of the perceptiveness of Jill's family and friends and teachers. The most revealing parts of the story could not have been unearthed without the thoughtful frankness and the continual indulgence of her parents and brothers, her friend and coach Dave McCoy, her close school friends Audra Jo Baumgarth and Linda Meyers Tikalsky, her physical therapist Lee Baumgarth, and former teammates and teachers like Kenny Lloyd and Aim Morhardt in Bishop, California. In addition I am particularly grateful to Winifred Valens, who helped bring shape to the voluminous material at every stage; to Janet Mason, who got the book off the ground in the beginning; and to editor Genevieve Young, who in the end brought it down to earth again.

The most outstanding feature of this entire "flight" has been the nature and quality of information supplied by Jill Kinmont herself. She has undergone some 300 hours of relentless interviewing and has in addition supplied detailed written answers to many thousands of specific questions, displaying a phenomenal memory and responding always with grace, humor and uncompromising honesty.

1

STARS WERE STILL BRIGHT SATURDAY MORNING WHEN Jill Kinmont left the ranch kitchen and started down the lane with a knapsack, four ski poles and a tightly rolled sleeping bag clasped in her arms. Her brother followed a dozen steps behind, carrying a pair of skis on each shoulder. The world was dark and perfectly still; it was early November, 1951, colder than usual, with promise of a good winter.

When the two young skiers reached the county road at the lower end of the lane they stacked their things against the wooden arch that marked the ranch entrance and then stomped around and beat their mitts together to keep warm. Above and behind them in the west, the scatter of stars was cut off by a ragged silhouette of High Sierra peaks.

A finger of light appeared in the east on Red Hill Road and thrust toward them uncertainly, wavering and dipping. The headlights approached and finally swung to catch Jill and Bob beside the arch. Bob was fourteen, short and stocky and rugged with close-cropped blond hair, a ruddy face and a shovel-shaped jaw. His sister was a year older, two inches taller, and slender. She held her head forward as if she were trying to keep herself down to her brother's height.

The headlights belonged to an old Ford sedan which squeaked to a stop as Bob stepped up to put his skis in the ski rack. In the car were Marc Zumstein, a ski patrolman, his wife, Ethel, and Jill's friend, Audra Jo Nicholson, whom the Zumsteins had picked up a few minutes earlier. Audra Jo said, "Jill, hi. Are you staying over tonight at the dam?"

9

"Yeah, Josie. Why don't you come along?"

"I'd like to, only . . ."

Jill finished the sentence along with her friend, word for word. ". . . only I have a date." They both laughed.

The highway climbed 3,000 feet in the first ten miles. Soon the desert shone white in the headlights and the road was framed between sideburns of snow. After an hour's drive, the Zumsteins' car turned off the highway and drove uphill to the end of the plowed road. The lights swept across an old six-wheeled army truck with a dozen skiers standing in the back and wraiths of steam rising from the exhaust.

The newcomers parked, piled out of the car, lifted their skis one by one from the ski rack and joined the others on the truck. It soon moved out, groaning uphill through a three-foot deep snow canyon that was exactly as wide as the truck bed. Jill and Bob were standing in the corner behind the driver's window. Jill was warm in back because of the people standing behind her and very cold in front because of the blustery wind that swept down through the trees and blew showers of ground snow into her face and down her neck.

An army-surplus weasel trailing two long ropes was waiting at the end of the truck's constricted roadway.

The skiers seemed to be in no great hurry to put on their skis, but when the driver gunned his motor they rushed to snap shut their bindings and grab for one of the ropes lying in the snow. The weasel started with a jerk and soon settled down to an easy pace on its wide caterpillar tracks pulling eighteen skiers behind it.

It was full daylight by the time the weasel reached the base of Mammoth Mountain, but the wind was up and the sky was a level gray. The mountain lay like a beast curled in sleep beneath a fine white sheet. Scattered pines and broad wedges of forest ran uphill from the flat where the weasel had stopped, but the crest was far above timberline, a broad backbone rising from steep flanks of unbroken white. The summit, just above 11,000 feet, was out of sight behind a great snow cornice that stood against the fast-moving sky.

10

Two long ski tows, one above the other, reached a quarter of the way up the mountain. Drifting snow had buried part of the #1 tow—the lower of the two—and someone was halfway up the towline shoveling it out. Bob skied over to help while Jill and Audra Jo headed for Mammoth's one building, a small cabin which looked like a trapper's shack. It was known as the Snake Pit because the snow level was often above the eaves in January, and skiers then had to tunnel down to reach the door.

The girls went inside to tighten their boots and find a place to leave the knapsack that held Jill's pajamas and toothbrush as well as lunches, extra gloves, sun lotion, goggles, and her knitting. A pot-bellied stove hissed in one corner. The floor was still brittle with ice along one side.

Audra Jo and Jill were juniors at the Bishop Union High School and they were both on the ski team. They spent much of their time together and strangers often assumed they were sisters since they were both pretty and rosy-cheeked with long blonde hair. Jill's hair was darker and shorter, with peroxide streaks at the front. Audra Jo, who was six months older, had big brown eyes and a lean face and a figure that Jill envied.

Jill was several inches taller and she worried about being skinny. She was in the habit of walking with a stoop because she felt too tall and yet she always marched around after supper with her shoulders back and books on her head because she thought this might do something for her bust. In addition, she made a point of putting away an ice-cream sundae every day after school, for weight.

"Say, guess who's coming up skiing today," Audra Jo said as she sat down to relace her boots.

"Who?"

"Linda Meyers."

"No!"

"Yes. She asked me what skiing was all about and I said she was just going to have to try it."

Linda was thirteen and lived next door to Audra Jo. The girls were still in the Snake Pit when she arrived with a pair of borrowed aluminum skis clasped to her bosom. "Hi," she said in a small, forlorn voice. She was chunky and woolly and looked totally unskiworthy.

Jill said, "Hi, Linda Mae. Do the skis fit?"

"Golly, I don't know."

Audra Jo found a screwdriver in the first-aid cabinet and Jill adjusted the bindings of Linda's skis to fit her large, wobbly boots.

Jill glanced at Audra Jo and their eyes held. Jill said, "How do you suppose we ought to go about this? I mean really, Jose, what do you think we ought to *show* her?"

"Gosh, Jill, I don't know. Let's sort of go up and see."

It was snowing now, but the trio put on skis and skied across to the tow against a bitter wind. Linda moved vigorously and her long blonde curls bobbed at the back of her ski cap. She said, looking up with wide, sober eyes, "Do you think I'll ever be able to ski as good as you?"

"What makes you think we're so good?" Audra Jo asked her.

"Well, you're both on the *team!*"

"Yes, but not by very much."

Linda seemed to think this was very funny. She giggled and threw back her head and stepped on her right ski with her left ski and fell over.

Jill said, helping her up, "A.J. and I only started two years ago. At Deadman Pass. Gads, I'll never forget it." That first time, the tow rope had twisted into the hem of Audra Jo's jacket and ripped out the entire front panel, including the zipper.

When they reached the tow, Linda grabbed the rope and her skis more or less straightened themselves out for her. Halfway up, however, the skis began sticking. They grabbed the snow and jerked free and grabbed again and refused to move at all. Linda wouldn't let go of the rope at first, but after dragging in the snow for 20 feet she gave up. Her two instructors were at her side when she climbed to her feet and Jill said cheerfully, "Well, you made it. Halfway."

Audra Jo demonstrated a beautiful snowplow, moving straight down the slope with her ski tips almost touching

12

and her tails pushed wide apart. Linda assumed a similar position, made several little turning steps until she was facing downhill, and lunged forward. Nothing happened.

"That's crazy," Jill said. "Push with your poles a little."

Linda pushed but her skis refused to slide.

"Just *go,* Linda. Any old way."

Long clumps of snow three inches thick were clinging to the bottoms of Linda's aluminum skis and they glued her to the slope. With considerable effort she managed to *walk* downhill, straight down, very slowly, step by heavy step.

Audra Jo whispered to Jill as they waited for their protégée, "This is miserable. She'll never get on skis again as long as she lives." Linda spent the rest of the day as a spectator.

After lunch Jill and Audra Jo worked for an hour punching tickets in front of the ticket booth by the lower ski tow. The tows were free to anyone who was young and serious about skiing; the youngsters, for their part, shoveled snow and punched tickets and carried cans of gasoline up to the tow engines and kept the Snake Pit in shape.

Later the girls went up to practice on the Face, a moderately steep hill alongside the tows. They decided to re-create the old cartoon showing a pair of ski tracks which suddenly splits apart to encompass a big tree, so they skied east from the top of the #2 tow until they found a gentle slope with a lone tree below them in the untracked powder. They started down side by side, each with one ski held up in the air. They parted just above the tree and managed to turn back toward one another again just below it. Their timing was perfect. They collided squarely on the lower side and went sprawling in the fresh and frigid snow.

Jill and Audra Jo were cold and tired by four o'clock and they went back with the first weasel. They soon passed another weasel, which had broken down in the middle of the trail. One of its tracks was laid out flat in the snow and a man was kneeling beside it, his bare hands black with grease. Several skiers yodeled or shouted at him. "Hi,

13

Dave. Whatcha makin'?" "Don't you know it's quitting time?" "Pa, you're going to freeze your fingers!" The man said nothing but he grinned and waved a wrench in the air before bending to his task again. He was Dave McCoy, who had discovered Mammoth Mountain and built the tows and rebuilt the weasels. His consuming passion was skiing, and he taught the local kids whatever they needed to know. Everyone called him "Pa," although he was only thirty-five. His skiing and teaching and building at Mammoth were limited to weekends and evenings, for he worked as a hydrographer for the city of Los Angeles during the week. He lived twenty miles away in a city-owned house at Crowley Lake Dam.

It was almost dark when the first truckload of skiers arrived at the parking area. Jill retrieved her sleeping bag from the Zumsteins' car, waved good-by to Bob and Audra Jo, and hurried to join Toni Milici, Mammoth's ski instructor, who was driving to the dam with his wife, Norma, and Kenny Lloyd, a classmate and teammate of Jill's.

Spending an occasional Saturday night at Crowley Lake Dam with the McCoy's was a privilege enjoyed by a select few of Bishop's promising young skiers, and Jill had been included since early the previous spring.

The McCoys lived in a small frame house on a plot which had been bulldozed in the steep hill above the dam. Parked in front were a jeep, the McCoys' 1941 Chevrolet and two older cars graced with thick hats of snow. Inside the fenced-in yard were treads and bogey wheels from a weasel, seven automobile tire rims, a tricycle, a wagon, a sled, two small bows and a cache of arrows.

Jill carried her own and Kenny's sleeping bags into the house while he took the skis off the car. She went up the back steps and through the kitchen to the living room, where she was immediately surrounded by children, cats and a dog. She wondered again how this little two-bedroom house could be big enough for Dave and Roma McCoy, their three young sons and two-year-old daughter,

14

and the animals . . . plus two to six teen-agers on a Saturday night.

Kenny exploded into the room with a shout and punched the sleeping bags out of Jill's arms. "Whadaya say, Ace?"

"Kenny! *Honestly* . . ."

"Hi, Punkin!" he yelled at the oldest boy, Gary, who was about nine. "Where's Ma?"

Roma answered from a bedroom. "Kenny? Is Jill there? Throw your things in a corner and make yourselves comfortable." The Milicis came in and the McCoy boys mobbed Kenny and the cats made unfriendly noises at each other behind the couch. Jill watched, enjoying the show but taking no part in it. Kenny started a pillow fight with Gary and it soon became a free-for-all that ended only when a lamp went down.

Dave arrived, bringing two more young skiers with knapsacks and sleeping bags. He was dressed in his usual black ski pants and black parka tucked in at the waist. He was blond, soft-spoken, intent and, at the moment, grimy. His sleeves were pushed up to the elbows and his forearms were smeared with grease. He pulled off his boots and massaged his feet. Then, since there was a lineup at the bathroom door, he washed at the kitchen sink.

"I don't want any soap in the string beans," Roma said, appearing in the doorway. "Hello, everybody, Jill, how was the mountain?" Roma was six months pregnant and resigned to the prospect of being a fair-weather skier. She was a slender woman, tanned and handsome, with long blonde hair that hung halfway down her back and was tied with a ribbon.

"Stormy," Jill said.

Dinner was roast beef and green vegetables with tapioca pudding and fresh-baked chocolate cake for dessert. Afterwards, while the women were in the kitchen, Dave wrestled with his three sons. He was soon on his back on the floor, cuffing them, grabbing them, holding them off, tickling them until they wriggled and screamed. "What's so funny?" he said. They ganged up on him and tickled him and he cried out, "Hey, no fair, three against one!" But when he crawled to his feet and turned to talk with Toni about his plans for a new warming hut at Mammoth, the kids let him go without protest.

Norma Milici and Roma brought their knitting to the living-room couch. Both were finishing sweaters for the ski team, black-and-white snowflake designs to replace the old sweaters that boasted BISHOP HI in big block letters. Jill joined them with a similar sweater of her own, but she was still on the back panel, just beginning to worry about decreasing for the armholes.

Dave stood at the rear end of the long kitchen table, leaning on it with both hands, studying some papers he had spread out on the formica top. He was physically impressive in the way a statue is impressive: strong, silent, serious, square-jawed, square-shouldered. He appeared to be a big man although he was probably not much over five-nine.

Dave and Toni came into the living room and there was some talk about waxing and a heated argument about racing styles to which Jill listened intently but silently. Dave stretched his hands in front of him, palms down, demonstrating the many different ways of turning a pair of skis. Then the Milicis left for Bishop and Roma sent her children to bed. Within half an hour the house was dark and quiet.

Jill lay in her sleeping bag on the living-room floor, warm and pleasantly aching from the day's workout. She wished she felt less self-conscious around Dave McCoy. She never knew quite what to say and he was too preoccupied to give her a clue. She did know that he never wasted words and never said anything he did not mean. A nod of understanding from Dave meant more than praise from most people. Also he was a man with a mountain of his own and he frightened her at times as a prince might frighten a page. He was a magnificent skier and a fine teacher and he was one of those rare human beings who really know what they are talking about all the time. He was the person Jill most wanted to know, and she was certain that he would find her totally uninteresting.

16

She had nothing to offer. No particular talent. No bright ideas, even.

Nevertheless, she had been accepted here at the dam as one of Dave's special group of serious young skiers. She felt honored. But she was anxious, for she did not ski as well as the others and she still was not thoroughly at ease with their language. By the time she had come to feel comfortable with words like *stem* and *christy* and *snowplow*, she had discovered that this was not the way Dave and his group talked. They called it a *wedge* rather than a snowplow. They talked of skis *working together* and of *hanging onto the hill* or *going into the air*.

Sunday was a fine day with high clouds and three inches of new snow on the mountain. Jill skied across the slope from the top of the upper tow to escape the racket of the engine and she stood for a long while looking west across a white wilderness at the sun-flecked Sierra peaks. Above was the pale winter blue of a sky swept with careless, hurrying clouds. She felt the bite of a light wind and was conscious of the mountain at her back, cold and beautiful and very big. She was oddly charmed by the thought that she was smaller on the mountain than a ladybug on a tree or a high bird against the sky.

She turned to find her brother above and behind her, looking out at the clouds. They stared at each other, almost smiling, and then skied together down into the sparse woods east of the Face, where they ran softly among big trees that stood roofed with snow like narrow pagodas. Jill was the more graceful skier but at times she seemed unsure. Bob was as solid on his skis as a steamroller and he always seemed to know exactly what he was doing.

Jill practiced hard the rest of the day, either alone or with Bob or Audra Jo. She saw Dave half a dozen times, working or skiing, and she wished she had the nerve to ask him why her turns weren't coming around the way they should. But he was always building or fixing things or he was on his way somewhere. There was always something on his mind. People usually did not speak to Dave McCoy unless they really had something to say.

17

But when Jill happened to find herself several places ahead of him on the lower tow, she waited for him at the top and asked her question.

"Don't worry about it," he said. "The main thing is, enjoy it. Relax. You tighten up too much. Do it like . . . well, here!" He made three quick, flowing turns and stopped to watch her follow his tracks. This time everything worked for her and he said, "Now, doesn't that feel better?" Then he took off, leaving a swirl of fine powder in the air.

Jil practiced all afternoon and when she passed Dave on her way to the weasel he said, "You really worked today, didn't you?"

She responded with no more than a brief smile, but when she reached home with Bob an hour and a half later she shouted from the kitchen door, "Hey, Mom, what do you *think?*" She flung her cap and gloves onto the table and slid the knapsack off her shoulders. "Pa noticed how hard I worked today. He even *mentioned* it." Bob greeted his mother from the doorway and went out to his room.

June Kinmont turned from the stove, took off her apron, sat on a chair in front of her bright-eyed daughter, and folded her hands in her lap. "Tell me all about it," she said.

Jill sat on the floor and unlaced her boots. "I was having trouble and Pa did a couple of neat turns for me and I sort of got the feeling and then I was in great shape." She grimaced as one boot came off and thudded onto the linoleum. "Oh, Mom, you should have seen him ski! *Wham wham wham.*" She made three jerky twists with her shoulders. "I get discouraged enough watching Kenny, but when *Pa* skis, wow! Is he ever powerful!"

"Did you ski on down behind him?"

"Yeah, about a hundred feet behind. Gads!"

June Kinmont laughed quietly. She was a slight woman with fine features and blue-gray eyes. She went back to her stove and Jill followed her.

Jill was describing Saturday's fiasco with Linda when her father and her younger brother, Jerry, arrived. Bill

18

Kinmont was hatless and gloveless. He put his flashlight on a shelf beside the door and set his burning cigarette on the windowsill for long enough to peel off one of his heavy Pendleton shirts. November was what he called two-shirt weather. "Hi, honey girl," he said. "How's old Mammoth? Is the snow belly-deep yet?"

Jerry said, "Hey, Jill, you know what? We just watered the ice!" Jerry was nine and was known as Little Beaver because of his front teeth and his general eagerness for just about anything.

"You what?"

"So we can skate tomorrow. Come lookit."

"It's a kind of surprise," Bill said, hooking his thumbs behind his big silver Rocking K belt buckle. He had a long, weathered face and an Abe Lincoln frame, both of which made him look as if he had lived on a ranch for a lot longer than three and a half years. "I got some fire hose and we rigged up a little pipeline and flooded the ice on the upper pond."

Jill clapped her hands and Jerry said, "C'mon, Jill, I'll show you. It's gonna be like glass tomorrow." Jill pulled on her jacket and Jerry led the way with a flashlight. "And we made a scrape thing, too," he added. "In case it snows."

The pond was only a hundred yards away, and beyond it was a wide view of the valley floor and the White Mountains on the far side. Bishop was out in the middle of the valley, five miles away, but it was neatly blocked from view by the rocky little mound of Red Hill half a mile east. Scattered points of light were visible north and south of town.

Jerry played his flashlight on a flock of sheep standing just below the pond in the north pasture; then he turned it on a homemade ice scraper that lay on the cement slab where the diving board had been bolted down during the summer.

"That's pretty neat," Jill said, rubbing her knuckles together and starting back toward the friendly lights of the kitchen. "But I'm in my stocking feet and my toes are freezing, Jer. And I'm starved. How about you?"

"Yeah, me too," he said.

To the right of the kitchen-dining room Jill could make out the roof lines of several guest cabins. On the far side and up in back was the "house," a long building containing three family bedrooms and a bath. In the darkness beyond was nothing but a barren, sloping piedmont called Buttermilk Country which rose toward the Sierra peaks above.

The Kinmonts ate dinner alone in their large dining room, which was a welcome experience after seven months of running the place as a public hostelry. The Rocking K Guest Ranch had been booked solid most weekdays and every weekend from the day the trout started jumping until the end of the deer season. Now at last the telephone was reasonably quiet, the cabins were locked up and the linen stored, and the wrangler had gone south for the winter with his wife, who was the cook, and his string of 25 horses. Jill thought of the first winter three years before when the ranch had been little more than a rundown oasis of willows and cottonwoods on 80 acres of sagebrush. The dining room had been roofed and made weather-tight and a bulldozer had finished gouging out the upper pond, but the only other man-made objects were piles of gray pumice bricks and stacks of lumber covered with tarpaulins. The family had lived in a small cottage down the lane where the three children shared a single bedroom. Since that time Bill had planted seven acres in alfalfa and had added a second pond, seven deluxe cabins, the "house," a commissary, a tackroom, three corrals and a roping arena.

On Monday Jill came home after school with two carloads of friends. They had all come to skate on the pond, although Jerry appeared with his Flexible Flyer and talked several of them into sledding in the south pasture. There was no snow, but Bill Kinmont had intentionally allowed the irrigation ditches to overflow. Ice was now gleaming in silver humps and flows and rivulets among the frosted hummocks of grass and the islands of crispy earth. It was a fast, rough trip and potential riders were not easy to persuade. At dusk some of the boys built a

20

small fire beside the pond and the skaters skated by its wavering light until six, when they all went home.

On Tuesday afternoon Jill and Audra Jo went riding in the bare hills behind the ranch shortly before dusk. Both girls had their own horses and both were careful to ride like cowboys and not like dudes—never touching the back of the saddle when mounting, keeping their hands off the saddle entirely while riding. They were dedicated rodeo fans and Jill had even talked about becoming a calf roper . . . until her mother informed her pointedly that the family had two boys already and didn't need another.

Due west of the ranch, biting high into the fading blue sky, was the side-heavy pyramid of Mt. Tom, back-lit by the late sun and etched with a silver-yellow light. To the left of Tom the sawtooth ridge of Basin Mountain reached up like a fat hand, holding in its palm a finely carved cirque laden with snow. The girls stopped finally and turned their horses. Below them was the ranch, dark on a dark plain, for the sun was gone from the spare brush and sage spotted across the ancient lava flows on the valley floor. They were higher than Red Hill and could see the town, flat and gray, patched with shadowy clumps and lines of willows and already pricked with early lights along Main Street.

On both sides of the valley solid rock rose to 14,000 feet—to the sharp Sierra summits behind them and to the worn and treeless heights of the White Mountains in the distance beyond the lights of town. The valley had been Piute country before the white man moved in with his stake and barbed-wire fences; it then became a valley of farms and orchards until the 1920's when the city of Los Angeles bought up everything for the water rights, letting the grain-fields revert to sage and bitterbrush while hundreds of thousands of fruit trees turned into stubby gray ghosts.

Jill and Audra Jo headed down the rocky trail, and by the time they reached the ranch the shy sparks of a dozen stars were visible.

21

2

MAMMOTH ALREADY HAD ENOUGH SNOW FOR THE season, but more kept coming. The day after Thanksgiving the road in to Mammoth became totally impassable and even the three weasels were useless. A week later a new storm dumped close to a foot of snow per hour for six hours. The snowpack settled to a depth of 16 feet on the level and Mammoth Mountain was abandoned for the winter.

So skiing again focused on McGee Mountain, where everyone used to ski before Mammoth. McGee was a steep, treeless slant of rock and earth and talus directly west of Crowley Lake. At the bottom was the McGee warming hut, a large, handsome cabin that had lately been used only a few weeks each year. On the hillside a hundred yards from the cabin was an outhouse, the most conspicuous feature of the landscape to be seen from any and every point along the two-mile stretch of highway that ran between the lake and the mountain.

McGee's first tow had been an $85 affair that Dave McCoy had run off the rear wheel of a Model A Ford back in 1939. Since the tow could be dismantled and dragged around on a toboggan, Dave and Roma and a few friends moved it whenever they found a better slope or better snow somewhere else. At first anyone was welcome to use the tow, but Dave had no money and he began charging 25 cents a day to cover gas and repairs. Soon he was building bigger and better tows, and he had two permanent ropes operating at McGee when the Forest Service finally permitted him to set up at Mammoth. The skiing terrain at Mammoth was far more extensive and varied and the season there was three months longer.

22

But now McGee had been half-dead for several years and Dave and Toni and two other Mammoth pioneers had to refurbish it. Fortunately, the two old tow engines had been left on the hill, each in its own tiny shack, and both were in fair condition. Kenny and Bob dragged rope and shoveled snow while another pair of young skiers strung and spliced the rope and got the engines running. By the middle of December two battered but sturdy rope tows were ready to go.

Slalom practice began at once and Jill was impatient to get to work. She loved the short, quick, precise turns which overlapped so neatly—in theory, at least—that the end of one was always the beginning of another. At every moment you had to know just what you were doing and just what you were going to have to do next.

Nine regulars from Bishop appeared for practice along with four from Lee Vining, a tiny town that straddled the main highway 25 miles north of Mammoth. They cut dozens of young willows along the banks of the Owens River near Bishop, stripped them, hacked them into seven-foot lengths and carted them to McGee in Dave's car. They hauled the willows up past the warning hut and then onto the hill by way of one or both tows, clutching the awkward bundles in one arm and spilling single poles down the slope. When they had planted about a hundred poles upright in the snow in groups of eight or ten, Dave began to set a course. He stood quietly at the top, leaning forward against his ski poles, sighting down the slope and apparently etching an imaginary line into the snow. He had no gloves and the sleeves of his black parka were pushed up to the elbows. He began sidestepping and side-slipping slowly down the hill, working his way from one cluster of stripped willow stalks to another, transplanting the poles as he went. Every few steps he would jab one or two into the snow.

Jill watched the growing line of willow sticks as it progressed down the slope. It was irregular, running straight down, veering suddenly, zigzagging, running downhill like a fence again. Technically, each pole was a *flag* and should have had a square foot of red or blue or yellow cloth at the top. A pair of poles set about 10 feet apart makes a *gate,* and a slalom course is nothing more than a long series of gates through which each skier, racing alone against time, must pass. Dave set a short course, about 35 gates. Most of the gates were *open,* which meant you approached the gate headed squarely between the two poles; the rest were *closed.* A closed gate is approached end on, with one pole standing behind the other, and may be entered from either side.

The first skier down the course was Kenny Lloyd. He was nimble and fast, jumping from side to side like a jackrabbit, yelling whenever he lost his balance, which was often. He seemed to be dodging willows rather than skiing. He knocked down two poles, fell hard and bounced onto his feet again.

The course contained two difficult flushes, which are lines of closed gates running straight downhill and set close together like fence posts. Jill fell in the first flush on her first attempt and took out five poles. She stood up and slapped the snow from her pants and helped replace the poles. She said nothing but she sidestepped angrily back to the top of the flush. Twice she went through the flags she'd missed and climbed back. Then she ran the whole course fast, fighting it all the way. Bob Kinmont had gone down in the meantime and he seemed to be having no trouble at all. He was wearing a hacked-up pair of skis he had bought secondhand from Kenny for $5 and painted bright pink. Audra Jo was in good form also, skiing slowly but very much in control.

Everyone worked long and hard, but after three o'clock they skied for fun. They came winging down from the upper tow, sometimes in a single, whipping line behind Dave, sometimes cutting in and out at random, always with a sporadic accompaniment of yips and cries and yodels. On the last trip before shutting down the tow engines, Dave said at the top, "You kids are sure full of the devil. Anybody want to go for a walk?" He glanced up at the unbroken slope above them which rose more and more steeply until it ended beneath a vertical wall of rock. The young skiers shared a few glances, but they started climbing with considerable spirit. They were beginning to think of themselves now as Mammoth skiers even though they were practicing at McGee and wearing BISHOP HI or LEE VINING sweaters. They had shoulder patches, black and gold, a small figure skiing down one side of a large M.

When they stopped climbing after twenty minutes, the point where the snow met the cliff above seemed as far away as before. Out below them lay the wide white valley and the spidery white arms of Crowley Lake.

Dave took off down the mountain without warning and a moment later the others plunged after him like a wolf-pack, exploding slow-motion bursts of snow at each turn. Jill was behind Kenny but she had her eyes on Dave, following him, working fiercely to capture something of his control and grace. She very much wanted Dave to approve of her and she knew that if she really worked he would say, "Well, you really worked today."

A new storm hit McGee and Crowley Lake so heavily that the road into the dam was lost under five to ten feet of snow and the main highway was blocked for 20 miles. Dave had been caught in Bishop and as soon as the highway was plowed he drove to the dam road and skied in the three and a half miles to his house. Roma's baby was due in a week or two and he was worried.

Dave packed his two-year-old daughter, Penny, in a knapsack and skied back out to the highway with her on his back, followed by Roma and the three boys, each on his own skis. He drove them all to Bishop where, at Bill Kinmont's invitation, they moved into a pair of cabins at the ranch. They stayed until after the baby was born. She was named Kandi Kay, the Kay being in honor of the Rocking K.

The season's first big race weekend was the California-Nevada Junior Championships in mid-January at Big Bear in the San Bernardino Mountains. There would be the usual downhill race on Saturday and slalom on Sunday, with awards given also for the best combined downhill-and-slalom scores. The competition would be rough compared with that offered by Bishop's traditional interscholastic

25

rivals, for it was one of four junior races sanctioned by the Far West Ski Association. The best performers in these four races would be sent east to represent the Far West at the National Ski Association's Junior Championships later in the spring. Jill had been at several FWSA races the year before but she had not done very well.

The Bishop skiers went south in two cars, five boys riding with Dave McCoy and three girls with the Kinmonts, whose Chevrolet station wagon was identified on each side by a large K set on a rocker. They left Friday after school and arrived long after dark.

On Saturday morning they found Big Bear to be a busy and sophisticated resort compared with Mammoth or McGee Mountain. Indoor johns and a snack bar and a chairlift and dozens of handsome women in elegant ski clothes. Jill felt out of place at first, but soon she began to recognize young skiers she had known at last spring's races. A Pasadena girl she had met in Yosemite called out as she was leaving the parking area with her skis on her shoulder. "Jill! Where'd you get that great sweater?"

"Hi, Barni. I made it. Can you believe it?"

Barni Davenport was a petite sixteen-year-old with vivid green eyes framed by spectacularly long eyelashes. She put her fingers on Jill's white-and-black sweater and traced one of the snowflake designs. "You're not kidding, are you?"

Jill laughed. "I just finished it in the car on the way down here." She felt a friendly pat on the head and turned to find Barni's father beaming at her.

"Jill," he said, "it's just not fair that the two cutest tricks in California are the same two who are going to walk off with all the medals today."

Barni said, "Oh, *Father . . .*"

"Well, I've got to go," Jill said. "My brother's waiting for me. See you later."

The best thing about Big Bear was the chairlift. Neither Jill nor Bob had ever been on a lift and they talked about it all the way up the mountain.

From the top they surveyed the downhill course and Bob said soberly, "It's kind of spooky."

26

Neither of them managed anything spectacular in the downhill competition, but in slalom on Sunday Jill placed second. The winner was Barni Davenport.

The boys' race followed the girls', and Jill studied each racer as he fought his way through the 12 gates that were clearly visible to her. She moved her shoulders as she watched, straining when a racer struggled to hang onto a turn and flinching whenever someone fell. The craziest skier on the hill was Kenny Lloyd, who came batting down the course with his arms and poles flying and one ski or the other off the snow half the time. He was never in serious trouble, however, and he placed second among the older, or Class 1, juniors.

Bob Kinmont was in Class 2 because he was not yet fifteen, and he was among the last of the sixty competitors to start. The course by this time was deeply rutted and icy and many of the boys were falling. But the moment Bob came into view Jill whispered aloud, "My gosh, I think he's going to win!" He wasn't fighting the ruts. He was thrusting out of each turn into the next, in the ruts and across the ruts with no trouble at all, smooth and steady and fast. He placed first in his class and his time was even better than Kenny Lloyd's. Jill met him below the finish gate, beaming. She said, "Okay, wise guy, how'd you do it?" He only shrugged, but after a moment a wide grin broke through and he tapped her on the leg with his ski pole.

At the California Championships in Yosemite the following weekend—this was also an FWSA race—Audra Jo finished second and Jill third in both downhill and slalom. The Bishop skiers brought home medals every week for a month, and on February 16, which was Jill's sixteenth birthday, Jill and Bob received identical letters from Los Angeles.

You have been chosen to compete in the National Junior Downhill-Slalom Championships to be held at Winter Park, Colorado, March 1 & 2, 1952, to represent the Far West Ski Association.

Jill shrieked and headed for the telephone. Audra Jo had been invited, too. So had Kenny. And neither of them was any more excited than Dave McCoy. National competition was a very big deal and an entirely new experience for everybody. The FWSA, which seemed so important in California, was only one of the National Ski Association's seven divisions, and it was pretty much a country cousin. The big skiers were all from Colorado or the East or Sun Valley.

Jill wondered what the chances were of coming away with anything better than a booby prize. Although competition was limited to juniors, which means skiers who were under eighteen at the beginning of the season, the stakes were high; the winners would be invited to compete in the big senior races which determine the selection of the Olympic team or the FIS team. The FIS squad represents the United States every four years, between Olympics, at races sanctioned by the Fédération International de Ski.

Jill was still daydreaming when the radio brought the news from Oslo that nineteen-year-old Andrea Mead Lawrence of Rutland, Vermont, had just become the first American skier ever to win two Olympic gold medals. Jill was deeply impressed. She was even more impressed when she realized that Andy Mead had been fifteen years old when she was a member of the 1948 U.S. Olympic squad.

Jill felt that her own time was running short; she was already sixteen years and several hours old.

The Winter Park trip was going to last five or six days, including a day of practice at Aspen, and money was a real problem. The skiers' parents contributed what they could and Kenny's father offered the loan of his brand-new Packard sedan, but the rest would have to come from the local citizens.

Bishop was a town of motels, gas stations, coffee shops and sporting goods stores strung out along the twelve blocks of Main Street, otherwise known as U.S. 395. There were some sheep and beef cattle in the valley and

28

a number of mines—tungsten, zinc, borax, pumice, silver —but the main business of the town's 5,000 inhabitants was catering to tourists and sportsmen. Everyone was pretty well informed about everyone else's business, and the word soon got around that Bishop's young ski stars had to have $500. The Lions Club and the Kiwanis passed the hat at their luncheon meetings. Another group made a game of fining members for infringement of silly rules they drew up on the spur of the moment. The *Inyo Register*, which came out every Thursday, made a strong pitch for funds, and the Chamber of Commerce came across with a check for $100.

Jill began to gather clothing and equipment immediately. She wrote out a check list which she carried around in her hand or, when both hands were busy, in her teeth. Red sweater, green cable-stitch sweater, two white-and-black sweaters, three turtleneck t-shirts . . . to start with. She pushed her stuffed animals and ski trophies to one side of her bureau top to make room for socks, a washcloth and towel, hand lotion, cold cream, brush and comb, and toothpaste. On her twin beds, which were always pushed together, she piled pajamas, wool shirts and three parkas. Her biggest problem was coordinating what she planned to wear when she wasn't skiing; whatever she chose, she had to make certain she had scarves and hair ribbons and lipsticks that would match them. She cut her lipsticks down to pink, red and orange. She drove to town once to take two pairs of ski pants to the cleaners and again for a new supply of hair ribbons.

Jill changed her list three times during the week, and on Sunday afternoon, the day before the trip, she tried to pack everything into the biggest Kinmont suitcase that could be found. She was not successful, so she pulled everything out again. Her father came in and groaned. He said, "Somebody going somewhere?" She decided definitely to leave out one of the heavy sweaters. Or perhaps she could take the sweater if she left two of the t-shirts; the third t-shirt she could wash every night. In the end, her luggage consisted of the suitcase, an overnight case, a packsack with such miscellany as goggles and shoe polish, and her

29

ski boots, which she carried separately on a boot tree. She did not forget her history, English and Spanish textbooks. Actually she had never yet done her homework on a ski trip but she always took it along.

On Sunday evening she polished her boots in her parents' room where her mother was ironing Bob's shirts and Bob was trying on his new long underwear. Jill took over the ironing board to press wrinkles out of a sweater and Bob pranced around like a ballet dancer in his long johns with the back flap down. She said, "Oh, Bobby, it's going to be a ball!"

"Except for what?" he said. He had caught an overtone of uncertainty although he knew she had no qualms about going on her first long trip away from home.

"Nothing, Bobby. Just that I'm nervous about all that Eastern competition. Maybe we're all going to look pretty silly."

"Maybe," he said.

On Monday after school the racers took off in the Lloyds' new green Packard equipped with a walletful of money, some of it borrowed, and enough lunches and assorted apples and oranges to last most of the way to Aspen. Dave was driving. His passengers were Jill, Bob, Audra Jo, Kenny, and Dennis Osborn, a Lee Vining boy who had helped string the McGee Mountain ropes.

They talked about school and skiing and how much money Dave would win on the slot machines when they stopped in Nevada. They went through a large bag of chocolate bars—except for Audra Jo, who was afraid her face would break out. The car was crowded and there was an eruption of protests whenever Kenny demonstrated his undeniably friendly nature. Jill said, "Maul, maul, maul! Kenny, keep your hands to yourself!" and everybody laughed. They ate at an excellent Chinese restaurant in Ely and spent the night in Wendover, Utah. They reached Aspen Tuesday night, skied there the next day, and completed their journey Thursday morning.

At Winter Park, which consisted mainly of ski lodges bracketing the highway, they found a cheerful letter from June Kinmont. Contributions toward their expenses were still coming in. She had added a postscript: "Bobby, did you buy a toothbrush and get your hair cut?"

Jill and Audra Jo checked into their dormitory, where they found Barni Davenport and two other girls from southern California. Barni was busy curling her long eyelashes. The room was finished in light pine paneling and furnished with six double-decked bunks, three on each side. At the far end of the room were two showers.

The three boys from Mammoth dumped their gear in their own bunkroom and made a thorough reconnaissance of the immediate area, inside and out. Then they tied together a number of sheets, climbed out an upstairs window and clomped down the wall outside the girls' dormitory. Barni took the trouble to open the door and shout at them, "*You* are *po*sitively *juv*enile!" For an answer they dragged a garden hose into the hallway and threatened her with inundation.

That evening Barni came into the dormitory with a bottle of horse liniment that someone had assured her was the best thing in the world for sore muscles. She took a hot shower and immediately rubbed in the liniment. It stung in her open pores like iodine and she moaned and cried and began bouncing from bed to bed trying to rub or beat or scratch the stuff off her skin. A little girl from Salt Lake named Monya wanted to go to sleep at eight, sharp, and when the lights were still on and Barni was still moaning at 8:10, Monya unscrewed a light bulb and dropped it on the floor. The other girls ignored her, so she unscrewed a second bulb and dropped it on the floor. Soon there was broken glass all over the room and all the light bulbs were gone. Barni stopped moaning and helped the other girls fill Monya's bed with eggshells and salt.

On Friday morning when the Far West competitors walked to breakfast, it was pretty nice to hear people whisper to one another as they passed, "Psst . . . that's the California kids." There were twelve of them, although two were actually from Reno. The Mammoth boys were always horsing around, and when the group stood for a photograph, Kenny draped himself between two of the

31

girls, grinning. Jill said, "Oh, Kenny!" Barni whispered loudly, "And to think we have to be identified with *those* California boys."

They were all on the mountain early and it was a sobering experience. As Jill said after watching some of the Colorado skiers practicing. "Geez, Pa, we're nowheres *near* these kids!"

While Dave was training with the boys, Jill and Audra Jo worked on downhill. Audra Jo was fast and loose and unafraid and she really seemed to know what it was all about. When the two of them stopped to study a particularly tricky or challenging corner of the course, Jill usually shook her head and said, "What do we do here, Jose?" The situation was the reverse of slalom, where Jill was the leader.

Later, when the whole group was checking out the downhill run, Dave gestured with his ski pole and said, "If you want to learn something, keep your eye on that boy coming out of the meadow up there."

The figure close above them on the trail made three quick turns and went off a little rise, leaping neatly into the air and leaning for a new turn even before he sank again onto the snow. It was Bud Werner, a Colorado boy from Steamboat Springs, and Jill could tell how good he was after seeing him just once, playing around. She studied him every chance she had, trying to figure what he was doing and how he was doing it. Dave said he would probably be the best skier in the United States by the time he was eighteen.

The downhill race began at noon on Saturday with twenty-eight girls starting and almost twice as many boys. The better skiers ran first and Jill was seeded away down near the bottom of the list. She hated waiting around and kept wishing she was already in the starting gate. Then suddenly she wished she had more time because the starter called out, "Jenkins up, Woolsey on deck, Kinmont in the hole!"

As soon as the other two girls had taken off, Jill moved gingerly up to the pair of little flagged sticks beside the

32

man in a sheepskin coat who scarcely gave her a glance as he bent over his portable telephone. She had run the trail several times but never without stopping; now she looked down toward the steep row of trees where the previous racer had just disappeared and she felt an uncontrollable shivering in her stomach.

"Thirty seconds!"

She closed her eyes and prayed that she might have a good run.

"Ten!"

Her ankles ached.

"Five . . . four . . . three . . . two . . . one . . . *go!*"

It was better once she was skiing, although her eyes watered. She stemmed hard down through the trees, trying to hold herself back, and she let her skis run when she reached the meadow. She had lost time, so she ran fast now, clinging to the snow, hoping she would remember what was below the next drop-off. It was too steep and she checked too quickly. She was on the snow, sliding head first on her belly. She struck a stump with her chin, spun around and came to rest with a pain in her tongue that made her gasp. Her skis were still on, so she climbed to her feet and was soon back in the race. She had bitten into her tongue and the blood was salty in her mouth.

Jill finished 26th out of 28. Barni hadn't even finished. Valerie Mullard, who was also from Pasadena, had slipped and jammed a ski pole in her eye. Audra Jo seemed to be the only Far West girl to come through without serious trouble and neither she nor the boys had run a very spectacular race.

The slalom on Sunday was not much better. None of the Mammoth group had ever seen a regular slalom with gates so far apart, which meant that they always picked up too much speed and then had a very rough time when they went slamming into the next gate. Jill's only thought was: There's just one thing I've got to do and that's to make it through the finish gate. She managed to stay on her feet for both runs and she placed 16th in a field of 35.

The winner, as everyone west of the Mississippi had predicted, were Bud Werner and his older sister, Skeeter.

The medals were awarded immediately after the race and the Mammoth skiers were very soon headed out of Winter Park. They were glad to get away. They all felt flattened by the weekend. The only thing not deflated was Jill's tongue; she couldn't eat solid food and she talked as if she had hot soup in her mouth.

Dave listened to the conversation for many miles and then said, "Okay. Now you know pretty much what you have to do."

"But Pa, that downhill was a *precipice* at the bottom!"

Dave shrugged. "That last schuss before the finish wasn't any different than schussing #2 back home."

Jill couldn't imagine coming straight down beside the #2 tow without a single turn to cut down her speed. She glanced at Audra Jo, who also had a *yeah-but-who's-ever-schussed-#2* look on her face. The car was silent. Everybody did know pretty much what he would have to do.

3

IT WAS A PLEASURE TO GET BACK HOME TO SIMPLE skiing without having to worry about anything more momentous than a few high school meets. Most of the skiing in March was at McGee, although the Kinmonts drove to the San Bernardino Mountains for the Snow Valley Giant Slalom where Bob, in his own cool, shy, unemphatic way, was something of a sensation. Giant slalom is a fast event with fewer flags than slalom, but it is more tightly controlled than downhill. Bob won the Class 2 race with a time that was better than anything any one of the older Class 1 racers was able to chalk up.

Bill Kinmont was beginning to succumb to a kind of racing fever himself, even though he did not ski. He had been ferrying his children and their teammates to races for a season and a half and he knew many of the regulars, both competitors and parents, from other parts of California. And at Snow Valley he went to a race committee meeting and agreed to help organize next year's complicated Far West racing schedule.

At McGee, Jill and Audra Jo taught Linda Meyers what they could and offered their sympathies when she cried, "I can't *stand* it when that Kenny Lloyd tries to help me ski!" They helped Jerry Kinmont, too, but he liked to go off by himself with a shovel and build jumps. He looked very serious, even with his huge freckles and his outsized ski clothes, and he always skied until his poles were dragging and he was too exhausted to straighten up. Marc Zumstein, who was Mammoth and McGee's one ski patrolman, had to pick him up one afternoon, skis and poles attached, and carry him down to the warming hut.

Jill and Bob often skied together now, following one

35

another down from the upper tow, working out on short slaloms or just playing around. They spoke little, but each seemed to know how the day was going for the other. Once when Jill claimed she was scared, Bob said, "You mean you're scared you'll knock down some flags. Who the heck cares what you look like? Go give it a try if you want."

Dave was always around, happy to work with anyone who needed help but never pushing it. His coaching, like his speech, was simple and to the point. *You're not over your skis. You're putting your arms up and down too much. You're back too much. You're not rotating.*

The kids didn't say much to Dave, but they all tried to live up to what they thought he expected of them. No one said, "I wonder what Pa would think," but there were certain things you did do and others you just didn't do. You were never lazy—at least not for long. You didn't reach for excuses. You didn't mind sweating something out if it had to be sweated out. You took what came along and you didn't bitch about it.

Jill often met Roma McCoy in town where they indulged themselves at the Malt Shop or bought Roma's groceries for the week or stopped at Dorrance's to try on a dress that Roma thought would look good on Jill. Jill cared a great deal about clothes; her things were always pressed and fresh and she never wore colors or patterns that clashed. She dressed as carefully for riding or working at the corral as she did for school or skiing. On summer evenings the ranch guests were certain to look up when she appeared in her white beaded moccasins and tight levis and fresh pink-and-white shirt.

During these excursions Roma sometimes talked about Dave's early career—he had gone to work in a mine at thirteen and had made his own first pair of skis at seventeen—and Jill asked one day about the accident. She knew the fact of it but not the details. Dave certainly never mentioned it. Roma said Dave had begun racing about 1937 and within a few years had won Reno's Silver Dollar Derby and several California slalom championships. But in 1942 he went through a hard spring snow crust at the Sugar Bowl and broke his leg in twenty-eight places. He lay in a Reno hospital for weeks with the leg unset, suspended in a big sling. One doctor had wanted to amputate. Finally they operated, pinning the bone fragments together. Dave wore a heavy brace for a year and then went to Los Angeles for bone grafts from his good leg. He continued to work and to operate his weekend ski tows, but it was 1946 before he tried to ski again.

Early in April a trail was finally broken through into Mammoth Mountain.

Mammoth was friendly and crowded and the girls had as much fun selling and punching tickets as they had skiing, for the ticket line was the social heart of the mountain. The boys had lonely jobs like hauling gasoline and running the tow engines. Their presence did not go unnoticed, however. Bob was a dead-pan comic who wore outrageous hats and once skied all day in a pirate suit. Kenny Lloyd usually could be spotted by the shirttail sticking out from beneath his undersized sweater or the shock of hair sticking out from under his fast cap—a tight fitting, helmet-like wool cap that tied under the chin. One noon he came schussing straight down from the upper tow with an empty jerry can swinging from each hand, yodeling and flying off bumps, and Linda Meyers said, "Gee, I'd like to try that!" Kenny took a wild spill right in front of everybody, and Jill said, "Are you sure, Linda Mae?" Linda laughed and nodded vigorously as Kenny rolled onto his feet, unchastened, without ever having come to a stop.

Dave was often tied up reconditioning his winter-ravaged equipment, but Roma always had time. Roma was back on skis, making up for a lost winter, and it was with her that Jill learned to feel comfortable about skiing at high speed.

Audra Jo missed this opportunity, unfortunately. She spent the first two weekends after Mammoth reopened dancing in an amateur review which was touring the valley to raise money for the March of Dimes. Then she spent an afternoon at Mammoth with Jill and Roma. All three were skiing well, feeling as gay as otters, slicing their way down the mountain on one another's tails with a sleek, careless grace that was a delight to watch. Each of the three took turns leading, and once when Audra Jo was out in front she started hamming it up: sudden little flicking turns, steep straight schusses, quick checks that exploded the snow at her heels. She had never skied better or loved it so much . . . until she caught an edge and did an eggbeater for 200 feet, cartwheeling, flying, crashing, sliding down the slope toward a line of big pines.

Roma and Jill were at her side within forty seconds. Audra Jo made a wretched face, partly in pain and partly in anger at her own stupidity. The verdict was not serious —a pulled ligament in her ankle—but it killed spring skiing for her.

And spring skiing, fast or slow, was the laziest and the most delicious skiing of the year. Mammoth was a warm, bright world with blue skies and fast morning snow that broke up into big crystals and sprayed from under turning skis like fine gravel. Jill skied in old jeans or shorts and a cotton shirt with sleeves rolled up. She enjoyed the luxury of having time to ski where she wished and time to stop for the view wherever one appeared. One noon she climbed, alone, from the top of the #2 tow onto the broad ridge that overlooked the whole ski area and the country beyond it. Just above the higher end of the ridge was the startling white of the great snowfields that slanted up to the summit of Mammoth Mountain. Out to the northwest was a rugged, forested wilderness. To the east, far away and far below, lay the entire upper end of the Owens Valley, flat, dry, snowless, another world in another season.

In Bishop, at the Rocking K, the apple blossoms had come and gone and the locust trees were in bloom and the lilacs were already fading. The ranch was open for the season and was filled with fishermen.

Soon it was light until 7:30 and warm until midnight. Jill began sleeping out of doors in a rollaway bed up behind the cabins. She and Bob took on a few of the ranch chores, mostly shopping and diswashing, and began to worry about final exams. They put away their skis then and admitted that winter was over.

After school was out and summer well under way, however, Dave McCoy dropped in at the ranch and said quietly, "You know, there's a very nice race on in a couple of weeks."

Bob grinned. Jill said, "Hmmm," and her eyes brightened and she began to wonder what the snow would be like and how warm the sun would be. The very name of the race made her want to go. Sonora Summit Summer Slalom. There would be some juniors, Dave said, although it was essentially an adult race for skiers from the Stockton area, which was 250 miles away on the other side of the Sierra. But the race should be a lot of fun and it promised to draw some pretty fair talent.

Jill said, "It's going to be the first *real* race we've been to. I mean, you know, not just *kids.*"

A Stanford graduate student named Dave Taylor was at Mammoth working on his slalom technique, so Jill and Bob and Dave and Toni Milici joined him. All five of them planned to race and they drilled every day for a week, concentrating on the hard morning snow.

The Mammoth quintet headed north at 5 A.M. on Sunday, June 29, in Dave's old black 1941 Chevrolet with five pairs of skis on top and a load of waxes in the trunk. An hour later they were skirting Mono Lake, where the treeless summer hills lay brown and dry in the early sun. All at once the highway climbed from summer to spring, running the year backwards. Little dust-yellow flowers of rabbit-brush soon were budding along the roadside and stains of new aspen green brightened the shallow valleys. After turning west across the cattle guard at Sonora Junction there were signs of April and March, then of winter, patches of gray snow with small mists rising from their edges. And finally, squarely trimmed snowbanks, for the road had been open for only two days.

Sonora Pass is over 9,600 feet, the low point of a high sweeping saddle that rises north and south of the road and falls off steeply to the east with a long view across the Nevada desert. The race was to be held on the Knob, which is an odd little conical hill on the south side of the road less than a mile west of the pass. Except for two parked cars, there was no sign of civilization anywhere when Dave pulled onto the plowed-out shoulder of the road just before eight o'clock. Jill wondered if they could have gotten into the wrong pass. It was two hours before race time, but even Dave had the lonely feeling that there wasn't going to be much of a turnout.

It was very cold, despite the sun, and the five skiers climbed from the car and ran up through the rocks and scrubby trees just north of the road to limber up and get some warmth into their feet and fingers. The steep, stony, wind-swept meadows here were almost clear of snow. Half a mile south was the Knob, on which blue, red and yellow flags were visible. Several figures were moving about on the flat at the bottom of the hill.

Dave McCoy led the way across to the hill carrying his skis and his huge box of waxes which contained everything from Sohm's Red and Østbe Klister to beeswax and rosin. Toni was behind him with the Coleman stove. They waved to several men in winter overcoats who were setting up two long tables in the snow. "Looks nice," Toni said to them, nodding at the hill. The course obviously had been set on Saturday and it looked exciting—a very tight giant slalom with about 40 gates.

Dave established his own headquarters beside a high, twisted stump. He pumped up the little pressure stove and held a match to it. The stove put up a long, involved protest, going *put putty putty put put* and threatening to die. Finally it gasped and settled down to a soft, dependable wheeze and Dave set a banged-up old coffee pot on top of it. Into the pot he dropped four bars of paraffin and fifteen mothballs. Mothballs, for some unfathomable reason, keep paraffin from wearing off the bottom of skis when they run on spring snow.

When the wax and mothballs were melted and stirred, Dave took a small brush and painted a thick coat onto the bottoms of all ten skis. Then everyone scraped the wax *off* his skis, leaving a thin, smooth film of paraffin. The

40

air was rich with the friendly odors of Tartan sun lotion and mothballs and hot wax.

A safari of cars pulled in from the west about nine o'clock, and skiers were milling all over the flat by the time the Mammoth contingent had registered and picked up its racing numbers. The turnout proved to be anything but meager—more than a hundred racers plus a surprising number of spectators from the Stockton Ski Club. About twenty of the competitors were women. A number of juniors were entered, all of them apparently older than Bob and Jill Kinmont.

"Who do you suppose is the girl to beat?" Jill said. Dave shrugged but a stranger overheard the question and answered it. "Carol Jones. She's *hot!*"

When Dave and Dave and Toni and Jill and Bob were satisfied with their wax jobs, each fastened his skis together, bottom to bottom, with waxed paper between them to protect the carefully finished surfaces. Then they shouldered their skis and started walking up beside the course. No one is allowed to practice on any part of a slalom course, but competitors are free to climb up or ski down close to it on either side.

Dave Taylor and Toni went their own way, and Dave McCoy climbed the hill with Bob and Jill, studying the course, deciding just how each gate should be handled. *Hang on above the flush or you'll come into it too fast. Enter it very high. Just before the hairpin there's time for a skating step or a good shove with your poles.* They walked down a few gates to check the line they planned to take and then resumed their slow walk up toward the start, which was at the very top of the hill in a little grove of stubby pines.

Near the top Jill put on her skis and made a couple of warm-up turns alongside the course. The snow was solid, with a corny surface of congealed ice crystals, and she felt she wasn't cutting into it well enough. Dave burred her steel edges with the file he carried in his knapsack, raising a line of sharp, almost microscopic teeth along the full length of each edge. This would make the skis

41

carve more deeply into the snow for the same reason that a knife bites deeper if it has a serrated blade.

Dozens of skiers were on the hill now, studying the course and testing the snow. Jill spotted Carol Jones and said to Dave, "Her turns are real nice and she doesn't sideslip hardly at all."

Dave replied, "You don't have to worry about her."

Waiting for the race to begin, Jill made a few short turns to see how her newly burred edges felt. As she checked at the end of her last turn, a man skied down from above and stopped beside her. He wore a very tight navy-blue racing parka with an Olympic patch on the front. His face was angular with high cheekbones and hollow cheeks and a jutting chin, and Jill recognized him as Dick Buek of the U.S. Olympic squad. She could not believe he was stopping on her account. He said offhand-edly, "You're going to win the race today."

Jill did not think he was serious but she said, "What about Carol?"

"She can't win, compared to you."

"Why?"

Dick Buek shrugged. He was leaning against his ski poles, standing in a loose, catlike manner, smiling.

"But how do you know?"

"From the way you turn," he said. He licked his upper lip and glanced around at Bob, who was behind him. He said, "You ski well, kid, but those flappy britches are sure going to slow you down." From his parka pocket he pulled a pair of garters. Bob put the garters on over his ski pants just below the knees.

Jill and Bob watched the first racers from several gates below the start. When Dick Buek bore down on them he was skiing so fast and free that he seemed to be playing some wild game. But coming out of the third gate his body jerked suddenly as he caught an edge, lost his balance and shot off toward a patch of unbroken snow and scrubby trees. As he was about to crash into the brush he lifted his downhill ski high in the air, did a running kick turn, came whipping back toward the

42

course in perfect control and shot down the hill again.

Bob said, "Boy, talk about a re*covery!*"

Jill thought, Well, if he can have *that* much trouble on *this* course, then maybe there isn't such a tremendous gap between Olympic skiers and some of the rest of us.

When she was finally at the top in the starting gate she felt good. Anxious, naturally, but not worried. She knew just what she would do in each gate. And it was a beautiful day . . . warm sun, quiet except for cheery voices and the occasional clatter of skis from lower on the hill. Good hard spring snow that was just beginning to loosen up.

The man with the walkie-talkie and the stopwatches said, "Thirty seconds," and Dave said, "Have fun."

Then it was "Ready!" and then, "Five, four, three, two, one, go!"

Jill ran fast and smooth. Her skiing had style, or at least she seemed to have a certain presence on skis. She moved neatly, without any of the fierceness that often shows in a racer.

When she pulled a sharp check below the finish gate, strange voices were shouting. "Beautiful run!" "Kid, that was terrific!" "Bravo!"

Jill said, "Thank you," although the run had been such a breeze that she didn't feel she had really *done* anything. She had in fact won the junior race by a very comfortable margin and handed in what was easily the best time for any woman of any age in any class.

All Dave McCoy said was, "You're on your way."

Later she asked him, "But, Pa, how come I won?"

"A fast start and then smooth and pretty turns with no slipping."

Bob also placed first in his class. Dave Taylor won the men's race with Dick Buek second and Dave McCoy third.

The Mammoth skiers collected their four awards from the Stockton people at a brief ceremony and then took off alone down the east side of Sonora Pass. Jill said, "Pa, do you know much about him? Dick Buek?"

Dave shrugged. "This year's national downhill champion. They call him 'Mad Dog.' " Jill also dragged out the information that Dick Buek worked at his father's ski shop at Soda Springs, near Donner Summit.

Later Dave said, "I first saw Buek at the Inferno on Mt. Lassen years ago. The course dropped from the top right down the southeast face, and the first eight racers, they all sideslipped or made turns back and forth. Dick was just a kid and he was off with his dad kind of looking at the fall of the hill. But when he came off that mountain he just pointed 'em straight down. No check, no nothin'. He just got smaller and smaller, and we all just looked at each other."

Jill Kinmont had something of a reputation for modesty, and it was deserved. But in Bishop on the 30th of June her demure behavior masked a strong desire to grab a megaphone and ride down Main Street like a town crier or perhaps like Paul Revere, posting all the citizens on the results of the Sonora Summit Summer Slalom. She never mentioned the race unless asked about it, of course, but her father suffered less than she from restrictive inhibitions of this nature. The word got around.

Until now Jill had skied when there was snow and raced when there were races, and that was about it. But Sonora had given her real confidence for the first time and started her thinking in a deliberate way about the art of skiing. To Audra Jo she said, "You know what, Josie? I've decided that I really *do* want to learn how to ski," by which she meant: learn how to ski very well, learn to race, learn what it takes to win. Audra Jo had no particular ambitions as a skier, but she loved to race and she was pretty much Jill's equal—better in downhill, not so good in slalom. Jill said, "Darn your ankle! You'd've done *great* at Sonora!" She added, "But next year we'll slay 'em. And Bobby too. You and me and Bobby and Kenny. We could really have a team next year!"

4

SUMMER DAYS ARE MOST BEAUTIFUL IN THEIR FIRST moments, and Jill was often out at dawn to watch the world light up. Mt. Tom stood ashen against the dark sky until the first sunlight struck. Then nearby crags on Basin Mountain, too, were caught. Soon the sun was slanting into the ranch through the dead and living branches of the ancient willows, and Jill listened for the fluffing sound of doves taking wing. Always there was the bright noise of running water, for a sluice brought mountain water from Bishop Creek and channeled it into the ponds and pastures. Teal and widgeon and mallards fed in the wet, sparkling grass.

Jill and Audra Jo both had summer jobs at the Rocking K, waiting on table at breakfast and dinner and making beds and cleaning cabins all morning. Jill was a very slow chambermaid, but she gained a reputation for efficiency in spite of herself because she was so light on her feet, always darting somewhere, barefooted, in her low-waisted jeans and cowboy shirt. The girls were paid to go fishing several mornings a week, since the upper pond was stocked with trout and the ranch was coming to be known for its big trout breakfasts. After lunch Jill gave Red Cross swimming lessons for five-year-olds at Keough's public pool south of town. She also drove to Joseph's Market regularly for the grocery order, hired out as baby-sitter for guests, and fed and combed and exercised Princess, her white-footed, white-browed chestnut quarter horse. She still found time for something extra like a short hike to the corral to watch the wrangler with some of his more unbelievable dudes or a walk to the old black willow in the north pasture where she could run and grab the rope

45

and try to swing up onto the back of one of the horses. There were 32 horses on the ranch now, as well as 45 sheep, eight calves and three steers for roping, a flock of bantam hens and two peacocks.

And there was always Jerry, who kept begging her to join him in his new barefoot game of stepping on bees. Jerry was a ten-year-old towhead with a thousand freckles. He had his own chores to do, but he spent a part of every day collecting for his "museum," which could be visited by anyone for a small fee. It was really a zoo, for it had live lizards, a magpie, dozens and dozens of frogs, and seven varieties of snakes, including a rattler. Plus minor exhibits like birds' nests and butterflies and spiders and arrowheads. When Jerry was stuck for cages he improvised, as Jill discovered one Sunday afternoon when she lugged the Dutch oven into the kitchen to boil spaghetti and found it already filled with the coiled body of a large black snake, very much alive and anxious to leave.

Some evenings Jill came rushing into the dining room late because she had been delayed getting back from Keough's. But when she was home early she took Princess out for a brisk run before dinner . . . and again managed to be late in the dining room. Every evening the dinner gong caught her at the ironing board or dashing from the shower or trying to button a blouse with one hand while pulling a shoe over her heel with the other. After a careful slash of lipstick and a comb whipped neatly through her hair, she would appear in the dining room with a gracious, unhurried smile that almost belied her breathlessness.

Life was not much calmer for the other members of the Kinmont family, each of whom regularly referred to the ranch as a madhouse. They seldom ate together, since each one had to grab a quick meal when he could. June Kinmont planned the meals, ran the dining room, handled reservations, kept the books and paid the bills, as well as mending clothes and answering the ever-ringing telephone. Bill had to work all day, be sociable at the bar all night with the drinkers, be up at four in the morning with the fishermen in order to make it up Bishop Creek to Lake

46

Sabrina or South Lake by six, and then listen to everyone tell him what a soft life he was leading.

But even in the middle of a frantic morning of work it was possible to steal five minutes for a walk to the pasture fence to look and listen or just breathe in the smell of willows and sage, of hay and wild roses. There were rich leather odors in the tackroom and the distinctive smell of oats.

At night when Jill got ready for bed and went out walking through the irrigated pastures in her pajamas, the fragrances were fresher still. She walked on tiptoe, slowly, sinking into the damp grass, trying to miss the mud puddles and keep clear of stickers. But always she slid into cool mud that chilled her soles and squished up between her toes; and always she returned with a harvest of foxtails and burrs on her legs. She slept outside, and sometimes she was asleep in a moment, not even aware of the sweet smell of the grass in the south pasture. Sometimes she lay on her back watching the stars, listening for the cry of a coyote, hearing always the small talk of running water and the soft rolling chorus of the crickets.

Jill went out three or four times a week, often double dating with Audra Jo. She was not told what time to be in, and neither was Bob. She used her own judgment, and if she decided to stay out later than 11:30 or midnight she telephoned home to say so. There was usually a dance or a ball game in town, or perhaps a good movie—"good" meaning Montgomery Clift. One night everyone drove out east to the airport and danced on the strip, letting the headlights send endless weaving shadows out across the desert. The next evening they drove along the canal road to watch the jackrabbits. Then there was a Saturday river party—hot dogs and marshmallows after drifting down the Owens River in inner tubes from Bishop to the swimming hole at Collins' Bridge.

Now and then Jill was allowed to have the station wagon for what she called "dragging the Main." She and Audra Jo would pick up two or three other girls and drive slowly up and down the full twelve blocks of Main Street

47

to see who was in town, who was going with whom, and who else in whose car was also dragging the Main. At times there would be a line of eight or ten or twelve cars parading watchfully for an hour or more in a procession that was almost funereal except for sporadic shouting and honking and laughter. The evening usually ended at the Malt Shop.

Jerry always wanted to go along when Jill took the car, but she did not feel that her social life profited greatly from his chaperonage. Often enough he would get to town on his own, find where the car was parked and set out after the occupants. Jill and Audra Jo ducked him, hid from him and left false leads at the Malt Shop, but Jerry always tracked them down and then tagged along. In the presence of male high school seniors he would call out, *"Jill! Hi, Jill! Jill, gimme a nickel will ya huh, Jill? Aw, come on, Jill!"*

Bishop's annual "Homecoming" was scheduled for the first week in September and local cowboys were already working out at the Rocking K practice arena on their days off. The Homecoming and Labor Day Celebration, which originated as a reunion for former valley residents, was now the big weekend of the year. Everyone put on cowboy clothes and turned out for three days of parades, street dances, barbecues, carnivals and—the main attraction—rodeos, both amateur and professional. The Kinmonts had been very much involved the year before because Bill had been president of the Homecoming Association and because Jill had been invited to ride in the parade with Gene Rambo, who was World All-Around Champion. This year they were becoming involved because of their roping arena and because Jill and Audra Jo decided to make a concerted bid for the role of Homecoming Queen. The title was earned by the sale of tickets for the amateur rodeo and Kids Day events, each ticket buyer being entitled to one "vote." Since the girls were equally popular and would be splitting the votes of their many mutual friends, they agreed that both would campaign exclusively for Jill Kinmont for Queen in 1952 and for Audra Jo Nicholson in 1953. Jill immediately squan-

48

dered a good part of her first month's salary on a new pair of Levis, a white, fitted shirt with tight sleeves and gripper snaps, and a powder blue Don Hoy hat. The white shirt was important if you wished to look like a roper and not like a dude, as were boots with walking heels, jeans that were not rolled up, and a hat with a modest brim, worn dead level.

On the last Saturday in July just about everyone in town showed up for a big dance at the Legion Hall, which was a barnlike place with folding chairs along all four walls. Audra Jo went with Bob Autry, an ex-schoolmate and skier who was in town for a few days on leave from the Navy. The dance was a good one and a long one, and Sunday was therefore a lazy, late-rising day.

Jill and Audra Jo had to work in the dining room that evening and they planned to go to the late movie at the Bishop Theater afterwards. They showed up as usual before dinner, dressed alike in snug levis and cowboy boots and western shirts. It was a slow evening, and yet Audra Jo found it difficult to keep up. Finally she sat at an empty table and whispered, "I've got to rest a minute, Jill. I'm sorry, but my *legs* have started aching for some silly reason."

Jill said lightly, "Dance too hard last night?" She added, "You haven't fallen off a horse or anything, have you?"

"No. I've been just fine, except I was awfully tired this morning." She rested for ten minutes and she felt worse. "No movie for me, Jill. I'm sorry."

Audra Jo went home early and on Monday she stayed in bed. When Jill went to see her she said she had driven home from the ranch Sunday evening at five miles an hour because she was afraid she was going to pass out. At the moment, however, she looked reasonably healthy— and very pretty—lying at ease with her long blonde hair spread across the pillow.

Word got around that Audra Jo was at home in bed, and more than a dozen friends came out to the house to see her Monday afternoon and Tuesday morning. Then her pains grew worse and she developed a severe headache. Dr. Scott came and, after a few routine checks and

49

questions, took a spinal tap. He said, "You're going to have to go to the hospital."

"But I don't *want* to go to the hospital."

Her mother said, "I'm sure Scotty wouldn't send you if he felt there was a choice." Dr. Scott was not only a friend but also an avid skier.

Audra Jo cried. And then she discovered the situation was even worse than she had thought: Scotty hadn't meant the Bishop Hospital but a hospital in Los Angeles. She sniffled and said, "But please, then, just be sure I'm back home for Homecoming."

The diagnosis was poliomyelitis, and Audra Jo Nicholson traveled 300 miles by ambulance to the contagious ward of the Los Angeles General Hospital. The following day she went into an iron lung.

The seriousness of Audra Jo's illness did not sink in for some time. Rationally, Jill knew what was happening, but the cold facts refused to fit with the friend she had worked and played and laughed with, winter and summer, for four years. Audra Jo was very sick, but the hospital was taking good care of her and would fix her up. It was that simple. Wasn't it? Of course, polio was something that might leave you having to wear braces, but *some*how everything was going to work out just fine in the end.

Jill understood and accepted the fact that no one could say yet whether the patient's chances were good or bad, but she refused to believe it when she heard there was a 50-50 chance that Audra Jo would die. And it was a long time before she could let herself believe that some form of crippling paralysis was certain . . . was, in fact, the best that could be hoped for.

Jill worked at the ranch as usual, waiting on table and helping with chores, and she was still teaching her young swimmers at Keough's. But everything was different and everything was sad. She had planned to join the McCoys on a camping trip but backed out. People kept asking her about Audra Jo and she hated that; every time she tried to answer, tears filled her eyes and she was unable to speak clearly.

The whole town of Bishop was concerned. People stopped at the post office with a vague feeling that the clerks must have some privileged connection with the outside world. "How is she today, have you heard?"

The Striplings—Audra Jo's mother and stepfather—sent daily reports from Los Angeles, but these were much the same for two weeks: *We just don't know yet; we just have to wait and see.* Audra Jo was in an iron lung and she was still alive and she was at least no worse today than yesterday.

After the middle of August—her birthday was on the 18th—Audra Jo began to improve; soon she was out of critical danger, although still in the iron lung. Jill could think of nothing to do for her beyond keeping her posted on the latest gossip. She wrote every day and Audra Jo soon knew who was just back from vacation, who was going with whom, what cowboys were in town already for the rodeo. Wilfred Cline was up from Lone Pine with his string of horses but the Bunker brothers hadn't shown up yet. Jill also kept her informed about how many Amateur Rodeo buttons she had sold in her campaign for Queen, although the whole thing seemed rather pointless now. Also, it was obvious that Janice Castagno was winning.

Red, white and blue banners were strung across Main Street for Homecoming, and the celebration was undoubtedly the biggest ever. The parade was longer than last year and the school band was louder and the floats were more inventive, but Jill felt she was looking on from a distance. The rodeo was where she missed Audra Jo the most. They had always stood together in the dirt by the calf chutes, hot and dusty and happy, ready to duck back under the bandstand in case a Brahma bull or a bucking horse should give them the evil eye.

Audra Jo was moved to a Los Angeles rehabilitation center called Rancho Los Amigos and Jill drove down with the Striplings to visit her late in September. Audra

51

Jo was cranked up in a hospital bed enjoying one of her first brief periods out of the iron lung, and her appearance stopped Jill cold: pale arms as thin as sticks and an odd little bandage low at the front of her neck. The bandage disturbed Jill because it looked so deliberate; cuts and scrapes occur at random spots on your body, but this bandage covered a wound that was neat and perfectly centered.

Jill said, feeling awful, "Hi, Josie. You look just . . . great."

Audra Jo *sounded* the same as ever. "How was the rodeo?" she said. "I can just *feel* how it was." She was smiling. "And the smell of it, too."

It was too late in the day to stay more than a few minutes, but Jill and the Striplings returned for a longer visit the following morning. This time Audra Jo was in an iron lung, which made her look 100 percent helpless— just a head sticking out from the end of a big tank-like machine. Jill thought: This is one of the worst things that could ever happen to anyone.

It was certainly not possible to feel that Audra Jo had somehow been singled out; the huge room was filled with iron lungs, dozens of them, and every one was inhabited. Some patients would be imprisoned in them for months, some for years, some forever. Audra Jo was already spending ten minutes a day out of the lung and each day she was able to remain outside a little longer.

Jill sat in a chair at the end of the lung. It required conscious effort to keep her eyes off the top of Audra Jo's head and to watch instead the reflection of her face in the large tilted mirror directly above it. Jill wanted to know what it felt like to be in the lung and how nurses could take care of her and how she could go to the bathroom and what would happen if the electricity should fail. She also wanted to ask how bad the paralysis was, but she could only talk about a lot of little things that didn't matter. How was the food and did she have any visitors and were there any good-looking boys in the ward and was the doctor young or old.

Audra Jo, on the other hand, enjoyed talking about

everything. "The worst was at the beginning," she said. "They took away my class ring and they put a band on my wrist. Like a label on a jar. And the best was when practically the whole Avalanche Ski Club came in to say hello." The Avalanche skiers were the most loyal Mammoth regulars in Los Angeles County.

"That's pretty great," Jill said. "Has Bob Autry been down?"

"No. In fact, I haven't even heard from him."

"Really?" This didn't feel like a particularly gay subject to pursue, so Jill said, "You been comfortable? I mean, what's it *feel* like inside that . . . uh . . . *thing?"*

Audra Jo raised her eyebrows in a way that looked as if she must be shrugging her shoulders. "The first time, as soon as they got my head through the collar, it felt like dropping in an elevator all of a sudden."

"I see you've got TV."

"Why, sure. And it's funny because the sets are fixed to make the picture backwards so it looks right in the mirror, and the nurses can't read anything on the screens."

Jill laughed for the first time since she had arrived in Los Angeles.

Later, when the Striplings left the two girls alone, Jill tried to explain her own feelings. The words wouldn't form. She said finally, "I don't know what to say, Josie. It's just that it's not *right."*

Audra Jo said, "I asked my mother *why*, when I'd always been good, *why* something like this should happen. When I'd been as good as I could, anyway. Why would God per*mit* this to happen? There's no answer, I suppose. Mother said there are just things that we can't question. And she said maybe it was because I could handle it better than some other people could. And she said she guessed a person just had to make the best of it."

Jill didn't answer because she was thinking what it would be like if you were stuck in a wheelchair for life and had to watch your boy friends drift away and had to find out you couldn't even dance and ski any more.

"I feel pretty lucky," Audra Jo said. "There's some little ones in iron lungs down at the end of the room somewhere and at night I hear them crying for their mothers. And there's two women here expecting babies soon, and they have other children at home, too." She frowned suddenly, studying Jill's face in her mirror. "Gee," she said softly, "what are you looking so worried about, for goodness' sake?"

Jill was beginning her senior year in high school and her faculty counselor asked her to what colleges she was applying. When she responded with a blank look he asked her if she planned to go to college at all. She said, "Well, yes. I mean, sure. Don't you think?" Then she added, half kidding, "Of course I'd really rather just ski."

"The truth will out," he said. "And perhaps, all in all, it's a valid point. You're only sixteen, so time is cheap." He was serious and Jill took him seriously. She nursed the idea and began looking for arguments by which she might influence and eventually persuade her parents.

A new warming hut had just been completed at Mammoth and Jill went up several evenings to help paint it before the snows came. The elegant, two-story building was several hundred yards east of the Snake Pit. On the lower floor were rest rooms, a ski shop, a first-aid room, an office and three small bedrooms. The upper floor was a cafeteria which had a huge fireplace with picture windows on both sides, facing the mountain. The chimney was magnificent. It was made of stones Toni Milici had collected for a house he never got around to building, and on the outside was embedded a mosaic of light-blue stones in the shape of an inverted arrow 20 feet high.

There was skiing before Thanksgiving, but the weekend hordes did not appear until the first Saturday in December. Jill was at the warming hut that morning with Bob and Kenny and Linda by a quarter after seven. About 8:30 Roma McCoy and Gloria Redman and the two girls moved out to the ticket booths in the crisp, gray morning, and as soon as one of Marc Zumstein's new ski patrolmen brought the cash registers, Mammoth was in business. Dave had gone up to the #2 tow shack with Don Redman to check out the engine. Bob and Kenny were trudging up the towline with jerry cans full of gasoline. A bright edge of sunlight was already showing on a high corner of the mountain.

Everything seemed to be functioning properly and the crowd was still thin, so Jill and Bob sneaked three runs on the lower tow. On their last ride up, the sun appeared with liquid brilliance on the high horizon above the top of the #2 tow. The warming hut and the lower slope were quickly flooded with light and warmth.

Roma and Gloria and Ethel Zumstein sold tickets and Jill stapled the tickets around the skiers' belt loops or onto their parkas. Linda and another girl were busy watching the towline, keeping an eye out for chiselers.

By eleven everyone who was going to buy an all-day ticket had already bought it, so Jill and Roma went skiing. They tightened their boots in the warming hut, picked up their goggles and a Cup O'Gold candy bar, stopped in at the bathroom, and retrieved their skis from the repair shop. Jill had two pairs of skis this year for the first time—slalom skis, which were light and limber but which chattered on hard snow at high speed, and downhill skis, which were heavier, longer and more stable, and which she was now breaking in. She followed Roma down the lower towline for a warmup run, and they managed four fast ones down from the top of #2 before lunch. Then a hamburger and potato chips and a Mission Orange pop before returning to spell Gloria and Ethel.

Jill had most of the afternoon free for skiing, and at three o'clock Dave came up with Don Redman. The two men led Jill and Bob and Kenny and Dennis Osborn all over the mountain. Linda stuck with them for a while, too. She kept calling, "Kenny, wait!"

"Don't talk so much and maybe you can keep up," he shouted back at her. "Now come on!"

"Kenny, I can't!"

The practical details of running Mammoth's tows and the new cafeteria were smoothed out that weekend, and from then on Dave spent most of his free time with the young skiers from Bishop and Lee Vining. He was a champion of no particular style or school; his object was simply to teach a sensible way of skiing. He studied each skier as an individual and suggested improvements if the person was in the market for suggestions. There were no rules or rituals and Dave was pleased that Mammoth had no star whom everyone wanted to imitate. There were hot arguments about where your weight should be and when to edge and when to keep the skis flat on the snow, but no one asked or cared whether a certain position was "Austrian" or "Parallel" or "French" or *what*.

Once when the question of style came up after a race, Dave said, "Look. How many techniques did you see here today?"

After considerable thought someone said, "An awful lot."

"That's right. Everyone does it his own way."

Dave worked in the same way with Jill, with Kenny and Bob and Dennis, and with his son Gary—with any youngster who was around and wanted to learn. Lots of them would never become racers, and that was fine. Each had his own special set of problems. One could never seem to think ahead about the next turn; another skied well but had no faith in himself; someone else was full of spirit but couldn't keep his skies working together.

It was also in Dave's nature to *do* things rather than to speak of doing them, and he settled arguments about technique by having a victim run through a few slalom gates and then stop to study his tracks. The evidence was all there, creased into the snow. The turn had started late and he was too far from the pole. Or it had started too early and he'd had to sideslip to get by. Or he had held it too long and wasn't set up for the next turn.

Over Christmas week Jill spent the better part of several days at the Striplings', for Audra Jo had been granted a brief vacation from the Kabot Kaiser Institute where she had gone to begin a long program of muscular retraining. She was too shaky to leave the house, but she could breathe now and she was free of the iron lung. She spent her time either in bed or in her new wheelchair.

The bandage was gone from her throat; she had a small round scar centered neatly between her collarbones.

Audra Jo's immediate worries, she told Jill, concerned clothing and schoolwork. She wanted to dress so her very thin legs wouldn't attract attention and so her clothing wouldn't pull when they put braces on her—there was some hope that she could be taught to get around with crutches and heavy braces. Meanwhile she was working hard on her school studies but was afraid she was too far behind to graduate in June.

Jill was less self-conscious than she had been on her Los Angeles visit and she asked, trying to appear nonchalant, just how much damage the disease had really done. Audra Jo told her she was totally paralyzed from the waist down, although feeling still existed as before, and she would still be able to bear children. She said, "Jill, it could have been so much worse." It was as if the patient were reassuring her friend rather than the other way around. "Look," she said. "When I was in the rocking bed . . . over in my ward there were some of us who could breathe without a respirator and some of us who could move our arms. I was the only one who could do *both*."

5

THE 1953 RACING SEASON BEGAN WITH A TIGHT
schedule of big junior meets, all of which would count in
the selection of the team to represent the Far West at
the Junior Nationals. The opener was a 40-gate slalom
with 109 competitors, held the week after New Year's at
Kratka Ridge in the San Bernardino Mountains.

Jill won the girls' race, but she was more impressed
with her brother's performance than with her own. Although she had been skiing with Bob regularly, it had
been a long time since she had stepped back for a critical
look at him. All fall he had been diving and tumbling and
playing varsity football and working out on the trampoline,
and he was nobody's little brother any longer. He was
short, but very well knit and powerful. He skied strongly
as if it were no effort at all, and he turned in the fastest
time of the day.

The Mammoth skiers wanted to win races, and they
worked at it all the time. They were sometimes the only
ones on the hill early on the morning of a race or at dusk
the afternoon before. They studied every course with care
whether it was a big race or just a few gates they'd put
up for kicks. On a single afternoon they could set a
slalom, ski it four or five times, tear out the poles and
set a giant slalom, and then argue their way up and down
the new course until it was too dark to see the ruts.

On the weekend after Kratka Ridge, Barni Davenport
won at Snow Valley, scoring for southern California. But
Mammoth monopolized the next four races. First place
awards in slalom or downhill went to Janice Castagno and
Jill and Dennis Osborn at Squaw Valley, to Kenny and
Jill and Bob at Echo Summit, to Dennis and Jill at Mt.

Rose, and to Kenny, Jill and Bob at Yosemite, where 156 entrants showed up for the Far West Divisional Championships.

The winners were invited not only to the Junior Nationals at Brighton, Utah, but also to the year's most glamorous race, the American Legion's Western Junior Championships at Sun Valley, which followed two weeks later.

At Brighton there were sixteen Far West juniors with Dave McCoy as their coach. They had new yellow parkas and plenty of spirit, and they scooped up nothing whatever in the way of trophies. Their best showing was a seventh place in the boys' downhill. Jill remembered Brighton mainly as the spot where Kenny sprained his ankle and where her own boots hurt so badly that she had to tear them open seven minutes before the race and wedge in little patches of lamb's wool and sponge rubber, which she always carried with her.

A week after Brighton Jill and half the team went to Sun Valley to watch the country's very best racers in action at the famous Harriman Cup races, and to put in six days of delicious practice before the Legion Juniors.

The Harriman Cup was the first big race Jill had ever seen and it promised to be a very fine show. Among the competitors were Christian Pravda and Stein Eriksen and several other of the world's great downhill racers as well as five U.S. Olympic skiers, including Andrea Mead Lawrence and a Los Angeles girl, Sally Neidlinger, who had skied at Mammoth a number of times. Sally had been temporarily paralyzed after breaking her back in Switzerland in 1952, but she was fully recovered and skiing better than ever.

Dick Buek also was around, as Jill knew very well, and she kept hoping she would run into him.

Dave McCoy gave his young California spectators just one assignment: to watch every move made by the really hot skiers. The kids had ringside seats for the slalom because they volunteered as gatekeepers to reset poles that were taken out or knocked askew. "Just watch the top racers," Dave said. "And don't look for style, because

59

when they're in a race they just *ski!*" He took motion pictures with a borrowed camera so they could all study the race back at Mammoth.

The great lesson Jill learned was that the winners never made little mistakes. No sideslip. No lost motion. They were never lazy for a tenth of a second. A hard shove with the poles on a flat between gates. Always into the flushes high. A fast finish on every turn, whipping out of one gate already set for the next.

What shocked Jill was the sloppy form of the women. Most of them skied like old ladies, practically doubled over at the waist so their butts stuck out. The graceful skiers were not the women but the men.

Jill wanted to ski the way the men skied. Pravda and Eriksen were unbelievably swift and sure, and she would have given anything for the privilege of following either of them down a mountain. Andy Lawrence looked more like the men than like the other women when she shot by, leaving scarcely a wisp of snow on the air. To beat *that* one, Jill told Bob, you've *got* to ski like a man. Mrs. Lawrence was beaten, however; although she won the downhill, Sally took home the gold H for slalom.

Pravda won the men's downhill on a startlingly fast and dangerous course, and Dick Buek was four fifths of a second behind him.

During the week of practice at Sun Valley, Jill spoke briefly with Dick several times and caught sight of him twice with Brynhild Grasmoen. Brynhild was a beautiful girl and a beautiful skier—she had won the Silver Belt at the Sugar Bowl a few years back—and Jill heard rumors that she and Dick were engaged.

In the Legion Juniors that weekend, Jill fell in the downhill, slid for what seemed like a quarter of a mile, and missed a control gate. She scraped to a stop more or less at the feet of Sun Valley's ski school director, Sigi Engl, who was very much upset and shouted to her, "You have no *beez*ness going so fast!" In the boys' downhill, Kenny took second place, the first Legion award ever won by a Californian. Toni Milici, who was expecting to become a father within a few days, telephoned from Bishop to congratulate him and promised to name his son Kenny Lloyd Milici—providing he didn't turn out to be a daughter.

Jill went to the competitors' banquet with Spencer Eccles, who was a little wild, like Barni, and Barni went with Marvin Melville, who was a gentle-mannered Mormon from Salt Lake City. Dick Buek sat at the speakers' table with Norma Shearer and Jill received from him only a nod of recognition.

When the awards were handed out, Jill was astonished to be called to the front of the room. She was presented with the Sportsmanship Trophy, which had been awarded on the basis of votes cast by all seventy-two competitors.

Back at Mammoth after ten days of Sun Valley, Jill found herself oddly depressed about skiing. She and Bob had both been winning California races and had wanted very much to see how they compared with the best skiers in the East and Midwest. Now they knew. Jill felt she was just beginning to get up steam, and yet here she was already at the end of an era: she was seventeen and about to graduate from high school.

Bob sensed his sister's mood. "You're pretty serious, aren't you?" he said to her one Sunday morning at the top of #2.

"I guess," she answered. "Most of the kids aren't, I know. Kenny, specially. Or maybe they're serious, Bobby, but they aren't *serious*, if you know what I mean." She was thinking: Bobby's a natural and he doesn't *need* to be serious. Or Kenny, either. But *I'm* serious.

Bob said, "For me, I like skiing fine, but there's no great big . . . I dunno."

"Challenge?"

He shrugged.

When Jill was punching tickets at the tow line that afternoon Bob came by and said, with a slight grin, "You know what people always say? People always say, *If Jill Kinmont hadn't fallen, she'd have won.*"

"You mean I ought to ski better."

61

"I just meant you're *fast!*"

"*Too* fast, you mean?"

"I just meant you've got guts and you really push yourself. Me, I never fall." Bob went up the rope grinning and left his sister with a slight frown on her face.

Jill heard someone in line saying, ". . . and the crazy jerk slammed his motorcycle into a car down near Concord and he's all broke up."

Jill said, "*Who* did you say was hurt?"

"Dick Buek."

She felt the skin along her arms and the sides of her neck tightening, prickling. "How bad was it?"

"Bad. Friend of yours?"

"Kind of."

"Well, you're not going to see him on the old boards again, that's for sure. It was a head-on smash and he went *in* through the car's windshield."

Jill could not have labeled what she felt but it was a dropping sensation and a sour one. She tried to think how she could find out more about the accident. She went on punching tickets and smiling at the customers.

Ten days later she learned that Dick had been so broken and torn that he'd been expected to die. Now the doctors said he would live but would never walk again. He had more than 250 stitches in his body. He was too weak to raise his head.

One Sunday evening Dave and Roma were driving down to Bishop from their house at the dam and Jill was with them. No one had been talking about skiing . . . in fact no one had been talking at all for ten miles. Dave said, quietly but suddenly, "Jill, I think you can probably make the next FIS team."

Jill and Roma chorused one loud, immediate reply. "*What?*" Dave's statement meant that he thought Jill could make it among the top half dozen skiers in the entire United States.

"Yeah," Dave said. "If you work hard, ski hard, keep on the way you're going now. There's no reason why not."

Jill tried to pretend that this was all a very nice compliment and nothing more, but she was nearly choking. "Pa, you're *kidding*," she said, partly because she wanted to be sure he wasn't and partly because she wanted to hear it again.

Dave did not answer, and after a very long silence she said, "Well, uh . . . then, what can I do? I mean like when there's no snow all summer and all. I'll do anything that'll help, Pa."

"There's not much to it," he answered. "Exercises, push-ups, run a couple of miles a day. And it wouldn't hurt to lay out a bunch of tires on the ground like they do for football training and jump from one to the next. But with two feet, with your feet together like slalom."

Actually it was too late to try out for next year's FIS team, but the 1956 Olympics was a real possibility if Jill could concentrate on skiing for the next two seasons. So she worked out a careful argument for her parents, and at supper one evening she said, "Hey, what do you guys think about me taking time off from school and just training at Mammoth?" Before there was time for an answer she quoted Dave's estimate of her ability and outlined a logical plan of action. She could live at the McCoys' when she was training and get a job in town when she was not. If she wasn't good enough in the Olympic tryout races, she would enroll in college at once. If she did make the squad, she would postpone school until after the Games.

June and Bill Kinmont were easier to convince than Jill had anticipated, and in the end she said, "Do you think I'm being foolish? I mean, I do want to try, but maybe I haven't got the ability."

Bill said, "Well, you've got plenty of *poss*-ability, honey-girl, and if that's what you want you sure ought to give it a whirl."

Jill collected a number of old automobile tires but she put off setting up a training schedule. Her free hours in April and May were consumed by dances and river parties and riding and by weekend skiing at Mammoth. Not to mention keeping a curious eye on the bulldozer that was trying to carve out a swimming pool just south of the commissary. Bill had drawn his own plans, based upon a standardized blueprint, and he was his own engineer and foreman on the job. As with everything else on the ranch, including water supply and power and sewerage, he had no need for outside contractors. He had worked for almost two decades as a manufacturer in Los Angeles, and his ingenuity was matched by his skill with machines and tools. Jill had seen him drive a thousand nails without ever a false ring or a bent nail.

Audra Jo came home for the summer and arrived in time to graduate with her class. When the seniors marched out onto the school lawn for the ceremonies and the band pumped out *Pomp and Circumstance,* she was there with Everett Skaggs pushing her chair. She was decidedly the center of attraction that evening at the Rocking K graduation party.

The summer felt like old times in many ways, for Jill went riding regularly and Audra Jo was at the ranch almost every afternoon. The evenings were soft and beautiful, as always. The White Mountains across the valley, so dead in the noon sun, came quietly alive in the low, late light, streaked with desert colors, pink and ivory and chalky lavender across the upper slopes and purple or russet in the draws and canyons.

Jill started her own swimming school at the new ranch pool, charging $1 per person per hour. She had three or four classes every afternoon and her pupils ranged in age from twelve down to four, with the exception of a talented two-year-old named Jimmy. Some of them were avid and some were reluctant. The shy or fearful ones she coaxed into the water, playing and splashing with them until they were thoroughly at home. She also gave diving lessons.

Jill liked to push Audra Jo's wheelchair and quickly developed a skill that no one else could match. She could move very fast without seeming to rush and she could turn or stop or start quickly and smoothly. She also learned, when crossing the street, to tilt the front wheels up only a split second before they reached the curb.

Audra Jo's first trip all the way down Main Street with Jill at the helm proved to be a big event, much to the surprise of both girls. At first Jill kidded around by exaggerating her little maneuver at the curb. Two women coming toward them gasped and exchanged a volley of shocked noises. Jill switched to another little trick she had perfected: she walked beside the chair, steering and pushing it with one hand and pretending to be totally unconcerned about either the vehicle or its passenger. A woman turned from a parking meter, shook her head vigorously and made a series of little clucking sounds. This kind of response greeted them a number of times, for people seemed to think Audra Jo should have been handled like a tea wagon loaded with china. Jill settled down to a sedate pace—because she was getting tired—and reactions were as odd as before. The chair was only two feet wide, wheels and all, but the pedestrians cleared the sidewalk for half a block ahead of them. They felt like a truck.

People began coming out of stores to stare or to say hello. Older women tended to be embarrassing, and some patted Audra Jo on the head as if they were about to say something like "Poor little doggie!" One very motherly type said in a rush of syllables, "Oh, how *brave* you are, you're such a *brave brave* little girl." Jill did not understand how Audra Jo could be so polite, so charming, to all these people.

Near Line Street, which crossed Main at the very center of town, old friends from Joseph's and Dorrance's and the Piñon Bookstore gathered around the chair, clerks and shopkeepers, customers, box boys, hairdressers, a waitress from the Malt Shop. Wheeling down the last half block of Main Street took nearly an hour and Audra Jo was relieved to get back to the car. She said, "I feel a little wrung out, Jill. I had no idea people would be so upset and so damp-eyed and all. I didn't expect all this . . . you know, all this *sorrow*. It doesn't seem to bother *me* that much."

Getting into a car from a wheelchair was still something of a trick because Audra Jo hadn't had much practice and her arms were still weak. She had what she called a sliding board, a piece of wood almost three feet long with a polished surface. The procedure was to open the car door, move the wheelchair as close as possible to the front seat, and use the sliding board as a bridge. Jill shoved the board under Audra Jo's left buttock and let Audra Jo push herself across. Jill then lifted the near end of the board and slid Audra Jo into the seat, trying not to pinch her bottom. The chair she folded and put into the back of the car.

The girls spent hours thinking up things Audra Jo might be able to do and then trying them out. They had the wrangler sit her up on a horse but that was much too scary. They wheeled down the lane and into the pasture. They drove to Mammoth often, and whenever they appeared Dave stopped work and took them for a ride in a jeep or a truck or weasel. He drove them over to smell the hot tar and watch the machines paving the road from the mountain out toward the highway. He drove them up onto the mountain and he drove them down to the Devil's Postpile and he drove them to Bodie, just north of Lee Vining, to see the beautifully weathered buildings of the old ghost town. Sometimes Audra Jo just came to the ranch to do nothing. Noontime there was hot and lazy with the sound of crickets. Once the girls spotted a red and white sailplane lying high above, against the blue, on the shoulders of the Sierra wind, fragile and small and silent.

Audra Jo was invited to Horseshoe Lake, near Mammoth, to meet her favorite actress, Ann Blythe, and watch the shooting of the motion picture *Rosemarie*. Jill wanted desperately to go along, but she had a swimming class scheduled and Bill Kinmont told her, "I know you don't get a chance like this every day, sweetheart, but once you've taken on a job you don't cancel out just because you'd rather."

The Rocking K was in the middle of its busiest summer and family life was necessarily chaotic. The five Kinmonts still managed an occasional meal together, however, and June always found time to wait on her husband, serving him an early lunch in the dining room or bringing him coffee or fixing crackers and cheese or something else in

66

the way of an hors d'oeuvre whenever he had time for a can of beer before dinner. She always sat with him then or later, at sunset, to talk over the day's frustrations and satisfactions.

Jill was tied up with her usual summer activities, but skiing was also on her mind and she launched herself on a modest training program. Fifteen push-ups twice a day, thirty deep knee bends, ten one-legged knee bends on each leg while standing on a chair, half an hour of roadwork. In addition she had twelve old automobile tires laid flat on the ground up behind the house. They were staggered, and she jumped with both feet into the center of the first and hopped back and forth down the whole line. She often shifted the tires, moving them closer or farther apart or straightening out the line. Sometimes she went through the tires hopping on one leg.

She was self-conscious about these morning and evening sessions because no other skiers in Bishop trained during the summer; nor did anyone she knew of in Los Angeles. But she was soon asking Dave what else she could do, and he told her. Deep breathing, long walks, half-mile runs, quarter-mile sprints, and developing abdominal muscles by pushing a bale of hay across the corral. "The tires are the best," he said. "For wind and timing and rhythm. Go through them fast; go through them slow; start slow and then pick it up. And don't space the tires even."

Jill gradually stepped up the pace of her training schedule and this, along with her responsibilities as a waitress and swimming instructor, gobbled up the summer days.

At Homecoming Jill and Audra Jo were in the thick of the crowd that jammed eight blocks of Main Street Saturday morning. They went to the big barbecue and the goat scramble and the greased pig contest and they looked in on the carnival with its octopus and Ferris wheel and tilt-a-whirl and merry-go-round and the booths that promised garish prizes for skilled tossing of darts and baseballs.

The rodeo itself took place Sunday and Monday at the rodeo grounds at the north end of Main Street. The whole valley took on a charge of expectation when the band struck up for the Grand Entry. The competitors circled the arena and lined up across the center for the Riding of the Colors. An American flag appeared at one end of the line and a California Bear flag at the other, each held high by one of the two pickup men. The music stopped, the drums rolled, and the two riders broke, taking off at a gallop in opposite directions around the edge of the arena, their flags snapping and cracking behind them. They thundered toward each other on the south side of the arena, head on, but they swerved, passed, spun around and came to a dead stop squarely in front of the grandstand.

Then began the real business of the day: bareback bronc riding, saddle bronc riding, team roping, calf roping, bulldogging, bull riding. Jill and Audra Jo still had their hot and dirty private box down by the chutes, although they were more alert than they'd been in the old days. Whenever an animal lowered his head and started moving in their direction, Jill screamed, "Duck!" and rolled the wheelchair madly back underneath the bandstand.

Audra Jo returned to Los Angeles immediately after Labor Day and Jill enrolled in two postgraduate secretarial courses at the high school.

One morning she was sitting on the couch in the dining room knitting to fill in the time between breakfast and the school bus. Her mother looked in from the kitchen and said, "Did you hear something a minute ago?"

"No. What?"

"It sounded like . . . well, the tractor. But I'm sure it wasn't."

Jill glanced out the door after a dozen more stitches. She could see part of the south pasture beyond the shallow end of the swimming pool, and she noticed something moving. She whispered, mostly to herself, "What's *that* coming across the field?"

What she saw was undoubtedly a man although he was walking in a strange, almost primitive manner. Both legs seemed permanently bent at the knees, and he moved with long, uneven strides, his arms loose and his hands hanging nearly to his knees. He vaulted the fence and came up the lane between the swimming pool and the upper pond.

Jill's knitting slipped from her hands and she cried out, *"That's Dick Buek!"*

Dick had never seen the Rocking K before, but he came straight toward the dining room. He was apparently healthy and obviously very much on his feet again. Jill sat back on the couch and picked up her knitting and tried to remember what she had been doing with it. Coming to see her was *the* Dick Buek, daredevil, Olympic skier, downhill champion, Mad Dog.

Dick knocked on the screen door and Jill let him in. He was wearing greasy levis that hung on his hips and a dark-blue ski sweater over a faded blue shirt. His straight brown hair stuck up at one side. His face looked just as Jill had remembered it except for the long curved scar that creased his cheek and added a distinctive coarseness to his features. His lips were thin and white, stretched across very large front teeth. Jerry Kinmont appeared at the door staring wide-eyed and biting the inside of his cheek.

Jill said, "Dick, hell*o*, where did you *come* from, how did you *get* here, this is my mother and, Mom, this is Dick, and this is Jerry, here."

"Nice to meet you," Dick said with an easy smile. His small, greenish-blue eyes narrowed when he smiled and seemed to turn up at the outer corners. "I left the plane down on the road, if that's okay."

"Oh, *really?* You . . . gee, sure that's okay. I mean as long as nobody hits it. But I thought you couldn't walk and you'd be in the hospital for years."

"I sneaked out."

"Will you have breakfast? A terrible thing is . . . I've got to leave for school in ten minutes."

Dick shrugged. "I'll drive you if there's a car."

June Kinmont said, "It's nice to see you, Dick. Would you like some coffee?" He shook his head. Jill said, "There's a john over at the commissary, Dick, if you want to wash up. Jerry'll show you."

Dick limped out the door at Jerry's heels, and Jerry returned in a minute to whisper in a loud, admiring voice, "Gee, doesn't Dick have a neat walk!" He gave a reasonably accurate demonstration while Dick was still out, bending both knees, swinging his arms and walking with an off-beat *thump*.

Jill was still pretending to knit, making little knots and undoing them. She whispered, "Mom, what do you *think* of him? Isn't he *in*teresting?"

June suppressed a smile. "He's a very unusual young man," she said. She was thinking not only of his gait and his clothing but of the fact that he was a good seven years older than her daughter and that he had a reputation for flying planes and driving motorcycles with the same blend of skill and abandon that he showed on skis.

When Dick returned, Jerry said with great enthusiasm, "Dick, you really got crashed up that time, didn't you?"

Dick described his accident: head, leg and internal injuries. They'd taken out his spleen and rebuilt a shattered kneecap. One of the operations had lasted six hours and they'd thought he wouldn't make it. His left leg had been badly mangled and it was now impossible to straighten it beyond an angle of about 115 degrees. He said it was easier to walk if he kept his good leg bent at the same angle.

"Did the doctors really say you couldn't ever ski again?" Jill asked.

"Yes, really, they said that."

Jerry said, "Because your knees won't work, huh?"

"Get me a piece of Kleenex," Dick said, and when Jerry brought it he crumpled it slightly and dropped it on the floor at his feet. He raised his bad leg off the carpet, leaned forward and spread his arms. Then he went down, balancing on his right leg, and picked up the Kleenex in his teeth.

Dick drove Jill to school and called for her again after her classes. "Hi," he said as nonchalantly as if he'd been chauffeuring her since kindergarten. "Want to go for a ride?"

70

"Oh, *yes*, I want to go for a ride."

They drove back to the ranch and ran down across the south pasture to the county road. The Piper Cub was just off the pavement and Dick walked around it slowly, critically. He kicked the tires and he ran the flat of his hand again and again along the wing and fuselage, stroking the fabric.

"Patches seem to be holding," he said. "Hop in."

The door creaked like an old porch swing. Dick helped her in, closed the door, wired it shut, and said, "Lean over and turn on the ignition." He spun the propeller until the engine caught and then ran around and climbed inside.

The plane moved forward toward the middle of the road and let loose with a blast of power which turned it 90 degrees and raised a whirlwind of dust. It taxied south up a slight grade and then roared forward, lifting off the roadway and circling east over the dump.

Jill had her face and both hands against the window. She had never flown before and now suddenly all the little familiar, isolated sections of the world of Bishop were there below, fitted together, tilting beneath her and all now of a single piece. Dick circled for altitude and Bishop became a flat patchwork painted onto the valley floor. Paved roads were pen lines. Dirt roads were white like the cracks in pond ice. The ranch was a splotch of dark trees on a tan desert.

When Jill looked up she caught her breath because the mountains were directly in front of the plane. They looked bigger and higher than they had from the ranch 5,000 feet below and she had to lean forward and look up to see the tops.

Close in under the jagged face of Basin Mountain the plane hit rough air. Dick banked sharply and headed back, flying straight out over the valley. When he was directly above Bishop he nosed down and said quietly, "Hang on, kiddo." Jill heard the engine whine and she squeezed her eyes shut as she felt her body being pressed heavily into the seat. When she opened her eyes the ground ahead had disappeared. A little white cloud came from above and dropped down past the nose. Then, with

71

a smashing shock to her eyes, something huge and dark and flat appeared from above and fell in front of the plane like a curtain and she began to float up out of her seat. Suddenly the horizon appeared and the engine quieted and her weight returned and everything was refreshingly normal. She glanced sideways at Dick and blew out a long slow breath. "So that was a loop, huh?"

They landed, parked the plane, and hiked up to the ranch.

The rest of the afternoon they spent at the swimming pool. Jill felt awkward at first because she couldn't think of anything to say. Then she realized that it was perfectly comfortable to be with Dick and say nothing at all. They were both standing in the shallow end of the pool and she became acutely conscious of the marks that Dick's accident had left on his body. She was careful not to stare at them: a little S-shaped scar on his shoulder, a long purple slash across his stomach, a crooked left leg that was half as thick as the right one.

"Go ahead and look," he said, his pale eyes squinting in the sun. "No charge."

She said, "You know, I felt pretty awful when I heard about your crash and all. Maybe I was extra upset because I've got a friend who won't be skiing any more. Or walking, even, and that's for sure."

"Automobile accident?"

"Polio. And of all the people in the world who didn't deserve that, she didn't deserve it the most, if you know what I mean."

"Was this someone you knew well, or just somebody you knew?"

"My best friend."

Dick pulled himself out of the water and sat on the edge of the pool for a long while, his shoulders hunched and his hands together between his knees. Jill was surprised to notice how stubby his hands and fingers were . . . and that the tip of one little finger was missing. He said, "I guess I know what you're talking about. Ever hear of Jimmy Griffith?"

72

"Uh-huh. He crashed at Alta or something. Good friend?"

"I skied with him at Sun Valley all the time. I don't know if I ever had a best friend, but if I did, he was it. He was U.S. downhill champion three years ago. He was training for the Games at Alta and he slammed into a tree and died in a Salt Lake hospital three days later. He was a hemophiliac."

Jill was listening as much to the sound of Dick Buek's talk as to what he was saying. He seemed cool and casual, but there were cracks and rough edges in his voice and when he looked around at her his eyes were glistening. She was surprised to find him this sensitive and even more surprised that he didn't try to disguise it.

"I can't believe there's a God," he said. "Not when something like that can happen. Jimmy had so God-damned much to give to the world. He was studying to be a doctor. And he has a little accident . . . it wasn't much, really . . . and he's dead. And here *I* am, with nothing. Tenth-grade education. So I'm going *no*where. And I do all kinds of crackpot things and I come out of it like *so what*. Why am *I* the jerk that survives? I can't under*stand* why these things happen."

Both were silent for a long time. Jill said, "You ought to know Audra Jo. She's a great person. She told me that the main thing was, it forced her to grow up. And she doesn't seem to be bitter about . . . oh, you know, about skiing, dates, dancing, walking, riding, going places. I don't know how she does it. *I sure* couldn't. How does a person manage something like that?"

"Beats me," he said and shrugged. Jill realized that he had in fact just gone through something similar . . . at least he must have gone through it when he was first in the hospital and they'd told him he wasn't going to walk again.

Early the next morning Dick left the Rocking K with a wave of thanks . . . and a shrug when Jill asked when he might turn up again. Jerry squinted into the sun to watch him take off and then strode up across the pasture with both knees bent and his arms hanging.

6

THAT FALL JILL WORKED AT MAMMOTH ON WEEKENDS checking skis and polishing boots for the rental shop and helping to paint the new porch at the front of the warming hut and the new sun deck on the roof. Every afternoon she followed her dry-land training schedule and was now up to 50 one-legged deep knee bends on each leg. She walked every day in the hills behind the ranch. She went barefoot to toughen her feet. She practiced slaloming down between clumps of sage on every slope and hummock she came upon. The physical effort she didn't mind, but her social life suffered. Training meant going to bed around nine most evenings and it meant no cigarettes and no beer. She was quite stuffy about it, as a matter of fact, for she didn't even want her dates to smoke or drink.

Bill Kinmont was up in the White Mountains three days a week as a guide, running a deer camp for hunters who were ferried in from the Rocking K by the owner of the local flying service, Bob Symons. On Columbus Day, after packing a 150-pound buck three miles into camp on his back, Bill was jolted with severe pains in his arm and chest. Symons gave him oxygen and flew him down out of the mountains. It had been a mild heart attack and it put Bill in the hospital for a week and ruled out all physical exertion for six months.

Later in October Dave McCoy resigned from the Los Angeles Water Department and moved his family from the dam into the old warming hut at McGee Mountain. Mammoth had become a full-time job and profitable enough that Dave could support his family on the proceeds. In November Jill moved in with the McCoys, taking along her skis and ski clothes and a pair of Levis and not much else. She even left at home a photograph of Dick on which he had written *Mad Dog trying to turn*.

The former warming hut had a lower story which Dave partitioned into four very plain bedrooms. And there was now a bathroom, which was a welcome addition. The main floor was still one big open room with windows all across the west side and a sunken fireplace at the south end. A kitchen had been built into the northeast corner and partly walled off by a long counter with stools in front of it. The stove was a big black affair which burned butane. There were several large rocking chairs and a couch covered with plastic. Roma had made ruffled curtains and ruffled lamp shades and a braided rag rug. Ski boots were always drying by the fireplace and toys were everywhere.

There were now six McCoy children—Gary, Poncho, and P-nut; the two girls, Penny and Kandi, and a baby, Randy, who was two weeks old when Jill arrived.

Jill slept on a mattress in front of the fireplace and she helped Roma with whatever chores needed to be done: housework, child feeding, trash burning, cooking.

On weekends Dave whipped out breakfast while Roma got the kids dressed in relatively winterproof clothing. Roma put together a lunch and everyone piled into the car for the 20-mile drive up to Mammoth.

Only Jill and Dave went to Mammoth on school days, and Jill worked in or around the warming hut until Dave was able to get out on the hill. On skis, Jill concentrated on slalom, studying whatever course Dave set for her, memorizing it, figuring just how she wanted to take each gate. She ran it three or four times and when she had trouble she climbed back up to study her tracks.

One afternoon Dave set Jill a 20-gate flush, a single line of poles requiring 20 tight, linked turns. Jill managed eight gates with finesse and after that she began having trouble. Dave was waiting at the bottom, watching. Jill said, before she had even come to a stop, "Pa, I was late in the gate half the time. What was I *doing*? I *tried* to keep high."

"You're turning too much. You don't want to hang

onto your turn so long. It leaves you out of position for the next one. Besides, it slows you down." He drew a snaky line in the snow with the tip of his pole, and next to it he drew an almost straight line which had the same number of curves, but very shallow ones. "And look at the distance you save," he said, staring directly at her, frowning, his jaw jutting forward. "When you make big fat 180-degree turns, what happens?"

"Yeah, I see what you mean."

"You travel twice as far. Why waste the energy if you don't have to?"

Jill ran the long flush again with a determined scowl on her face. She was perfectly capable of making nice, tight, slight turns and she wanted Dave to know she could do it twenty times in succession without a slip. In the 15th gate she fell.

"Hey, don't be so serious," Dave called up to her in a serious voice.

Jill sat in the snow, ashamed for a moment, and then she remembered how *serious* Dave always was about having *fun*. She lay back in the snow and laughed.

"Let's go down and have some soda pop," he said. "I'll race you."

One Saturday the boys spent all morning with Dave building bumps east of the Face on a run they called Bowling Alley. They shoveled and packed until they had constructed a series of high rolling hillocks and a whole range of smaller, sharper bumps. After lunch the boys and Jill and Linda started pounding down across the bumps, first slow and easy, then faster and faster. Off the first bump and land on the downhill side of the second. Into the air on the first and land on the downhill side of the third. Prejumping every bump in order to *keep* from flying into the air. "Always keep your skis flat on the snow as much as you can," Dave said. "They're fastest when they're *on* the snow and *flat*."

In slalom practice, one of the most difficult lessons was learning to carve each turn precisely. Every unnecessary bit of pressure on your edges slows you and tires you.

Snow spraying out from beneath your skis may make a lovely photograph, but it is a sign of unwanted, wasted motion. The same principle holds in diving, as Jill had learned long ago from watching Bob and her father: the better the dive the smaller the splash.

Dave taught her important little tricks about weighting her skis, and these were not easy to master. She was thoroughly familiar with leaning forward, pressing her tips into the snow for control when beginning a turn or when checking. And she knew from unhappy experience that too much of this good thing could make the tips dig in and throw her. But she felt awkward about leaning *back* when coming out of a gate in order to reduce friction and pick up speed. It was also hard for her to ski with her weight dead center, which was a good position if she wanted to knock out a train of quick little turns.

The only continually unpleasant thing about skiing was the awful business of boots. Jill had spent a considerable amount of time searching for the right boots, but her feet still ached whenever she laced them up. She always had blisters or sores at the points of her ankles or just above the backs of her heels. She made little sponge rubber triangles and felt doughnuts to protect the sore spots. She wore thick, soft socks. But she never dared lace her boots really tight. Standing in the starting gate she sometimes had the unhappy feeling that her feet were swimming in her boots, no more than vaguely connected to her skis.

Buying skis was just as complicated as buying boots, although the results were more satisfying. Jill had seven-foot Stein Eriksen downhill skis and very limber Northlands, about four inches shorter, for slalom. Dave did not go for the usual stiff ski that would distribute the skier's weight along its entire length. He believed in a flexible ski that would put greater pressure on the snow near its center and therefore carve into the snow somewhat in the manner of a figure skate on ice. The ski also had to have a soft tip that could more or less *feel* its way, riding over the snow rather than shoving against it as a rigid tip tends to do. "It's like a blind man in the woods," he said. "With a heavy cane, all he can feel is rocks and trees. If he has a limber stick he can feel twigs and bushes and even the tall grass." It was not easy to find limber skis and it was not easy to find skis without expensive edges made of spring steel. Dave wanted Jill to have edges of mild steel which could be easily burred with a file before a race, giving them a feathered edge under the boot so they would grip better on ice and very hard snow.

The Mammoth skiers went into the 1954 season in good form, and Dave never missed a chance to show them something new. On the way to Big Bear the highway dips and rises through rolling hills south of China Lake, and Dave said, "Watch what we're doing. Can you feel how we lift off the springs going over the knolls and press down in the troughs? If you just *ride* it that way you're going to go into the air and lose contact with the snow and lose control. But if you can make your springs rise up in the troughs and sink on the high spots, then you're able to level out the terrain for yourself."

At Dodge Ridge in mid-January, Bob Kinmont won the boys' slalom and downhill, both. The girls raced the same slalom course, and Jill won with a run that was four seconds faster than her brother's. Second place went to Linda Meyers, which was even a greater surprise. Linda had fought her way desperately through every gate, and when she heard she had placed second to Jill she blushed and grinned and her eyes shone as if all her best dreams had come true. She stood in front of Jill, beaming and fidgeting with Kenny Lloyd's class ring, which hung from a gold chain around her neck. "Boy, I really came down that thing full bore," she said.

Linda was about five feet five now and still a bit chunky. She had been pushing herself constantly and, like Jill, had become good enough to race within two years of first learning to ski. She still skied with more doggedness than grace, but she had come a lot further in a short time than anyone had realized until this weekend.

Jill and Bob won or placed in race after race. They earned sports-page headlines in Los Angeles—the third

78

week it was just KINMONTS AGAIN—and they were the leading racers chosen to represent the Far West at the Junior Nationals at Jackson, Wyoming. Jill was also invited to race at Aspen in the *Nationals*—that is, the national *senior* championships, which was probably the most important single race in the country. She was excited about Aspen, of course, but it was Jackson that concerned her; no young skier with dreams about Olympic competition could afford not to win or place in the Junior Nationals.

Jill decided to focus on downhill during her last week at Mammoth, and she spent an entire morning on the Face, deliberately taking on all the rough spots she could find. After lunch she rode up the tow with Toni Milici while Dave stayed below on the sun deck, watching. At the top they stood together silently looking out toward Deadman Pass and the rugged mounds of snow-covered lava just west of it. Jill bent over, wiped the snow off her ski tips, and slid her skis quickly back and forth to free any ice that might be stuck to the edges. Toni said, "Jill, you're looking pretty hot. Why don't you schuss it?"

Toni was only teasing her, and she knew it, so she returned the tease by taking him seriously. She looked around at him, nodded, picked up one ski and skated off straight down the mountain. Toni whispered *"Jesus!"* as he watched her pick up speed, running parallel to the #2 towline and taking the brutal shock of the bumps in her knees. Her form wasn't much—hunched, with her arms out and her feet apart for stability—but she obviously knew what she was doing.

She was making 45 or 50 miles an hour by the time she reached the smoother, shallower slope halfway down along the lower tow. She made one long fast turn to the right and then whipped to a stop ten feet from the sun deck. She glanced at Dave and turned to look up at Toni's miniature silhouette high above on the mountain. She waved one pole and laughed as she skated over to the bottom of the tow. Dave remarked the exploit with a nod and a one-sided grin.

After that Jill schussed everything she could find.

Straight down the Face again. Straight down Bowling Alley. Down through the woods, down across bumps, down over the icy corners scraped bare by the weekend crowd. She schussed easy slopes and rough slopes and sane drop-offs and crazy pitches. Whatever she might run up against at Jackson or at Aspen, if she could compare it with something she had already run fast and hard at Mammoth, then it wouldn't seem like so much of a gamble. She clocked herself at 55 miles an hour down the Face, and some of her runs were undoubtedly faster than that.

On February 27 the Kinmont family left at 4 A.M. on the 750-mile drive to Wyoming, arriving the following afternoon. Jackson was a little western town with wooden sidewalks and arcades, and it was built around a square. Strung across the main street was a great banner which said WELCOME JUNIOR SKIERS.

The five girls and ten boys of the Far West team were put up at a motel near the chairlift at the base of Snow King Mountain, and they immediately transformed a heated garage into a waxing room. Waxing was a chore usually performed in the evening. The bottoms of the skis had to be chipped and scraped clean with a pocket knife or a scraper. A base wax was ironed on with June Kinmont's battered and wax-stained traveling iron and then buffed by hand or with a cork. A second coat was ironed on over the base, and then a third coat and perhaps a fourth. If snow conditions changed or if there were an afternoon race, skis were waxed during the day. Wet skis had to be wiped with a shirt or sweater and allowed to dry before Dave could paint on the hot mixture he regularly concocted in his bent old coffee pot.

The temperature at Jackson was consistently below zero and on the first morning both Jill and Bob returned to the motel to put on a second pair of ski pants. The chairlift was a primitive and creaky thing that appeared to have been strung together from parts of an old mine tramway. It was long and steep, with a vertical rise of 2,000 feet, and the view from the top was spectacular. Out to the west was the white bulk of the Tetons and

80

directly below was the town, a grid of straight streets with an irregular perimeter that gave it the look of a waffle made without enough batter.

There were six days of practice before the race. The Far West skiers stuck together most of the time, criticizing each other and discussing in detail how to run the new mile-and-two-tenths downhill course which had been laid out the previous summer especially for the Junior Nationals. Once they had the downhill memorized, Dave had them concentrate on slalom. The official course would not be set until the day before the race, but each of the seven regional teams set its own practice course. The Far West skiers were accustomed to varied runs full of interesting hairpins and flushes and corridors and open gates that swung the course back and forth across the hill. Dave noticed with some alarm that the local skiers and the competitors from the East were practicing on tight, linear courses with the flags running downhill in a nearly straight line. This kind of course could change the whole pace of a race. Dave set a similar slalom and made everyone work on timing.

Riding up on the lift the day before the downhill, Jill turned and called to Bob, who was on the chair behind her, "Dave thinks I look okay, Bobby. I mean he thinks I ought to do pretty well if I feel good and if we can hit the right wax and all." To Bob this was just a roundabout way of saying *I'm going to win, y'know*. Bob himself didn't think in terms of winning races. He liked to race and he liked the tuned-in feeling he had when everything was working. Either you ran a course right or you fouled it up, and he always wanted to run it right.

The downhill was on Saturday, a day that was sunny and clear but so cold that it pinched Jill's nostrils at every breath. Before the race the teams from the seven divisions of the National Ski Association paraded on the flat and a band played for a formal flag-raising ceremony.

Jill was slightly anxious and was aware of occasional sharp pains from blisters at the backs of her heels. She was the sixteenth racer to start. Her stomach fluttered as she stood in the gate but a wink from the chief starter made her smile; he was Dick Movitz from Salt Lake City, a veteran of the 1948 Games, and he knew better than she how it felt to stand there waiting for the *five-four-three-two-one-Go*. Dave McCoy gave her a grin and a wave just before she shoved off.

The run began with a series of short pitches which sent her very fast down into a long, sloping meadow. Next came a knoll and a steep drop with high bumps at the bottom, after which she shot out across the flat below at a speed that would have scared her a month earlier. The later turns and the final open hill down to the finish line were no problem, although she almost fell from simple exhaustion as she wheeled to a stop beside the big blackboard where the results were posted. The best time so far was Teresa Schwaegler of Yakima, who was away ahead with a time of 1 minute 19.1 seconds. A moment later a voice on the public address system said, "Jill Kinmont, FWSA, 1 minute 22.2 seconds." Jill skied laboriously over to the sidelines. She spotted her mother in the crowd and waved a glove at her without smiling.

None of the remaining girls did as well as Jill, so her second place held. In the boys' downhill Bob Kinmont placed twelfth.

Sunday's race was a two-run slalom, with awards based on the total time for both runs. There were two courses set side by side a hundred or more yards apart, both of them fast and difficult but without any deliberately tricky combinations. There were no spots where a reckless skier might shave off a whole second by taking a chance, so the race would likely go to a consistently fast and precise competitor who was able to save just a few hundredths of a second in each and every gate.

Jill climbed slowly up alongside the first course, studying, memorizing, lining up each pair of flags in turn with the care of a dart thrower sighting a target. And when she ran, finally, she started fast and took each gate exactly as she'd planned. Her timing was so right that she forgot about timing. She was conscious only of the rhythm of her body and the feel of her skis carving into the snow and the look of what was going to be her line through the gates ahead. She finished neatly with a quick turn and a sigh.

Jill's time on the first run put her ahead of all the girls and most of the boys. Bob was half a second faster and his teammates accused him of worrying more about keeping ahead of his sister than about beating the boys.

Jill was tense waiting for the second run, but there was really less at stake now than there had been before. She knew what she could do and how to do it, and she was already in the lead. She spoke to no one. She closed her eyes and thought her way down the second course many times. She was nervous in the starting gate, but once under way she felt fast and at the same time wonderfully unhurried.

Her total time for two runs was 89.8 seconds. None of the girls could match it, and neither could the first nine boys, who were among the best. The tenth boy to come down was Bob Kinmont. Jill was waiting for him, and when he finished she beat him joyfully on the shoulder with her mittens. His total time was 88 seconds flat, and it gave him first place in the boys' slalom.

Jill's reaction to her own win was mainly a sense of relief. She had survived the obligatory first round. She was now an acceptable competitor in any race and certainly one to be reckoned with. She reflected upon the fact that she had just turned eighteen and it was less than two years until the 1956 Olympics, at which time she would still be nineteen years of age. She said calmly to herself: "When Andy was nineteen and I was fifteen, she won all the gold medals in Europe, and that is just what I have decided to do."

7

THE NATIONAL DOWNHILL AND SLALOM CHAMPION-
ships were scheduled the very next weekend at Aspen,
Colorado. They were combined this year with Aspen's
traditional Roch Cup, which included giant slalom as well
as slalom and downhill. Jill found a ride directly to Aspen
while the rest of the family and Dave returned to Bishop.
Dave and Bill Kinmont, who was now chairman of the
FWSA's Junior Competition Committee, would drive to
Colorado a day or so later.

Jill checked into the dormitory at Aspen's Roaring
Forks Inn late in the afternoon and Barni Davenport was
there to greet her, sitting cross-legged in the middle of
her bed in ski pants and a t-shirt, combing her hair. "My
God, Jill," she said at once, "wait till you see the *'women'*
racing in this thing. They have legs like *this*." She en-
circled an imaginary elephant's leg with her hands and
looked up, her eyes green and bright under beautifully
curled lashes that Jill wished she could imitate. "That's
be*low* the knees. And with knickers and knee socks on
. . . *brother!*"

"I get the picture, Barn, but can they *ski?*"

"They have absolutely *no fear*, Jill. They aren't a bit
afraid of the downhill, and it's the hairiest downhill you've
ever seen. I'm out of my *mind* to be here!"

Jill didn't feel it was going to be exactly a breeze, either.
In fact, the very idea of racing in the Nationals was a little
unbelievable. She had never before raced in any kind of
national senior competition and the Harriman Cup was
the only one she'd ever seen. Now she was entered in
what was probably the most important single race in
the United States.

84

She went out for a walk and was wandering down Aspen's main drag for the first time in two years when she spotted a familiar figure—Dick Buek, still walking with bent knees but taking long strides and looking less awkward than he had six months before. He carried ski poles and used them as if he were skiing. Jill waited until he saw her and then she felt so shy that she said only, "Hello."

Dick stopped in front of her and leaned forward heavily, resting his chin on his poles. "Pretty nice going at Jackson," he said.

"Thanks. How's the leg?"

"No sweat."

He seemed to be on his way somewhere, so she said, "Well, we'll see you around, huh?"

"That's right." He nodded and shuffled off.

The next morning she ran into him again and he asked her to ski with him. She was delighted, although she wondered how he would make it with his bad leg.

After one run—she'd had no opportunity to talk to him until it was over—she said, "Look, I'm going to leave if you don't promise to make at least a *turn* or something between the top and the bottom." His speed had surprised her to the point of making her wince, for every bump must have torn painfully at the scarred tendons. She was also surprised at his style, which was totally different from her own neat, deliberate actions. Dick skied so casually that you felt he must be thinking about something else . . . and quite possibly he was.

Later, when they parted, Jill said, "I guess you're planning to race *any*way, so I won't say anything. But couldn't you really wreck your leg, the way it is?"

Dick shrugged. "No problem. I brought my cast along and I'm going to put it back on for the downhill so I won't stretch anything out of shape. Have a great run yourself." He loped off down the street bearing his skis lightly across his right shoulder but maneuvering his poles like a crutch with his left hand. Jill felt unsettled and did not know whether this feeling was due to admiration or exasperation or affection.

At the lodge café next morning Jill spotted Andrea Mead Lawrence, who was wearing a big parka that hung to her hips and was obviously pregnant. Her long dark-brown hair was tied back with a ribbon and made her look like a young girl. In the middle of breakfast Mrs. Lawrence strode over to Jill's table and said, "You did a fine job at Jackson last weekend. Congratulations. Great going." She had a low, masculine voice that was friendly but matter-of-fact.

"Thank you," Jill said with a shy smile.

Throughout the rest of the meal Jill was perfectly calm and cool, but later she said to Barni with explosive enthusiasm, "Boy, was I surprised she knew who I was! Fantastic! She's never seen me before. Gads, she really is too much, isn't she!"

The three days of competition were to begin Friday with the giant slalom, followed on Saturday by the National Downhill Championship and on Sunday by the National Slalom Championship.

Friday was a depressing day, cold and foggy. Forty-five women were entered in the race, and Jill was given the choice spot, running number one, in recognition of her victory at Jackson. This added to her embarrassment when she fell and barely managed to keep from sliding past a pair of flags. She fell a second and then a third time. She placed 14th and Barni placed 12th.

In the men's event, where the competition was very rough, Dick Buek took fifth place. When Jill heard this she had a lumpy and confused sensation of pride and wonder, and she was not alone in remembering the medical verdict of eight months ago.

Jill had no alarm clock, but two alarms let go in the dorm shortly before seven on Saturday morning. She crawled from her bunk reluctantly and dressed—long, two-ply red underwear, two pairs of socks, white turtle-neck sweater and black Bogner stretch pants. She went sockfoot down the hall to the bathroom, comb and toothbrush and towel in hand. Then came the uncomfortable chore of padding her ankles with sponge rubber and pulling on her boots, which she laced very loosely. She and Barni hiked over to the cafeteria near the lift to meet Dave, who had come in Thursday evening. They all talked about the weather—it was a good day—and joked feebly about the threatening one-and-seven-tenths miles of downhill racecourse awaiting them. Jill felt uneasy and ate nothing but toast and hot chocolate.

Dave said, "That's not enough food before a big race."

"Maybe not, but I'd rather keep down a slice of toast than lose a whole breakfast."

After breakfast they all worked on their skis, although Dave had already done most of the job for the two girls. The skis had stood outside all night, each pair neatly clipped together with waxed paper between. About 9:30 the competitors began tightening their boots and picking up their racing numbers. Then up the lift at ten.

The day was clear, sunny and very cold, with six inches of fine new powder. Jill was the third racer to run and she felt quite at home on the course except for one knoll that she took on the wrong side. She had forgotten what was below it and she ran off into the untracked powder on the far edge. She sweated out the rest of the run and her legs were spaghetti when she slid through the finish gate. She turned in the third best time of the day, earning a bronze medal for herself as a downhill racer in her first national senior competition.

In the men's event that followed, the best downhill racer in the nation proved to be Dick Buek, who raced with his left leg in a cast and pretty well undermined the considered prediction of at least two orthopedic surgeons.

Many people said, as if it were a matter of secret potions and magical powers, "But how could he possibly do it?" Jill often thought, and once said, ". . . because he can ski, that's how."

As soon as possible after the race Jill changed skis and went up to study the courses which had been set for Sunday's two-run slalom. The whole slope was smothered with moguls—those mounds and humps and loaves of snow which are left when thousands of skiers follow the same deepening grooves day after day—and the moguls were rock hard everywhere and icy in spots. The edge of Jill's skis seemed to be made of butter and she said to Dave, "Pa, I've got to do something. These skis don't hold."

"Then we'll fix 'em."

So Dave spent the evening filing Jill's edges, honing them razor sharp and then burring them slightly under the foot.

Sunday morning was bitter cold again but visibility was fine. Jill had both courses clearly in mind and the first one memorized in detail. While lying in her bunk before breakfast she had rehearsed many times the line she planned to take in the first run. There were 42 gates and no major problems, but it would be fairly rough because some gates were set right across the tops of big moguls and some were set deep in the gullies between them.

Jill climbed slowly up alongside the snapping red and blue and yellow slalom flags. She wanted very much to come into the pre-Olympic season next year with a title, but she knew she was going to have to hit something better than the comfortable speed she felt at ease with. When she reached the start she studied the faces of the other racers. *They* seemed to have no qualms whatever.

Andy Lawrence was forerunner, in spite of the fact that she was almost seven months pregnant, and she opened the course with a beautiful run which Jill was able to watch all the way.

As the starter began his countdown for Jill, she said aloud, "Well, good luck, Old Jill," and glanced around for a last reassuring nod from Dave. Once moving, she fought the course all the way, skiing too fast between gates, having to turn too sharply, sliding low in the tight gates and maintaining a form she knew must have looked like a hooked trout up on the rocks. She was fighting mad— at herself, at the course. Several gates from the bottom she lost her grip on her right ski pole, which dragged from her wrist and slammed against a slalom pole, knocking her off balance.

She finished ungracefully with a grunt of effort and a

groan of disappointment. She had tried too hard. Nothing had felt *right;* things hadn't been *working.*

She was leaning forward on her poles just below the finish flags, trying to catch her breath, when she heard a voice at her ear: *"Congratulations!"* It was Andy, and Jill turned to frown at her. Jill said, with no false modesty, "Oh, it was the sloppiest race I've ever run!"

Andy answered, "You may have thought it was sloppy, but you certainly didn't waste any time."

Dave, who had just come down along the side of the course, skied over and said, "Great. You made it look like you know how to ski." Bill Kinmont was there, beaming, and he said, "Honeygirl, you've got it made."

When the first run was completed, Jill Kinmont was leading the field by a margin of three seconds, a gigantic margin in a national slalom championship. Dave told her, "You have three seconds on the other girls. Now for the next one . . . just ski it smooth and pretty; all you got to do is stand up."

Jill smiled and said nothing. She thought of what Bob had told her once: *People always say if Jill Kinmont hadn't fallen she'd have won.*

The second run went well, neater than the first and not as fast, but fast enough. Jill's time—the total for the two runs together—was the best time of all and it earned her a gold medal as women's amateur slalom champion of the United States. She was awarded a second gold medal as national *open* slalom champion since she had beaten all the professional skiers in the race as well as the amateurs. In addition, she had a pair of bronze medals for her downhill performance and a pair of silver medals for having the second best combined downhill-and-slalom score in both the amateur and open classes.

Jill had mixed feelings about the fact that she and Dick had just become two of the year's four national ski champions. Dick's victory was something totally different from her own. She was a dark horse making her first splash, so to speak. He was an old hand who'd crashed and burned and—everybody said—been put on the shelf; he'd turned up again, bent out of shape but asking no quarter, and done the hardest thing of all, made a comeback, come all the way back up to the very top.

Jill had trained long and hard for this victory but she was not at all convinced that she deserved it. She said quietly to Dave before the banquet, "But the *really* big ones weren't racing, Pa. Andy's having babies and the rest of the U.S. team is in Sweden. Jannette Burr and Katy Rodolph. And Skeeter Werner. And Imogene Upton had to go back to college."

Dave was grinning, studying her curiously with his pale-blue eyes. "Fair enough," he said. "You'll have your chance. And you've got just about everything working for you. Your technique's great. Physically, you haven't a flaw. You've got the spirit for it. And on top of all that you're a real cool one and you're never going to panic in a pinch."

"And what have I *not* got?"

"You've got everything but confidence, and that's just because you're still young. You need a lot of competitive seasoning, and you've got plenty of opportunity, now, for *that*."

"But my *skiing*, Pa . . ."

"There's nothing going to improve your skiing outside of some more victories."

8

Friends in bishop congratulated jill warmly when she stopped over at the Rocking K between races, although most of them were a week behind in the sports news. The latest *Inyo Register* had a four-column front-page story about Jackson with photographs and the headline

JILL, BOB KINMONT WIN NATIONAL TITLES

Jill was off in the morning for the Harriman Cup races at Sun Valley, where she roomed with Barni and Barni's friend, Ann Roberts. On the first evening she asked Barni how to curl her eyelashes and Barni taught her.

Dick Buek was in Sun Valley but he hurt his bad leg in a wicked spill on the racecourse. When the girls heard about it, Ann asked Jill how well she knew Dick.

"He's a good friend, Annie. I mean . . . you know . . ."

Barni said, "I know." Her bright green eyes were fixed on Jill. She raised her eyebrows, and her lips curved as if she were about to break into a grin.

"Well, yeah," Jill said. "But that's not like I was going to *marry* him or something." She whistled. "Gads, can you picture my folks if I brought Dick in and said *Meet your future son-in-law!*"

Ann said, "Well, anyway, Jill, I think you're very courageous to let yourself become so fond of him."

"Am I *that* fond of him? I mean, is that what people think? Because I'm not just sure *what* it is I feel about him."

On the evening after Dick's crash Jill said to Barni,

"Let's go over to the hospital." But she didn't move; she only added, "Geez, I wish I had enough nerve."

"Nerve?" Barni started to laugh. Instead, she said softly, "What *is* there about the Mad Dog . . . ?"

Jill shrugged. "I don't know, really. I feel as if I don't know who he *is*. His life is so different from my life. How the heck can *he* be interested in *me*? I wonder how he is."

"Go up to the hospital and find out."

"Barni, I can't just barge in."

"Well, Spence Eccles just broke his leg, so let's go up and see *him*. Then maybe you can just happen to bump into your friend."

The two girls visited Spence at the hospital and Jill soon excused herself and wandered down the corridor with a heavy air of attempted nonchalance. She walked past Dick's room and saw that he was blanketed with baskets of fruit and boxes of candy and was happily engaged in fond conversation with Norma Shearer. She returned to Spence's room and said to Barni, "I guess we shouldn't be late getting back."

The Harriman Cup was the first race in a long while that Dave McCoy hadn't been around with encouragement and advice. The downhill went poorly. Jill spilled twice and placed 17th and wept at the finish line. Barni was 10th.

Jill went back up the lift to the Round House, which is a large circular warming hut halfway up the slope of Mt. Baldy. As she walked inside she saw Dick, fresh out of the hospital. "Hey!" he shouted at her across the room. "How'd it go?"

"Second . . ."

"That's *great*. You did well." He stumbled to his feet, grinning and thrusting the handles of his ski poles under one armpit like a crutch.

"Second from last."

"Oh."

Jill made her way to him through the crowd and was pleased on two accounts. First, because Dick was so happy when he thought she'd done well. Second, because she had

92

been able to handle her small joke with aplomb and a straight face.

The next day Jill managed a 12th place in slalom, the result of a terrible first run and a beautiful second run. All the gold medals went to Jannette Burr, with time to spare.

Jill felt dejected about the whole weekend and was still low when she met Dave Monday evening at the house below McGee Mountain. She knew Dave had missed becoming a big skier because of his crash years ago at the Sugar Bowl, but she had always felt that some of the kids he'd taught to race might make it. She wanted to do this for him, what he couldn't do. Now she had just been on her own at a big race for the first time and had let him down.

"Thing's didn't go well, did they, Pa?"

"But you can do it," he answered. "I think I know what the trouble was."

"Pa, I still don't know how fast I can really go. I feel so slow when I just ski it pretty and nice."

Dave hadn't seemed to hear. He said, "You know how I always lead the way when we go some place new? I been thinking; maybe following me all the time isn't such a good idea. Even at home."

"How do you mean?"

"You get spoiled that way. What you should be learning is to trust your own judgment. This goes for all of us, but maybe you specially."

"I learn, though, by skiing behind you."

Dave frowned but said nothing.

"You want to know something?" Jill said suddenly. "I really *hate* not *win*ning."

Her dislike of not winning was more than just wanting to stack up a good record before the Olympic tryouts. And it wasn't simply wanting to win for Dave, or for old Dad's sake. Mainly, it was just that it was nice to be skiing so well and to be in such good shape that when you came down a racecourse you came in first.

Another thing: although she was always embarrassed for fear it would show, she loved all the attention that fell her way every time she earned a gold medal. She was dimly aware, in addition, that she wasn't too sure whether she could ever stand up against the truly big-time racers like Andy, who would undoubtedly be back on the race circuit next year, or like Jannette Burr, who seemed to be winning everything in the meantime. But the more attention she got the better she felt about herself—quite different from Bob, who seemed to have all the self-assurance he could ever use and didn't need an audience.

Jill placed fourth that weekend in the National Giant Slalom at the new Reno Ski Bowl on Slide Mountain. Then she went with Bob and Dave to Sun Valley to practice for the American Legion Juniors.

Dick Buek was living and skiing at Sun Valley, and he found Jill shortly after she arrived. "Busy tonight?" he said.

This was the first time he had ever literally asked her for a date. She said, "Not really. What's going on?"

They spent the evening at a club in Ketchum with friends of Dick's who worked at Sun Valley. The next day after skiing they walked to Sun Valley's "Opera House" to see a ski movie. They had to detour around a funeral procession that was about to take off from the resort's chapel, 100 yards from the theater.

"Isn't that too much!" Dick said.

"What?"

"All these ignorant jerks who dress up in black and say sanctimonious words across the top of a coffin. All that fuss and big tears, and they pretend they're doing it for the poor bastard that's lying there dead. He doesn't need anything from them; he's well taken care of, wherever he is. The only person they're really sorry for is themselves. It's just too much."

"The funeral?"

"The self-pity."

Jill saw Dick every day after skiing or in the evening, and she began to notice the esteem with which he was regarded by many of the seasoned racers. Skiers often stopped him for a word or for long enough to recall some crackbrained exploit of his. In a crowded room, people made way for him . . . not obviously, not even consciously, but with unconsidered deference. Many times that week Jill heard him addressed as "wild man" or "idiot" or just "you crazy bastard" . . . and the words were usually spoken with love.

Twice after dinner Dick took her to see Scottie at his repair shop in Ketchum. Ed Scott was an old friend of Dick's and a true craftsman. He didn't "repair" skis; he remade them. Dick was one of his great admirers, as were many of Sun Valley's veteran racers and instructors.

Scottie was a soft-spoken man in his forties, tall, balding, with a thin face and rimless glasses and reddish hair. From him Jill learned a little about repairing skis and a lot about Dick Buek. Dick had had an uncle who was killed diving from a high tower into a shallow tank of water. Dick himself had dived off the cliffs at Acapulco because, if the local boys could do it, Buek certainly was not going to chicken out. His father had been uneasy about him and had made him promise never to go in for auto racing . . . and he never did. Dick was a far-out nut worshiped by other nuts, particularly by the wild ones who didn't have nearly as much on the ball. He was also dogged by female skiers. And everyone—friends, nuts, girls—always told one another that Mad Dog was going to kill himself.

The evening before the race, Dick decided that Jill's downhill skis weren't carving well enough and he sharpened the edges for her.

Dave McCoy gave the skis a serious look the next morning. "What happened here?" he said.

"Oh, Dick fixed them for me."

"He did, huh?"

Jill thought Dave was going to say something more, but he went silent. She knew that her skis, like her training, were Dave's province and not Dick's. She felt guilty. She said, "Pa, could you do me a favor and go over my edges again?" Dave ignored her.

Jill won both the downhill and the slalom with no great strain, but Bob Kinmont had an off weekend and fell in both events.

Four months of racing had given Jill a sound knowledge of her weak points. She knew what she had to work on for as long as the spring snowpack lasted, and she went at it methodically. She rode fast down every kind of terrain she could discover on the slopes of Mammoth Mountain and Dave set slaloms for her that were purposely too fast or too slow or too steep or too tight. May was warm and lovely and she skied every day except Mother's Day, when she went home to the Rocking K. "It's a sacrifice," she said with a grin, "but for you, Mom . . ."

The days were long—sunup before seven and still light enough to ski at eight in the evening. Jill wore white shorts and a halter and socks rolled as low as possible. She worked constantly on her racing technique, although skiing long and hard in friendly weather among friendly skiers never impressed her or anyone else as being a great chore.

Jill loved being physically so very small on the monstrous bulk of the mountain, and at the same time being master of it. She went to the top with Dave once, following in his snowsteps up the shadowed and ominous snowfield. Dave shouldered her skis as well as his own and she carried both pairs of poles. She soon felt at home with the slow rhythm of climbing. She liked the taut feeling at the back of her legs and the sensation of muscles being warmed from within. She liked the way the thick sole of her boot supported her like a small floor when only the toe was in contact with the hard, slanting snow.

Standing ready at the cornice, with her skis on, Jill felt a quick chill of fear. But she pushed off, dropping onto the top of the snowfield and carving her way down, fully and neatly and powerfully in control, free and able to use the mountain precisely as she wished. She cut a fine track down across the forbidding pitch beneath the cornice, an incisive S-curve that would freeze tonight and glint in the early sun tomorrow, visible from as far away as Deadman.

One day Jill and Bob had an entire afternoon together on the mountain. They were hot and were totally with it:

96

every run was *right,* every run was like a bird, like flying on your own wings. They could do *anything.* They hopped off ridges just for that sweet, shaky feeling, like a falling elevator. They leaped into the air from bumps and sharp rises, trying to outdo each other, sometimes turning their skis in the air or dropping their tips to land neatly on a steep slope below. They were possessed, flashing and streaking with impossible skill and spirit, beautifully lost in a world that was somewhere apart from the world of friends and strangers below who watched them with wonder and perhaps with reverence.

As summer approached and bare spots began to show through the wet gray snow near the warming hut, Dave dragged portable ski tows halfway up the mountain where the snow was still cool and grainy and fast.

But Jill had to leave Mammoth and the house at McGee Mountain in June while there was still snow. The moment school was out the Rocking K was jammed with guests and she had thirty swimming pupils at the pool. Her classes lasted all afternoon, and she waited on table at dinner and breakfast. She still had time for several evening dates during the week and never missed her dry-land training—"slalom" practice with her tires, one-legged knee bends, cross-country running and a routine of special exercises that she and Dave had worked out.

Linda was now a dedicated skier and asked Jill to show her what she could work on during the summer. Linda had heard about the tires and had done some running and calisthenics herself, but she was surprised when she came to watch Jill work out. The tires were what really got to her. They were spaced so far apart that Linda didn't think she could have jumped from one to the next with a running start. Jill bounded through them like a young kangaroo and said, "Okay, you're next."

Linda tried to repeat the performance, and felt like a hippopotamus chasing a gazelle. She said quietly, "Now I know what I'm going to have to do if I want to become a great skier. You really have to put *everything* into it, don't you?"

97

Audra Jo was at home for a summer vacation before starting college at UCLA and spent many afternoons in her chair at the Rocking K pool. Better than that were the trips up and down the valley. Bob Kinmont had bought himself a car, a creamy yellow MG, and he was happy for Jill to borrow it when he couldn't take off himself. So Audra Jo got to see more than a dozen of the lakes that lie in the high country on the near side of the Sierra crest. The open MG was particularly appreciated when they stopped because Audra Jo could sit there and flirt with boys who didn't know she was paralyzed and therefore weren't self-conscious about her.

One evening before supper when all the Rocking K guests were on the commissary porch or over at the pond, a small plane came zooming down out of the sky headed for the center of the pond. Jill breathed an angry sound through her teeth and said in a low, level voice, "Oh, *brother!*"

The plane pulled up at the last minute, clipping with its wheels the dead white branches that stuck up above the green bulk of the willow trees beside the pond. Bleached chunks of dead wood fell into the water and the ducks rose in terror. Uncle Bob Lamkin, a family friend who had come over for supper, covered his eyes with his arms and said in a loud voice, "Somebody get a shovel and let's trudge out there and scrape poor old Buek up off the desert."

Jill waited for Dick to appear on foot. As soon as she had an opportunity she took him aside and said, "Look, Dick, when you fly in and knock the branches off the tree, well, I think that is a bit too low, so I would appreciate it very much if you would fly a little bit higher, because it bothers the guests."

Dick said, "Yes, ma'am," and made a short bow. "But don't sweat it," he added. "As soon as we're married we'll fix a place with a strip right between the pool and the house so I won't have to rattle the cottonwoods just to say hello."

"What did you say?"

"I said we'll have a landing strip . . ."

"I mean you said as soon as we *what?*"

"Well, it's perfectly obvious, Jill, that you and I are going to make the big move."

"Oh, *Dick*. Don't try to be *funny*." He was teasing about the plane, but Jill knew he was quite serious about everything else. She said, "Dick, I hardly know you."

"You mean you haven't gotten to see me very often. You know me very well indeed."

"You're making a lot of silly statements."

"True ones, however."

"Dick, the gong's going to go off and I've got to be up at my tables."

Jill was still clearing away dishes in the dining room when she heard Dick take off. Forty minutes later Uncle Bob Lamkin came huffing up to the commissary with Dick ambling along in his wake. Uncle Bob tried to look as if he were a complete physical and psychological wreck, but the lilt in his voice betrayed him. He called out, as he approached, "Did you see what that nut *did* to me? Jillie, did you *see* us?" Jill shook her head and Uncle Bob was obviously disappointed. "He flew *upside down*. With *me*. With me *in it. Me, 210 pounds!* Plus a tub full of gas. In this dinky 65-horse Cub he's got."

Dick said, "He means I sort of clipped the ridges. I had to make all the ridges, with all that *lard,* because I had to use the updrafts to get some altitude."

"He did *too* fly upside down," Bob said. "Boy, did I ever say the wrong thing. We finally got up there, and I mean right up there above the Rocking K, and I say, very professional and cool, Say, can they ever stunt an old Cub like this? And he says right back, just as cool, Hell, yes, all you got to do is point the nose down and give her full throttle. And, boy, our nose is already down and our throttle is already full and I freeze to the strut I'm hanging onto and he goes and *loops* the thing. Right out there over the dump!"

Dick went into town in the morning, and when he returned Jill was over at Audra Jo's listening to some new records. He drove to the Striplings'. Jill introduced him to Audra Jo and said, "We better get back to the ranch."

"But I just *got* here!"

"I know, but I've got all these kids coming for swimming lessons in about twenty-five minutes and I have to change and all."

Dick carried Audra Jo to the car, swung her neatly onto the seat, and drove the two girls west toward the ranch. "Want to go for a ride?" he said to Audra Jo. She looked skeptical but Jill said, "Oh, he's a great flyer."

"And it's a nice plane," Dick said. "I found it for practically nothing and patched it up and it's like new. At least it will be when I get my 90. It needs more power." He turned onto the county road. "You've *got* to learn to fly," he told Audra Jo. "If you had an Aerocoupe . . . it's all hand controlled and you don't need legs at all. You'd be great!"

Dick parked beside the plane and Jill started for the pasture. "I'll walk up to the house," she called to them. "Meet me at the pool when you get back."

An hour later Dick and Audra Jo appeared at the swimming pool. "Jill, it was mag*nif*icent," Audra Jo said. "But don't you dare tell my mother."

Dick left the ranch reluctantly, promising to be back—and he was, at the end of the summer, in a biplane. His new plane was a bargain he'd picked up at an auction, a staggerwing Beechcraft which he landed out at the Bishop airport.

"Guess where I'm off to," he told Jill when he took her up. The Sierra and the Whites were both dusted with snow down to the 12,000-foot level.

"The Andes, probably."

"Not that. The winter's practically over already in Chile. I'm going in the Army."

Jill said, "Oh," which was all she could say. What she *thought* was: How come the Army ever took crazy old busted-up Dick Buek?

"I don't mind. It's a good thing to have that out of the way before we're married anyhow." Jill frowned and he

100

said, "Don't give me that kind of look. I'm not going to spirit you off at midnight and shock the pants off of old Dad Kinmont or anything. There's no hurry about it."

"Boy, you *are* crazy," she said.

9

THE SUMMER HAD BEEN A VERY PROFITABLE ONE FOR the Rocking K and Bill Kinmont was able to pay off all but $14,000 of the ranch's mortgage. He printed up a giant postcard with a color photograph of the ranch and the information that it was located

> In the heart of California's High Sierras. Deluxe individual cottages, beautiful dining room and cocktail lounge, fine string of riding horses, expert instruction, private trout, bass and blue-gill lakes, heated swimming pool, ideal for family vacation.

Immediately after Labor Day Jill went to work behind the counter of the Malt Shop, which was at the very center of town. She planned to work until the snows came and then move in with the McCoys at McGee Mountain. She found that some hours at the shop were frantically busy, but there were also pleasant doldrums. When business was slow she brought out her knitting or perhaps talked one of the boys into helping her wind a new hank of yarn. At other times she tried to do the work of two soda jerks and a waitress all at once. She had no steady boyfriend, but she dated regularly and it was not easy to sandwich her social life between her Malt Shop obligations. One evening she had to wear her levis under a formal dress so she could clean up the Malt Shop at midnight on her way home.

Jill Kinmont, eighteen-year-old Malt Shop waitress, was in the local news far less than was Bob Kinmont, class president and star quarterback. She was even eclipsed by a younger generation of Kinmonts and McCoys when the ski season opened with the Junior Alpine Races at Mammoth. Jerry Kinmont, who was a dogged eleven years old with a flat-topped haircut, thousands of freckles, and gleaming braces on his teeth, won the Class 4 downhill and was runner-up in slalom. Poncho McCoy took the Class 5 downhill and slalom and Gary McCoy placed second in the Class 3 slalom.

The next week it was Jill who was suddenly very much in the news. Her picture was spread across the November cover of *The Skier,* which called her racing record "unprecedented," and she was invited to Los Angeles by the Helms Athletic Foundation to receive the 1954 Andrea Mead Lawrence award honoring her as America's foremost junior woman skier. Her photograph in the Los Angeles *Examiner* was three columns wide.

The award ceremony at the Wilshire Ebel theater on December 3 was exciting but rather formal. The best thing about it was that it was held on Friday night and Jill had the rest of the weekend to visit Audra Jo, who was enrolled at UCLA as a freshman but was living at the Kabot Kaiser Institute.

KKI was on the beach at Santa Monica, a massive, eight-story former hotel that had been made over into a massive, nine-story rehabilitation center. The extra floor had been sandwiched in beneath the high ceiling of the once-palatial second story. The whole place looked run down and dismal with ragged curtains on the windows and crinkly, peeling paint on the walls, but there was an Olympic standard swimming pool on the ground floor with a special lift which could lower patients into the water for hydrotherapy.

Audra Jo was upstairs in a double room. "Hey, you're *famous!*" she said when Jill came in.

"Not really," Jill answered. "How are *you?* How's college?"

"I'm fine. And college is fine except for English composition."

"Why?"

"The professor asked me in for a conference and what he wanted was for me to write about polio and about how traumatic it was—*he* thought—and how all my friends deserted me or something. If there's one thing I don't want to write about, it's *that*."

"But did you?"

"Of course not. He tried to be subtle about it and hinted something about my skiing and he said, Write me a story with real irony. So I wrote about what modern science gave us: *smog*. And how we could control it by piping it down to the border in big pipes that had screens so they wouldn't suck in the birds along with the smog."

The two top floors at KKI were essentially a number of hotel rooms for patients who were self-sufficient or for friends and relatives, so Jill stayed upstairs with Audra Jo Friday and Saturday nights. She followed Audra Jo everywhere—to meals, to therapy, out on the boardwalk—and she saw a great deal of her friend's fellow patients. They were of all races and occupations and ages and their specific complaints ranged from amputation and paraplegia to polio and multiple sclerosis and cerebral palsy. They shared in various forms of games and torture, including occupational therapy, stretching, hydrotherapy, ultrasonic therapy, speech therapy and workouts in the swimming pool.

The variety of injury and illness was appalling to Jill, but there was so much to see and ask about that she didn't dwell on it. She did feel a moment of panic, however, when she went into a rest room and found there a partially paralyzed girl trying desperately and with no success whatever to get herself onto the toilet seat. The solution, of course, was obvious and simple; the girl who said her name was Bobbie, asked for help. Jill helped her and then wondered why she—Jill—had been upset.

Immediately after Jill got back to Bishop, she and Bob each received a letter from the international competition committee of the National Ski Association. Jill skimmed the first paragraph and shouted. They had been invited, along with eight other women and fourteen other men who were also considered likely prospects for the 1956 Olympic team, to a three-week training camp at Sun Valley, starting the week before Christmas. Five other

Californians had been invited: two Olympic veterans, Katy Rodolph and Dick Buek, and three other "youngsters," Ann Roberts, Lewis Fellows and Dennis Osborn. Why Kenny Lloyd had not been asked was a mystery.

Telephone calls began to come in from newspapers and from *Life* and from the ski magazines. *Sports Illustrated* turned up at Mammoth with an endless stream of questions. What were Jill's plans? "Really, I don't *have* any." How and where and when had she learned to ski? "I copy Dave McCoy. He taught me everything I know."

The week before Sun Valley was still a school week for Bob, but Jill and Dennis Osborn worked with Dave at Mammoth, training for the training camp. At the end of the week Jill and Dave and Dennis climbed to the top of the mountain and made a fast last run, dropping from over 11,000 feet down to 9,000; an endless succession of quick, hard, carving turns all the way down. At the bottom Dave said to Dennis, "She could learn to ski if she'd just keep trying."

Jill and Bob took off in the family station wagon eight days before Christmas with Jill at the wheel. Bob slept until somewhere in mid-Nevada. When Jill changed places with him she said, "We're nearly out of gas. Be sure and stop." She dozed off until halfway between Ely and Wendover, where the car coasted to a stop with a dry tank. Bob walked and hitchhiked 25 miles before he found an open service station.

During the rest of the long trip to Idaho, Bob and Jill spoke infrequently, but they said more to one another than a casual eavesdropper might have guessed. Bob wondered why Jill took skiing so terribly seriously, although he respected her determination and admired the results. She wondered why he was so casual about the whole business and she was envious of the fact that he scarcely trained at all but still managed to ski about as well as she.

Bob said, "You know, I watch you sweating out those tires up in back of the kitchen sometimes and I think that everything I've gotten I've gotten for nothing."

At Sun Valley most of the trainees had already checked

in, although Dick Buek hadn't shown up and probably wouldn't since the U.S. Army was not in the habit of granting ski leaves. Bob and Jill were both worn out and turned in after a quick supper. Jill was given a room with Ann Roberts and Bud Werner's sister, Skeeter.

The Kinmonts were out on Baldy early the next morning. Jill felt that the mountain had gotten shallower and smoother since her last visit. A few days before she had felt totally competent on her familiar and beloved Mammoth Mountain, and now she was pleased and a little surprised to find that she felt just as good on Mt. Baldy. After two runs she confided to Bob, "I've never felt this great before. *Everything's* under control." She was still out of breath and leaned forward on her red-handled poles so that a wavy blonde forelock hung down to her eyebrows. "There's nothing can bother me at all, Bobby. Anything that comes up, I can handle it."

Bob was leaning forward also, staring at the snow. The corner of one eye caught the bright yellow of his sister's sweater. He straightened up and tapped her ski pole with his own. She smiled and wrinkled her nose.

"Now I know I can *be* somebody," she said, and she added silently to herself: I feel like the best woman skier in the world and by God I think I can beat anybody.

The first official training camp meeting was held that afternoon in the Lodge office. Everyone sprawled on the thick carpet or sat against the wall, and Jill found herself next to the boy who was already being referred to in sports circles as *the* Buddy Werner.

The first order of business was to fill out a questionnaire—name, address, birth date, ski club, 1954 racing record and related items. Buddy finished his questionnaire long before Jill, who was studiously listing all her medals and was only up to the middle of March, 1954. Bud bent forward and turned to study her face: turned-up nose, wide blue eyes, cheeks flushed from the cold, and short gold-blonde hair. He glanced at what she was writing and said, "My God, look at the *races* you've won!" He had a cracked voice, somewhat raspy and uneven but at the same time slow and gentle. He seemed to be conscious of trying to speak softly.

Jill went on writing, using a new line for each event, and soon she had to turn the page over and write on the back. "How about *you?*" she asked without looking at him.

"Me?" He was still squinting at her list, his thin, straight eyebrows bent slightly in a frown. "One race. Just one race all year while you've been cleaning up."

She looked at his questionnaire and read his single entry. *Holmenkollen gold medal.* She said, "Gads, what do all my races mean when you go and beat the best skiers in the whole *world!*"

"And how about that birthday?" he said.

"What?" She looked up. He had a lean fair face flecked with freckles, and his thin, chapped lips were stretched in a wide smile. Jill saw a small St. Christopher medal at his neck.

"February 16, 1936. If you'd been born ten days later we'd be twins."

"Really? I guess that makes me an older woman, huh?"

Skeeter and Bud Werner and Jill and Bob Kinmont began skiing together and often ate together at the recreation hall and lunched together up at the Round House. Skeeter was two years older than her brother and the two of them seemed to be even closer than Jill and Bob.

Bud Werner had already been called America's greatest hope for the 1956 Olympics. Jill Kinmont was now being described in the press as a "new star" and a "glamorous young champion." Both of them came by their reputations honestly enough. Both displayed admirable modesty. Both reveled, nevertheless, in the publicity. Both felt relieved of any necessity to impress the other.

What pleased Jill most of all was the discovery that Buddy Werner always had a lot of fun on skis. He had as much fun as Dave always *said* people should have. At the same time he was deadly serious and worked at it constantly. He made every turn count, even when he was clowning. When the whole crew was given a day off from

107

training, just about everybody hung up his boards for the day except Bud and Jill. They were on Baldy early. Bud stood poised at the top of the run, very trim in his red sweater and skin-tight ski pants. He had his parka tied around his waist, rolled carefully so his FIS patch would be visible in back. He said to Jill, "You go first."

"No. *You* go."

"Come on!"

Jill was not used to going first and didn't like to go first, but she scowled and took off. She pretended she was following Dave, and the trick worked. Bud was at her heels and at the bottom of the canyon they spun to a stop in a cloud of powder and Bud said, "My God, you're skiing good today."

Jill felt magnificent.

The training schedule was crammed with practice and meetings and slalom coaching and chalk talks and theoretical discussions about how to cause two straight boards to follow a curved path. There was plenty of expert opinion, all of it male, and the discussions quickly became analytical, critical and heated. There was much talk about the *locked knee position,* in which the downhill knee is tucked up against or behind the uphill knee, and there was great emphasis on *prejumping,* which meant jumping up off the snow ahead of a big bump so as to land just beyond the crest and thus avoid being thrown into the air and out of control.

There were five coaches, including wise old Barnie McLean, who had been captain of the 1948 Olympic team, and Christian Pravda, world downhill champion whose superb skiing made up for his inexperience as a coach. Pravda was Jill's idol. He was a small, sturdy man with a rough and friendly face and a large nose, although he looked like a giant fly when his huge golden-brown goggles were in place. He wore a small red Tyrolean eagle centered on the front of his sweater. His timing in slalom was flawless. In downhill his speed was frightening.

Out on the mountain, however, Pravda could be a problem. His English was sometimes pretty wretched and his temper was such that none of the girls dared ask him what it was he'd been trying to say. They tried to do what they thought it was he might have told them to do. Half the time he would just say "Follow me!" and take off down the mountain. The difficulty was that, as Renie Cox told Jill, *"No*body keeps up with Christian." Renie and Jerryann Devlin and Betsy Snite always lost him at the top and only caught up with him at the bottom long after he had arrived.

Jill, however, did learn from Pravda, and she learned by following him. When Pravda said "Follow me" she followed. The other girls thought she shouldn't try. The fact was that neither of these thoughts occurred to Jill Kinmont, who forgot all about form and control but kept on Christian Pravda's tail all the way down the mountain. Consequently, Pravda told the other girls she was always skiing out of control.

Whenever Jill had a choice she skied with the boys. And she stayed with them. She stayed with Ralph Miller and she stayed with Bud. Pravda watched her one morning and said to Renie, "She skis with the boys. She's going to kill herself skiing like that."

It soon became apparent that Bud Werner and Jill Kinmont were the stars of the show. They were not supposed to be, but it so happened that everyone paid attention to them all the time. Also, they were both avid learners. Some of the other racers felt distinctly left out, and they murmured agreement when one of the girls said, "This training camp looks like it was set up to help Bud Werner and Jill Kinmont, and they're the only two who don't need help."

When the photographers from *Life* and *Sports Illustrated* showed up, they zeroed in at once on Werner and Kinmont. They were not obvious about it, but there was no doubt as to the number of pictures they took—there was always that little sound, that soft, mechanical voice of the shutter that said *sssick*.

Jill had been five days in Sun Valley and felt as if she had known Bud Werner since childhood. He was constantly attentive, and it seemed only natural that he should follow her all over Sun Valley and that they should soon find themselves eating together all the time, sitting together on the bus over to Baldy, skiing together, spending hours together in the waxing room of the Challenger Inn. Bud always helped her scrape her skis at the end of the day and then repainted them for her, laying on a few careful strokes and then dipping the brush again into the pot of hot wax he held with a pair of pliers in his other hand. He checked her edges for gouges and loose screws and he lacquered them with Faski, which gave the steel a green sheen. He was always careful to lacquer the sides of the edges as well as the bottoms.

Once when they were alone in the waxing room Bud said, "We can be the greatest, you know," and Jill answered soberly, "I know." This was a claim, or an admission perhaps, that neither could have made to anyone else. But they were both that confident, and they could say easily to each other what would have sounded like arrogance to other ears.

"You know, Jill," he said, "once we both pick up a couple of gold medals over in Italy we're going to make a pretty neat couple."

"Where are we going to live, Buddy? Do you think Sun Valley would rent us the Round House?"

"I don't know, because the kids are going to have to learn to ski at Steamboat."

"Mammoth."

"Well, we can fight about that when the time comes."

10

Jill was skipping into breakfast in very high spirits two days before Christmas when she saw a soldier, the sight of whom stopped her absolutely cold. It was Dick Buek, seated at an empty table and talking with an employee who was apparently an old friend. He looked thoroughly out of character in the uniform of the U.S. Army.

Jill was with Skeeter and Renie and Betsy. Whoever was behind her bumped into her and she made a silly, embarrassed smile. She called across to Dick, "How are you?"

"Fine. How are you?"

"Fine."

Dick went on talking with his friend and Jill kept moving, more or less sideways, to get in line for breakfast. She had decidedly mixed feelings. Life in Sun Valley so far had been perfect, and here suddenly was Dick, who didn't fit into the pattern anywhere.

Dick was older than most of the avid young racers and had turned up late and he now was just not part of the group. Nor did he care to be, apparently. Jill did not know what to do about him, particularly since she was very close to being in love with Bud Werner. Consequently, she did nothing. But she ran into Dick again that afternoon and he said, "Come on down to Scottie's after supper." So they drove the few miles to Scottie's shop in Ketchum. The evening was very short, however, as all evenings had to be where training was rigid and nine o'clock was official sack time.

Jill Kinmont's attitude toward men had a great deal to do with skiing. She had full respect for qualities like

111

affection and humor and intelligence and taste, but physical ability and coordination meant even more to her. She could not honestly look up to a man who did not ski well. In fact, no man stood much of a chance with her unless he was, first of all, a better skier.

This criterion was of course no problem for Dick or Bud, and when Jill compared them she thought of other things than skiing. For Dick she felt much warmth and great admiration. She was always comfortable and confident and at ease with him. Yet he was incurably wild, careless, restless, and he was never going to change. He was a knight in rusting armor and he would be just too much to take. As a husband, at any rate. Bud, on the other hand, had the same kinds of goals and the same kinds of tastes as she had. He even worried about and blushed about the same kinds of things. Also, he was a goodhearted, wholesome sort of guy and the elder Kinmonts would adore him. But Jill did not know Bud as well and she was not certain just what his feelings for her were, or hers for him.

"Buddy's neat, isn't he?" she said to her brother when they were lunching together at the Round House a few days after Christmas.

"Great skier."

Jill brightened. *"Isn't* he, though! And he just never falls."

"I know, and . . ."

"But if he does fall then he's back on his feet in a second."

"Yeah. Down and . . . *bang* he's up again!"

"But I meant not just skiing, Bobby. I meant he's all for the other guy all the time."

"He's all for Jill and he's all for Skeeter and he's all for Buddy."

"Bobby, he's *not* just . . ."

"Sure he is, and why not? You don't get to be a great skier by being Big Brother to everybody. You've got to be a very self-centered guy, and Buddy's a very self-centered guy. You've got to be an egotist to go out and do what most people can't."

112

"He's no more self-centered than I am, Bobby. And he cares a *lot* about what people think of him." Even as she spoke she realized that this was not exactly the antithesis of egotism. And she remembered something Bud had said about Renie Cox . . . that she was much too *nice* to be a skier, that she was not *competitive* enough.

Jill said, "Bobby, if you think Buddy's an all-for-me-nothing-for-you kind of guy . . ."

"I don't."

"Deep down inside maybe he is, but he always has . . . look, he hates to lose, Bobby, even in a time trial, because it means a lot to him. But he's the first guy there to throw his arms around the guy that won."

Most of the boys, Bud in particular, had become greatly concerned about a new style of turning which involved an exaggerated weighting and unweighting of the skis. They called it the "new way" or the "up-and-down" technique. Jill had never heard of it, and she paid little attention because her skiing felt right to her and both Bud and Bob kept telling her she looked good. Skeeter and the other girls tried to ski the new way, but they couldn't get onto it and this worried them a great deal.

The last week of training camp was devoted largely to a series of time trials and informal races. Jill had trouble with the slalom courses and she began to wonder if she really was as self-sufficient as she had thought. She began to listen to the always warm discussions about up-and-down turning and leading with your inside shoulder and rotating your body at just the right moment. After three consecutive poor runs in the time trials, she went to the coaches and said, "All right, tell me what's *wrong*."

They were happy to give advice when asked, and they were loaded with it. There were a dozen things wrong with Jill's skiing. She thought of retreating, but by now she was convinced that she probably ought to learn the new way because everyone else, including the best of them, was learning it.

One afternoon Jill was nearing the bottom of a new slalom course, racing, worrying about how fast she dared

113

enter a flush . . . when she was assaulted with the cry, *"Knie zusammen!"* The rest of the day went the same way. "Knees together!" "Keep your weight *downhill!*" "Don't rotate the shoulders so much!"

Jill was sure the coaches were trying to change her style. *Now*, of all times, just a month before the beginning of the most important racing season in her life. But she was so confused and so unsure about what was going on that she didn't even have the single-mindedness to get angry.

By the middle of the last week her timing was off and she found herself repeatedly sideslipping instead of carving. The only help she got at the end of a particularly lousy run was the maddeningly cheerful reminder, "You'll be okay if you can just make it a little later with your rotation!"

The daylight hours out on Baldy were beginning to feel like a burden, and Jill appreciated more than ever the relatively private hours of late afternoon and evening. She spent as much time as possible with Bud, although there was no real sense of privacy because they had come to listen instinctively for the *sick . . . sick* sound of a shutter shuttering. They were both still of necessity on stage before the great American public, a nasty aggravation which both of them enjoyed thoroughly.

One evening Jill and Bud and Bob and several of the girls were relaxing in Jill's room before dinner. They were all talking except Bob, who was bent over his guitar. Someone was searching frantically for a lost shoe. Jill was standing in front of a mirror combing her hair and Bud came and sat on a bed to watch her. He said, "Jill . . . ?"

She turned and smiled.

"Jill, tell me something. Have you ever been in love before?"

She stopped, her comb in the air. The noise and confusion in the room was suddenly unbearable and she walked over and sat beside Bud on the bed. "No. I don't think so," she said and began combing her hair again. "Why?"

114

"I have. Quite a few times."

"Really, Buddy? I thought people only fell in love *once.*"

"The girl I'd been going with . . . I mean in Colorado . . . she gave me this St. Christopher." He pulled open his shirt collar to reveal the small silver medal.

"I always thought, Buddy, that the person you fell in love with was . . ." She took a long breath. "Was the one you married. I've never told anybody that I loved him."

"You haven't? I've told that to several girls. But I don't just toss the words around. And I want you to know that."

"Oh?" She put down her comb and turned to face him, smiling and staring openly into his pale-blue eyes.

"Chow time!" someone said. Jill made a quick sigh and Bud shrugged and everyone filed down to the rec room for dinner.

Jill still saw Dick Buek for an hour or two almost every evening, and they usually spent the time at Scottie's. She received a few puzzled glances from friends who saw her with Bud and then with Dick, but no one was tuned in to her dilemma.

Although Dick had been formally invited to the training camp and had finally talked his way into a leave of absence from the Army, he stayed away from the camp entirely. He watched them from a distance now and then, these bright young comers who represented most or all of what would be the next Olympic team, but he skied with his own friends and he spent a lot of time flying. He treated the young stars to a memorable few minutes one day when he buzzed Baldy in a rented plane and flew under the chairlift.

On the last day at Sun Valley Jill and Bud skied together on Baldy. At the bottom after a good run Bud said, "Jill, why don't you come train with us after the Snow Cup?" The Snow Cup was one of the big early races, a traditionally long and steep giant slalom in the Wasatch Mountains at Alta, Utah.

"Buddy, I don't know. Something bad has happened to

my skiing up here and I've got to fight just to get back what I've lost. I think maybe it would be the wrong thing for me."

Bud frowned and scratched his chin on the handle of his ski pole. "I guess you're the one who knows what you've got to do." He gave her a puzzled, searching stare. He said, "Jill, I love you." She bit her lip but made no response. He said, "Please come, Jill."

Back home after Sun Valley, Jill skied badly and Bob, too, was having trouble. Jill began to wonder if she could win big races any longer. Her form was shaggy and her timing crude. Dave was very much upset. He said, "I can't help you, Jill, but there is a cure. Stop thinking and just get out on the mountain and ski. And by *ski*, I mean just *have a ball*."

Jill spent an occasional day or evening at the Rocking K, but she was living with the McCoys at McGee Mountain. She was strongly aware of Bud's absence. She talked about him with her mother and with Roma and with Linda. And she received a letter from him asking her point-blank to join him and half a dozen others for informal training at Aspen in early February. They would all live in an apartment and share expenses and they would compete with each other and ski every day from dawn till dusk.

The chance to go to Aspen was a dream which could come true. Jill had only to say yes. When she told Linda, Linda said, "Oh, *go!*" Jill shook her head and Linda said, "*I'd* go, Jill. *I'd* go. Go ahead. Go to Aspen!"

"Linda, I can't go. I can't afford to get involved."

"What do you mean? You're in love with the guy, aren't you?"

"I don't know. I mean, I don't know what I mean. And anyway, the way they like to ski, it just throws me off."

Dave was strangely silent when Jill talked about Bud. He appeared to have no reaction, positive or negative, to anything she could tell him about either Bud's personality or his skiing. Jill was disappointed, but she

116

realized that she was very much Dave's skier, his friend and protégée; he had reason to be less than enthusiastic about her interest in Bud Werner. Dave wanted absolutely *nothing* to get in the way of her goal of getting on the U.S. Olympic squad.

Jill, knew, too, that she could manage a lot more hard practice if she stayed at Mammoth. She knew Dave could help her regain her old form and timing, and she knew Mammoth was clearly the place for her final polishing before the Olympic tryout races.

Jill wrote Bud that she had to stay at Mammoth.

Then she took Dave's advice and went skiing just for the sake of skiing, although it was several days before she could stop thinking about what she was supposed to be doing, separately, with her shoulders and feet and knees. Soon she was setting up problems and challenges for herself and began to work out not only with Dave but with Kenny Lloyd and Dennis Osborn and with the Zumsteins' daughter, Charlotte, a former junior champion who had been away from home for several years. The quartet set up crazy, demanding slaloms and got out shovels and built wicked bumps which they then came down into at high speed. Sometimes they took off deliberately so they would get accustomed to handling themselves in the air. They found sharp dips and gullies that were even harder to handle than bumps. Then they dragged over the slalom flags again and worked on rhythm and speed and pacing.

Life came out with a short feature called "Cram Camp for Skiers." Jill's reaction was a long joyful murmur "Oh . . . oh . . . *look!*" What she saw was a large photograph of Christian Pravda negotiating a slalom gate and a small photograph of Jill Kinmont coming through the same gate in precisely the same way. Her attitude in the gate was a facsimile of Pravda's. There was also a full-page photograph of Bud in the air on a downhill run with his skis a good seven feet off the snow.

Letters were coming thick and fast from Steamboat Springs. Bud wrote "I love you," and Jill found it extremely difficult to appear casual when she arrived back

117

at the McCoys' late in the afternoon. She always let two or three minutes pass before asking, "Any mail today?" She wanted to say the words *love you* when she wrote him, but she still felt shy and careful about it. To her, these words were like a vow. She wrote, "I really miss you, Buddy."

By the third week in January Jill had fairly well regained her skill and confidence and, with them, her poise. Her only sustained loss was some of her old sense of privacy on Mammoth Mountain, for reporters or photographers were coming in every few days. Jill Kinmont was news and the forthcoming Snow Cup giant slalom was news, for it was the last important race before the Olympic tryouts and everyone looked upon it as a dress rehearsal. The next U.S. women's Olympic team would undoubtedly come from among the Snow Cup contenders, and sports editors were betting it would include three or four members of the 1952 team plus Jill. The tryout races themselves were to be the big invitational events in February and March—the Nationals, the North Americans and the Internationals, which would be held in New England, and the Harriman Cup at Sun Valley. The selection of the U.S. team would be based mainly on performance in these particular races.

The reporters learned less about Jill from Jill than they did from Dave, and Jill herself learned things she hadn't known about herself. "She's got a smoother style than most women," Dave told an interviewer in his usual unemphatic manner. "And she's got grace, too, so she'll last longer as a racer than most. Her technique's steady and sound and she's less apt to get in trouble. No jerky motions, no fighting the hill. We've always stressed trying to finish up on your feet more than anything else."

During the last few days before she left for Utah, Jill was again thoroughly at home on the mountain, skiing fast and strong and ready to take on all comers. For a while she had been fighting the mountain, beating at it, tearing it up, giving it everything she had to the point of pain and exhaustion . . . and now she was a friend of

118

the mountain, comfortable with wind and snow and speed and steep terrain.

She tried to tell her mother what it was like. "You're going down and the snow is there and you're all a part of it, kind of, and it's noiseless. You go down and carve nice turns and go into the air and come down and catch and hold. And there's always unknowns. Do I hit the downhill side of this and feel that nice feeling like you do when you *do* hit the downhill side, or do I hit the flat and go up the other side and *bam,* the mountain slaps you right in the face, or do I keep control of the mountain and land nicely, and softly, and go on to something else I'm not sure of and then make *that,* too? The control you have of what's happening is so nice. And it's so gentle. And then at other times coarse and rough and beastly, kind of, and you end up fighting like a dog to stay with it."

11

ON THE LAST TUESDAY IN JANUARY JILL AND KENNY and Dennis spent the evening at the McCoys' at McGee Mountain, packing and checking their skis. They all stayed for the night and early the next morning they piled their skis and knapsacks and boots and waxes into a beat-up old Plymouth and took off with Dave for Bishop. On the way into town they stopped at the Rocking K to wish the rest of the Kinmonts good luck on their weekend trip to Kratka Ridge for a big junior race. Bob would have much preferred the Snow Cup, but he had a history test on Friday morning and he couldn't get out of it.

Bill Kinmont said, "Have a great run, honeygirl," and June said, "Before you leave town, Jill, be sure and stop by Spitznagel's and sign that insurance policy."

"Oh, Mother, don't be silly, I won't be hurt. But I'll stop. And, Bobby, do good things down there."

"Good luck and be careful," June said.

The next stop was the Zumsteins', to pick up Charlotte. In town, Jill walked over to Spitznagel's while Dave was exchanging the borrowed Plymouth for his own 1953 Pontiac which he had left at a garage for repairs. Finally everybody and everything was more or less ready and Dave and his four Snow Cup hopefuls set out for Utah.

The trip was a breeze compared with driving to Sun Valley or Aspen. They stayed overnight at Wendover, Utah, and were in Salt Lake City the next morning, Thursday. Sixteen miles south of the city they left the flat valley and turned east up the steep and narrow V of Little Cottonwood Canyon.

Alta had once been a mining town but it now consisted of nothing more than three lodges plus spectacular alpine

120

ski country up on the south side of the canyon. The air was sharp and cold and the snow was a lovely, fine dry powder that would spin and sparkle into the air if you merely gave it a swipe with your ski pole.

The Mammoth skiers checked in at the Peruvian Lodge for lunch and immediately went up onto the steep run below Germania Pass where the race was to be. The race-course was marked but they skied everywhere, trying to get the feel of the terrain.

Between skiing and supper Jill wrote a note to Audra Jo:

We arrived in Salt Lake about 12:00 noon and skied this afternoon. The course looks great! Just hope I can stand up. Skeeter, Andy and Buddy are to arrive either tonight or in the morning. Oh boy. They have a double chair here, too. Mmmm!

P.S. I'll try to write when "The Bud" shows up.

Friday and Saturday were sunny and cold with several inches of new snow each morning. Jill skied mostly with Dave but she followed Andy and Skeeter and Nancy Banks on several runs. The racecourse was a mile and a quarter long and fairly steep. The competitors helped pack it and then skied down alongside, stopping to study each hump and curve and each pair of flags, sometimes sidestepping back up to replot their lines. The first two thirds of the course, except for a very tight, steep start, was set on a fast open slope along the west side of Rustler Mountain. Then, above a gully known as the Corkscrew, the course squeezed left through a grove of trees where it lifted suddenly over a four-foot rise, ran across a short plateau, and fell precipitously down toward the Alta Lodge on the narrow valley floor. The sharp bump above the Cork-screw was obviously the spot to watch, a stark test of skill and strength and perhaps of daring. It would be impossible not to go into the air, and it would take some pretty spectacular skiing to make time on that section of the run. But it was just another racing problem as far as Jill was concerned; Dave had said she'd be fine as long as she controlled her speed coming into it.

121

Jill came down alongside the top half of the racecourse behind Katy Rodolph, and she was pleased to find herself coming up on Katy's tail all the time; her skis were running faster than Katy's and carving better.

She stopped above the Corkscrew to study the bump, and she had lots of company. Andy and Skeeter were there, close enough to Jill so that she could hear them talking. Andy said something about prejumping and added that the race was going to be won or lost right here.

On her next ride down Jill came into the narrow section fast, riding just to the left of the marked course. She checked hard with a snowplow well ahead of the bump. Even so, her knees slammed up against her chest when she struck the rise and she was in the air for 15 or 20 feet on the lower side.

Jill liked the course and she liked the mountain and she was skiing well. She knew that she *could* win. Everything would have to go right. If something happened, she wouldn't make it. But it was possible. Bud had told her he always knew he could win . . . and unless a racer had at least this much confidence he wasn't likely to make it.

Jack Reddish, a Salt Lake skier and Olympic veteran whom Jill had once met with Dick Buek, stopped her on her way over to the lodge. "Just bought your picture," he said.

"What do you mean?"

"On the front of *Sports Illustrated*."

"No!" Jill had expected to see herself in the magazine, but certainly not on the cover.

Reddish said, "Yeah," and Jill's edge of doubt finally crumbled when Kenny Lloyd greeted her with "Here comes old Glamour-puss!"

Bud asked Jill out for dinner in Salt Lake with Skeeter and the Lawrences and Sally Neidlinger, and on the way in he bought her the January 31 issue of *Sports Illustrated*. The cover had nothing on it but the name of the magazine, the date and price, and a gorgeous color photograph of Jill Kinmont in a yellow sweater with skis on her shoulder. Inside was a three-page article called "Apple Pie in Sun

122

Valley" with eight photographs. Jill skiing. Jill chatting. Jill and Bud. Jill and Pravda. Jill and Bud again. Jill in the warming hut. Jill puffing into a ski mitten. Jill and Bob and Bud and Skeeter skiing together on Baldy.

Jill grinned shyly and tried not to reveal how much she enjoyed looking at the pictures of Jill Kinmont. She frowned, however, when she read the short text, because she was afraid she could not live up to the article's assessment of her. She remembered something Dave had said in December: *We've never cared for publicity; we'd rather earn it first.*

There was one thing that Jill appreciated even more than the magazine story, and that was being accepted as something of an equal by Andy and Skeeter and Sally. She had never before been included in a social affair of any kind with Andrea Mead Lawrence or with any of Andy's good friends. She wished Audra Jo were along. Jill and Bud sat across the table from one another; many times their eyes caught and held in a warm, happy stare.

The skiers did not get back to Alta until eleven o'clock, and Jill felt guilty as she tiptoed into the dark dormitory. She should have been in bed by nine on the night before a big race, and she hoped that Dave didn't know what time she'd finally made it. She climbed into the bunk above Katy Rodolph's and ran the course in her mind twice before falling asleep.

Sunday morning Jill came in to breakfast with the other racers but she was so keyed up that she felt sick to her stomach. She skipped the food and went down to the ski room where her skis were ready for their final waxing.

Once she was outside and away from food she felt better than she could ever remember having felt before an important race. She was at ease, confident, strong and anxious to get moving. Alta had lost the good weather of the past three days, but so what? You don't sweat the little things like gray skies and a blustery wind. It was actually an exciting day with spots of sun showing now and then on the north side of the canyon and great flurries

123

of powder snow whipping into the air or streaking out from cornices up on Rustler.

By race time there were thousands of cars below in the long parking space and the mountain was crawling with spectators. A cold wind was blowing down the slope from Germania Pass, but the snow on the course was like pressed velvet, hard enough that it wouldn't rut yet soft enough that skis would hold on it.

The women's race was scheduled before the men's, as usual. Andy and Skeeter were supposed to run among the first five, but they were late reaching the start. Jill was sorry because Andy, of course, was the one to beat, and because she wanted to see how both of them made out. Jill was not at all nervous in the starting gate, although she wanted to get going. Dave said quietly, "Just make it smooth and pretty." Andy appeared a few moments before Jill took off and said, "Hey . . . have a great run!" At the last moment Jill looked over at Dave, who winked and gave her the high sign. She felt as if she owned the world, or would very shortly.

Jill started with a surge of power, crouched low in the straight-away, and then barreled down through the fast, swooping turns on the upper part of the course with a wind at her back. The snow was faster than she'd expected, and she found herself low on a gate, slipping still lower and nearly falling as she struggled to hang onto the hill.

She had recovered by the time she shot down toward the trees and the left turn above the Corkscrew where she had always checked during practice. This time she did not check because she had already decided that the racer who let his skis run here was likely to win. She got ready to prejump the four-foot high knoll, but she was moving too fast and she started her jump two or three seconds late . . . so instead of prejumping, she lifted just where the snow surface itself rose up to the stubby plateau.

She had flung herself high into the air and was flying . . . off balance and aware only of the blur of trees coming up at her from below. She fought to get forward over her skis and raised one arm to protect her face from being

124

smashed against the tree trunks. She missed the trees and screamed at two spectators who were now directly in her path. She crashed onto the snow, slid and spun and tumbled another 50 feet and slammed into one of the spectators, carrying him on down the hill, thrashing and cartwheeling. In the middle of this final tumble, Jill felt within her body a sudden dull vibration. As if something had gone *toing* . . . except that there was no sound. And there was no pain.

When she stopped sliding she had the odd feeling that parts of her were somehow not connected. She thought immediately, maybe this is the way you die.

But she saw vaguely familiar faces and said, "Oh, my God . . . what have I done?"

She recognized Sally Neidlinger. She said, "I can't move."

"Of course you can't move. This guy's still sprawled on top of you."

"No, it's more than that. I don't know what's the matter and I'm scared." She felt a hand supporting her head and looked up to see Dick Movitz bending over her. She started to sob and thought, Oh, no . . . here go the Olympic tryouts and everything!

There was apparently a doctor among the spectators and Jill heard him saying sharply, "Don't move her! Don't move her! Get a litter. Get splints."

Jill said, "I can't feel anything." She was whimpering and trying not to. There was no feeling of cold snow beneath her and there should have been. "I can't feel anything." She discovered she could move her head, and then kept moving her head because it was the only thing she *could* move. She saw her hand lying out at one side in an odd position and had the horrible impression that her arm must have come off. Her arm and hand did not seem to be a part of her any longer.

The ski patrol arrived with a toboggan. Sally and Dick and several others lifted her with great care—just enough so that the Stokes litter could be slid beneath her. Jill said with some alarm, "Sally, I can't feel you touching me!" Something, she now knew, had made her unable to

125

move or feel with most of her body. Whatever this something might be, she wondered if it might keep coming up, whether it would come up still higher, into her head. "I can't feel," she cried again.

She was put in temporary traction, tied to both ends of the litter with strips of unbleached muslin which were pulled snug under her chin and apparently cinched around her ankles. Pieces of cardboard were fitted against the sides of her neck and her cheeks to keep her head from moving.

She asked Dick Movitz to find Dave.

The race had been stopped, but it began again after Jill, in her litter, had been lifted onto the toboggan and moved off the course. Someone shouted, "Hey, here comes Andy!" Jill said, "Quick! Sit me up so I can see her go by. I want to see how she does. Sit me up!"

Nobody would move her.

Charlotte Zumstein appeared and touched her cheek gently and said, "Jill, where are your folks?"

"Down at Kratka Ridge, and don't you tell them what's happened. Don't you *dare* tell them."

Dave arrived in time to help walk the toboggan gingerly down the mountain and then up a shallow slope to the first-aid room in the basement of the Alta Lodge. Andy was there and the first thing she said was, "Gee, Tiger, what were you *do*ing?"

Jill mumbled something about having been a bad girl. Sally said Jill had been ten seconds ahead of the field when she crashed.

Jill was worried and puzzled and afraid. She felt as if her arms were gone. She said, "Andy, would you mind going to the hospital with me?" Then she said, "Who won?" It had been Andy, Katy and Skeeter.

There were traffic jams and a bad automobile accident on the narrow, icy road that climbed the steep ten miles up Little Cottonwood Canyon to the ski area, and it was hours before the first ambulance could get in. A cold and damp and dreary wait. Meanwhile, the first-aid room was filling up as the result of eight bad spills during the race. There were soon half a dozen loaded toboggans laid out

126

on the floor, plus Kenny Lloyd with his arm freshly splinted, and the man Jill had hit, who had several broken ribs.

Dave and Andy went with Jill in the ambulance to Salt Lake, but all Jill thought about was staying awake. She was convinced that she would die if she didn't. She said aloud, "Don't let me go to sleep because I know I won't wake up."

She had other worries, however, the moment she was wheeled into Emergency at the Salt Lake General Hospital. They stretched her out on the floor and a doctor approached her with a big pair of shears. "Don't you touch my ski pants!" she said.

"I'm sorry . . ."

"You're *not* going to cut my good Bogners off me!"

"I've no choice."

"Well, all right, but go down the seams, then, so they can be sewed back again."

They couldn't find the seams on her bright red sweater, however, and they slit it right up the front.

The doctor began poking her with a pin and saying, "Can you feel this . . . can you feel this?"

"No," she said, again and again and again.

The world that was beginning to close in about her was made of a white ceiling and lavender tubes of light and a swarm of horribly serious faces and a vague, floating medley of disembodied voices that didn't go with the faces.

"Immediate surgery is indicated."

"What are you waiting for?"

"We can't operate without the parents' permission."

"Look, we've gotten a message to them, but they're on the road or in the air somewhere in southern California."

"Nevertheless, we need a personal release from the girl's parents."

"I'm her coach and I said I'd take full responsibility."

Another voice far away said, "It doesn't matter anyway. She won't last."

Then the room resounded with Dave McCoy's voice. "You *operate!*"

127

Jill said, "Pa? They think I'm going to die?"

Dave pulled out his copy of *Sports Illustrated* and waved it in the doctors' faces and said in a voice that sounded to Jill like Abraham Lincoln's, "Are you going to let this girl go without even *doi*ng anything!"

12

THE REST OF THE KINMONT FAMILY HAD STAYED WITH the Davenports in Pasadena Saturday night and the two families were together at Kratka Ridge most of the day on Sunday. Bob and Jerry were racing, and so was Barni Davenport's sister, Jackie. The big news was that Bob won the downhill by *nine* seconds, which meant he was certain of being invited to the Olympic tryouts in the East. Linda Meyers was making a name for herself, too; she won the girls' slalom.

At the award ceremonies Bud Davenport came up to June Kinmont and said, "The Forest Service has just taken a message for you from somewhere near Salt Lake City. Jill has been in an accident."

June took one long, slow breath before she answered. "What is it? A broken leg?"

"It was worse than that, but the connection was terrible," Bud said. "I don't think we should tell Bill."

June was very calm. She told Bob as soon as he had received his medal, and added, "We'd better not tell Dad until we get down out of the mountains, because of his heart. It's eight thousand feet here and the air's too thin." She pulled her jacket tightly around her shoulders. It was beginning to snow.

Bob stood in front of his mother, pale and staring. "Are you sure?" he said. "Who told you this? It *can't* be. The *try*outs start in a couple of weeks, Mom. It's not *fair*. It's just not *right!*" He went off to see if he could confirm the telephone message.

Bud guessed that Jill had hurt her back, and June thought immediately of Sally Neidlinger's accident three years ago. She said, "That's awfully serious, but at least . . ."

Bob returned with the information that it would be useless to try to telephone Salt Lake City from the hill. His mother said, "Bobby, it's apparently her back or something."

"I know," he answered bitterly. He was furious. To him skiing had been just one of those great things that you do, and if it hadn't been skiing it would have been something else. But to Jill it was everything. She'd put in groveling years of work just to really *make* it, and now when she'd finally earned the chance to do her stuff, the chance was snatched away and crumpled up.

Bill Kinmont waved from a short distance away and strode across the snow toward them. "Boy, what a great race, Bobby," he said, clapping his son warmly on the shoulder. "You know, this is probably the luckiest day of your life."

Bob stood silent for a moment and then turned away.

It was snowing hard now and both the Davenports and the Kinmonts quickly packed into their cars and headed down out of the mountains. The Kinmonts stopped when they reached the valley and June told her husband and Jerry that Jill had had a serious accident. They drove on to Pasadena and telephoned Salt Lake from there. Two hours later Bill and June Kinmont were at the Burbank airport waiting for the next flight to Salt Lake City.

Bob and Jerry stayed with the Davenports. Barni was not at home, but her two younger sisters tried to be cheerful for Jerry's sake. Everyone knew Jill was badly hurt but no one really knew *how* badly.

Jerry Kinmont disappeared soon after his parents and Bud Davenport left for the airport, and he was finally located hiding behind a chair in the dark of the dining room, crying. He never stopped crying until he fell asleep.

In Salt Lake City that Sunday evening the first hospital bulletin listed Jill's condition as *critical* and stated that "early X rays indicated the upper portion of Miss Kinmont's back has been fractured." The local *Time-Life*

130

bureau concluded that there was a measure of comfort in this report because "it had been feared her neck was fractured."

About this time, while June and Bill Kinmont were still in Burbank, Jill was being wheeled in to surgery. She was face down, fully conscious, and they gave her only a local anesthetic. At the side of her eye she caught the flash of light on the blade of a small scalpel. Then she heard the little knife going *ch ch ch ch ch* down the back of her neck and she felt warm blood on the skin along her collarbones.

The anesthetist said, "How are you feeling?"

"Just fine, except kind of drippy on the neck."

The operation was a long one and it ended with the boring of two shallow holes in the top of her skull.

When they wheeled her out she saw Dave hunkering outside the door. He stood up, looking worn and gray. She said, "Hi," and he smiled momentarily. She traveled far, far down the hall, and her mother and father were there and she said, "Hi, Mom. Hi, Dad." The next thing she remembered was a number of very small, pink ballerinas, some of them dancing and some just floating in the air.

She slept until morning, and when she awoke she felt as if she were drifting away somewhere. She was vaguely worried but couldn't follow the thought long enough to make anything of it, and when her parents came to see her she was relatively cheerful. She was also an impressive spectacle for she lay in traction, face up and motionless with wide bandages at the back of her neck. A bottle-fed tube ran into a vein in her left arm. Another tube ran from a suction pump into her nose and down her throat. A catheter—a hollow tube inserted into her bladder—connected her to a urine bottle at one side of the bed. An oxygen tank, with a mask dangling from it, stood close to her head. She was meanwhile being stretched lengthwise by steel tongs which had been fitted into the holes bored into her skull; 35 pounds of sausage-shaped iron weights hung from a cable which ran over a pulley behind her head and was wired to the tongs. She was lying on

131

a Stryker frame, a canvas-covered metal frame supported at the head and foot by a kind of axle which allowed her to be turned regularly like a roast on a spit. Two hours face up, two hours face down. In the latter position, an opening in the canvas gave her an unobstructed view of the floor.

Jill's condition was still *critical.* She felt no particular pain except that the back of her neck was stiff and swollen. She didn't even have a headache. Slight feeling had returned to her arms—a vague, tingling awareness—but she had no sensation whatever in her body below the shoulders. The tongs biting into her head were no more painful than a deep scratch, but whenever she thought about the way they were hooked into her skull she began to feel sick.

Things got better as the day wore on . . . which is to say, someone talked the doctors into letting her have a few selected visitors even though she felt sleepy and occasionally drifted back into dreams. Bud came in, silent and serious. His voice, when he finally said, "Hello, Jill," was scarcely audible. After a short while he nodded and backed toward the door. "I'll see you again before I go east."

Jill said, "Aren't you going to kiss me good-by?"

He leaned forward dutifully, despite the forest of tubes and wires, and gave her a peck on the lips. "Practically twisted my neck out of shape," he said with a quick, shy grin. "Well, so long."

Andy's visit was something else again. She stood with one fist on her hip, surveying Jill's medical sideshow. "What are all the tubes? How are they treating you? What's this flip-flop business?"

Kenny turned up briefly with his arm in a sling, and his overwhelming *"Whataya say, Ace?"* rang through the corridors.

Jill had a beautiful tan and her attire, she thought, was quite sexy; she was not allowed to wear any clothing, so her shoulders and arms were bare and the rest of her body was covered only with a sheet. Her greatest annoyance was that her field of view was limited to the ceiling directly above or the floor directly below. Except for a kissing friend like Bud, she saw very little of her visitors. She quickly learned to recognize her parents and Dave by the sound of their footsteps, and when she was face down she could easily distinguish the regular nurses and doctors by the look of their feet. Dr. Patterson, for example, always wore white buckskin shoes with big brown bloodstains on them. When Jill was on her back she had to be content with following the cracks in the green ceiling and despising the exposed green pipes and what she could see of the florid window draperies with their maroon, green, yellow and white ferns.

Her head was rigidly fixed by the tongs. Consequently it always rested on the middle of her brow or on one spot at the back. These areas were getting sore, so Dave sat with her most of Monday night, supporting her forehead with his hands when she was face down and holding up the back of her head when she faced the ceiling. He left before dawn, planning to return to Bishop so he could bring Bob Kinmont and Roma back for a visit.

Her father held her head, too, but she couldn't stand the cigarette smell on his fingers. She even asked him not to smoke in the room because of the odor.

When Jill awakened Tuesday morning her room was so full of flowers that it looked like a funeral parlor. Five stacks of letters and telegrams were piled against the wall, plus two packages, each of which contained a stuffed animal. It was a very Christmaslike morning.

Best of all was a call from Dick Buek . . . even though June had to take the call because Jill could not be moved to a telephone and there was no phone in the room. Dick was in Germany and had just heard about the accident. He wanted to know just what the injury involved, how Jill was right now, and how long she was likely to be in the hospital in Salt Lake. He said he was trying in every way he could to get back to the States to see her. He'd told the Red Cross he had to get home at once because his fiancée was dying.

There were dozens of letters from friends and hundreds from strangers. Many of them contained dollar bills, even a few fives and tens. Jill was puzzled that so many people she did not know should be concerned. The people of Salt Lake City sent gifts and words of cheer and many offers of a temporary home for Jill's parents. They lent Bill a car and Jill a television set. Bill kept saying, "Nobody asked what they could do to help; they just helped."

The Junior Chamber of Commerce, which had sponsored the Snow Cup, donated the gate receipts from the race to help meet hospital expenses.

"I thought I had in*sur*ance!" Jill said.

"You did," her father answered.

"Well . . . ?"

"Well, it wasn't quite enough, honeygirl."

What Bill Kinmont thought and did not say was: accident insurance in the amount of $700 just about takes care of sandwiches for the ambulance crew. The bank in Bishop was at the moment setting up a new mortgage on the Rocking K—$25,000 instead of $14,000—so there would be some ready cash available. Dr. Powell had already told Bill, "She'll need a nurse with her twenty-four hours a day for a long while, three shifts. As far as medical expenses in general are concerned, it will take $20,000 just to get things started. But don't worry about it."

Bill had no idea how costs might run once things got "started," but he knew exactly how much $20,000 was. He could translate it at once into man-hours, bar sales, construction costs, capital gains or net profits on P-38 parts sold to the Army Air Forces. He had worked for his father in a small manufacturing plant during the 1930's and had taken over the plant himself when his father, mother and sister were killed in an automobile accident. The business had thrived on war contracts and had converted to the manufacture of industrial machinery in 1945. Three years after that Bill had sold the plant and bought the ranch in Bishop, so all his money was now tied up in the Rocking K. He and June and the three children had an investment of labor and love tied up in

134

the ranch, too, and he was reluctant to consider the possibility that it might have to go.

At the moment, which was midmorning of Tuesday, the first of February, Jill was receiving letters and messages by the bundle from Bishop. Todd Watkins, who published the *Inyo Register,* telephoned regularly so that he could keep the town posted on her progress. St. Timothy's had conducted a special prayer service at 7:30 that morning. The local radio station broadcast special *Jill Kinmont* bulletins, and the stores in town were putting out collection jars labeled HELP JILL UP THE HILL. The money was for the Far West Ski Association's Jill Kinmont Fund.

A fresh nurse came on duty and went very busily in and out for about ten minutes until Jill noticed that the room's fragrance seemed to be fading away. "Is somebody carting off my flowers or something?" she said.

"They're using up your oxygen. We have to keep them out of here."

"If anything, they're *giving* oxygen."

"The hospital believes otherwise."

It was flip-flop time again, and two orderlies named Bud and Clark came whistling into the room on schedule. Jill got a good look at them as they worked over the Stryker frame and decided they were both pretty cute. They placed on top of her a canvas-covered frame similar to the one on which she was already lying and they secured her neatly inside this sandwich after pinching off the catheter and arranging all the tubes so they wouldn't tangle. Then, while a nurse held up the weights attached to her head, Clark barked a brief order—"Prepare to blast off"—and Jill was flipped 180 degrees with admirable dispatch. The frame she had been lying on was now on top and was removed, and she was free to stare at the floor for two hours.

A skier named George Hunt, whom Jill had met at Mammoth, appeared with a bottle of Chanel #5. Since she could see only his feet, he stretched out on the floor, partly under the bed, and they had a pleasant face-to-face chat.

135

Another advantage of being face down was that letters or newspapers could be placed on a low shelf under the bed and she could read with ease as long as someone turned the pages for her. The face-up half of the day was made more palatable by the borrowed television set and by a small tilted mirror above her head which enabled her to see it.

News clippings about the accident were many and varied although the choice of adjectives to modify the subject was somewhat limited: Jill Kinmont, the plucky young skier . . . The spunky eighteen-year-old Bishop, Calif., blonde . . . The spunky little lass . . . Plucky Jill Kinmont . . . A spunky young woman . . . Spunky Jill Kinmont . . . Plucky Jill . . .

Jill said, "Isn't it *funny,* Mom, the way they write these articles?"

The accounts of the accident were constantly surprising. Her flight through the air was never less than 50 feet and in one newspaper it reached 100. Her speed had doubled, she had crashed into everything from tree trunks to whole crowds of spectators, and she had "practically won the race" several times. One reporter even attributed bird-like qualities to her: "Had she turned in mid-air and headed towards an open gate, she might have made it and won the Snow Cup."

Jill also came upon at least a dozen reasons for the crash, none of which she recognized. Dick Movitz said that snow and wind conditions had changed drastically and the course had turned icy. Dave said the wind had been blowing a layer of ground snow down along the run and kept Jill from seeing how fast she was traveling. She was pleased, and a little amused, to find everyone so anxious to discover excuses for her.

Dr. Patterson came around Tuesday evening in his blood-spattered white buck shoes and spent most of the night working on a small problem in hydraulic engineering. Jill asked what he was trying to do. "It's just a matter of getting the waterworks to work," he told her. He was trying to set up what he called a "tidal drain" so that her bladder would automatically fill with a mild solution of

136

acetic acid and empty again at regular intervals. This would keep the bladder pliable and help avoid the severe urinary problems that inevitably accompany paralysis. His problem was one of figuring where and how high to hang the various bottles so that the drain would operate automatically and still not interfere with the flipping of the Stryker frame every two hours. From that evening on, Jill always called him "Dr. P."

On Wednesday they pulled the needle out of her left arm and began giving her real food for a change. She was fed by a fat and sloppy nurse with bad breath whose conversation was ever-pleasant, ever-present and effervescent. "Are we ready for our big dinner?" she said gaily, spoon-feeding Jill a gooey, undercooked soft-boiled egg. "Now we mustn't frown. We must remember that, as a food, *egg* has *ev*erything." One of the interns stopped at the door and the nurse told him how many ways her mother had of fixing eggs. Since she believed in looking at the person with whom she was speaking, she dumped a generous spoonful of undercooked egg down the side of Jill's neck.

Dave arrived in the afternoon with Roma and Bob. He moved with an aggravated quickness Jill had never seen before and his footsteps were stomping ones. When he spoke with Roma his voice was abrupt and when Roma mentioned this, he jumped on her.

When Bob came in he glanced at all the contraptions and said, *"Ye gads."* He seemed shocked but also very curious.

"It's kind of a circus," Jill said. "How do you like the bed?"

"Sort of neat. But they sure got you tied down."

"And how do you like the TV? It's all switched left for right so it looks normal in a mirror. Hey, what's going on at Mammoth? Are you going to be in shape for the tryouts?"

Bob shrugged. He stood beside the bed, fingering the acetic acid bottle. "I'll make it," he said. He was not at a loss for words as much as he was at a loss for feeling. He was still angered by the accident and still bewildered.

He thought, I'll be skiing for you, y'know—and Jill knew this—but he said only, "I'd like to get on the team. I've even been training!"

The next visitor was Jerry, who had come from Los Angeles with his aunt Beverly Lewis. His first train ride. He said, *"Ow! Ice-tongs!* Right in your *head!"* He was profoundly impressed by the stacks of mail that came for his sister and spent most of his time standing on a stool holding up letters for her to read.

13

OFFICIALLY, JILL'S CONDITION HAD IMPROVED FROM *critical* to *poor*, and everything seemed to be looking up. The oxygen tank and the suction machine were still there, but both appeared to be unnecessary. Intravenous feeding was a thing of the past. Dr. Evans, the orthopedic surgeon with the bushy mustache, had offered some very optimistic remarks about the future.

Slight feeling seemed to be returning to her upper arms, but she could feel nothing in her legs or trunk or hands. Many times she tried to move her fingers and her toes. She tried to feel. She tried to figure out what it felt like *not* to feel. There certainly was no positive sensation of her body being absent or vacant or cut off. What she felt below her shoulders was a vague heaviness which reminded her faintly of the way a leg feels when it is "asleep." Along with this came a *glowing* sensation which gave her the impression that her hands and legs must be warm. She remembered having felt armless while waiting for the ambulance, but once she'd had a good look at her arms in the operating room that particular sensation had never returned.

After supper Dr. Powell looked in, smiled, and nodded at Bill Kinmont in a rather meaningful manner. Bill and June joined him in the corridor a few moments later. "I don't want to frighten you," he said in a frighteningly subdued voice, "but I must tell you that the mortality rate for this type of injury is very high." He paused uneasily, as if about to speak again, but he only licked his lips. And then he left.

For Bill and June Kinmont this was the most unnerving moment of all the unhappy moments so far. Through all the hard hours since Sunday afternoon they had grieved and worried about many things, but it had not occurred to them that Jill was ever in danger of dying.

And why had Dr. Powell dropped this little shocker *now*, almost three days after the accident and the operation? Had some new threat and danger cropped up? Nobody could tell them. Everyone said, "Things are going along just fine."

Life seemed to have two levels that were scarcely connected. On one was the sun-tanned skier laughing at Jerry and worrying about how her hair could be washed with those tongs sunk in her head. On another level was a patient whose body could scarcely function, whose condition hovered between poor and critical, and whose chances of dying, statistically at any rate, were excellent.

June Kinmont stopped weeping in private about Jill's legs and hands, for she now had been dragged down to a more essential concern. The stark prospect of a spirited young girl being caged for life in a lifeless body was undeniably less stark than the prospect of death. Jill had not been killed, and this was something for which to be devoutly grateful. June remembered a guest at the Rocking K who had a daughter with a head injury and extensive brain damage. The woman had always said, when asked, "She's doing as good as can be expected," which meant that nothing could be expected because there had been nothing left to work with. June also remembered the young girl she had seen skipping gaily down the corridor in a bathrobe two days before; a nurse had mentioned casually that the girl had a brain tumor and would be dead within two weeks. June said to her husband, "We can be thankful our girl is as well off as she is."

There was nothing June could do for her daughter now as far as physical care was concerned, but there were still hundreds of small tasks and errands she could perform. She read Jill's mail to her and answered some of the letters. She cut out newspaper stories and she went shopping for lipstick or hair ribbons or a magazine. And she knew that her simple presence was the most eloquent way she could find of saying, "I am here; I love you."

She had never been a demonstrative person and neither had Jill. There had always been a good-night kiss, but affection was usually expressed with a pat on the hand or a warm smile rather than with hugs and kisses. June remembered Jill at the age of eighteen months sitting up straight in the front seat of the car, not about to snuggle up to anybody.

June also believed that personal grief was something best borne in private since her tears could help no one. If she felt unable to smile, she stayed away from her daughter's room. The rest of the time, however, she was cheerful and fresh and neatly combed. This was all she could do for the present, and until there was more to be done she would spend all her time at it because it was the most important thing there was. She was a very ordinary mother, she thought, without anything to qualify her for coping with the present extraordinary situation. But as time went on she began to discover many small realities that were easier to accept and emotions that were easier to comprehend because of what she had already learned, without realizing it, from Audra Jo Nicholson and her mother.

On Thursday, four days after the accident, the reporters were let in. The swirl of activity was a circus and a maelstrom. It was quite something to be *queen* again, even if you had to be stretched out motionless on a slab to make it. But it was disturbing to be asked questions that the questioners seemed to have answered already for themselves.

"How often do you ask yourself, *Why did it have to happen to me?*"

"I never thought of it."

"Well, I'm *sure* you *did* think of it. When was the first time?"

"Were you really going sixty miles an hour?"

"Twenty-five or thirty is more like it."

"*Fifty*, then, maybe?"

"How can you take it, just *lying* there, and still smile?"

"How long till you'll be skiing again?"

"Gee, *I* don't know what's going to happen or not happen."

"How come you're so brave? Where'd you get all that spunk?"

The reporters were finally herded out and the photographers were given five minutes. They had been slinking around the corridors all day and now they exploded into the room firing their little puffs of brilliant light.

Five minutes lasted a long time. "Nurse, *please*, just this *one* shot." *Pfoo!* "Hey, Jill, baby, *smile!* And now the two of you."

Jill heard her father's voice in the hallway. "Don't worry, she'll get well. And if she wants to get back on those boards again, it'll be okay with us. We don't hold skiing responsible for this accident. It's something that just happened. Bobby and Jerry haven't quit skiing because of it, and we hope no one else does, either."

And a strange voice: "Mrs. Kinmont, just one question. How can you let your son go east to race when your daughter's just broken her neck? Doesn't it kill you to see him go?"

"It doesn't happen to be my decision."

The next morning Jill read in a newspaper: *I'm gonna run it again, said spunky Jill Kinmont from a traction bed, declaring she wasn't through.*

No one appeared to be disturbed by the gap between the facts and what was said to be the facts. In almost two days Jill had been able to move nothing but her eyes and her face. She had no feeling below the shoulders except for some sensation in her arms. She knew, whenever she really thought about it, that she must be in serious and lasting trouble.

But everyone insisted upon talking about the day when she would be back on skis. She even began to talk this way herself. Newspaper accounts were glowing with hope. Friends spoke with an air of wise confidence. June Kinmont talked about Sally's recovery from her broken back. Dr. Evans again gave them all hope that Jill might

142

eventually regain the use of her hands. Dr. Powell was of no particular help since he came in every morning and said, "How are you? You don't look very sick," and left. Jill's hands never moved, but one of the nurses told a reporter in a learned voice, "Her condition may only be temporary. She's moving her hands now more than when I came on duty this morning." Jill tried to move her fingers and tried to move her toes, and she kept trying. But they would not move.

Jill's immediate problems were of no medical significance whatever but were very much on her mind. She had always cared about being clean and combed and neatly dressed, and this concern became highly frustrating when other hands were fixing her hair or putting on her lipstick. She was being given a daily sponge bath, but it would be weeks or months before she could hope to get to a hairdresser. Her hair hadn't even been washed for almost a week and it was beginning to feel itchy and to look, she thought, decidedly unkempt. She said to her doctors, "How can I *possibly* get my hair washed with all this hardware on my head?"

Chris, one of the special nurses, would have done the job hair by hair if this could have helped, and the chief nurse, Wiggins, would have pitched in, too. Someone discovered a dry shampoo, which proved to be a total flop. In the end Jill settled for simply combing and brushing and then tying into two ponytails.

Other minor problems were working out rather well. It was important to her that she appear as normal as possible, even in bed, even when suspended face down; and visitors were constantly mentioning how healthy she looked. She fretted about losing her tan, so the nurses scrounged a sun lamp for her. She had a collection of more than a dozen eight-by-ten photographs and these were now taped onto the wall where she could see them at least part of the time. Cards and letters were stuck on the opposite wall. A clothesline was strung up for her growing collection of twentieth-century artifacts, which included two wooden monkeys, a plastic pirate pistol, a

143

doll on skis, a rag monkey, and a menagerie of stuffed animals: large monkey, grinning cat, small fluffy white dog, big fluffy white dog, another monkey, rabbit, big floppy duck, lion, another rabbit, and a horse.

A local glass company sent a mirror measuring 18 by 30 inches. It was mounted to swivel in a frame so Jill could watch either television or the doorway of her room. The mirror was most convenient for talking with visitors, although some visitors were unnerved when they stood at the head of the bed looking straight at what seemed to be a window behind which Jill was apparently standing.

The best thing about the mirror was that Jill could see more than just the eyes and foreheads of people who were speaking to her. She could see now what all the faces were wearing: her mother's open-collared print blouse, Jerry's baggy gray sweater, Dad's dark jacket and shirt, Dave's light jacket and plaid shirt, Roma's short-sleeved black sweater and the two bracelets clinking on her wrist. She could also see her own body, which was for some reason a comfort. She discovered it was easy for her to feel that her legs were in the position they were actually in as long as she looked first. But if her legs were then moved without her noticing, she continued to imagine them, even to "feel" them, in the original position.

Mail was down to about fifty letters a day. One letter was addressed simply to "Jill, Salt Lake City," and another to "The Girl Who Broke Her Back in the Ski Accident." There were letters from the governor of Utah and artist Norman Rockwell and an encouraging note from golfer Ben Hogan, who had been told he might not walk again after his automobile accident but who came back to win the National Open. There was a short, affectionate note from Bud Werner every three or four days.

By the end of the first week Jill's condition was still *poor*. Her parents had spoken with the internist and with the orthopedist and with the neurosurgeon and with the urologist and with the physical therapist, and they still had the uncomfortable impression that they hadn't really been informed as to just what were the blunt facts about

Above: Jill at the Rocking K; left: with Audra Jo. Below: Linda Meyers and Dave Mc-Coy.

Left: Dick Buek. *(Franz Berko.)* Right: Jill skiing down Mammoth. *(Stephen Lukacik.)* Below: Jill and Bud Werner at Sun Valley, December, 1954. *(Joern Gerdtz.)*

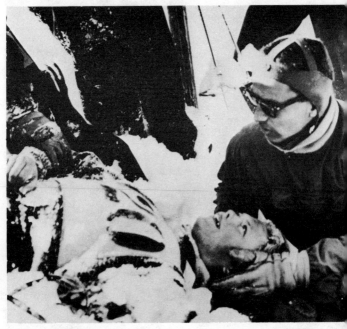

Dick Movitz holds Jill's head immediately after her crash at Alta. *(John H. White.)*

(The photograph at the right and those on the following pages are by Burk Uzzle.)

Jill with her father and mother.

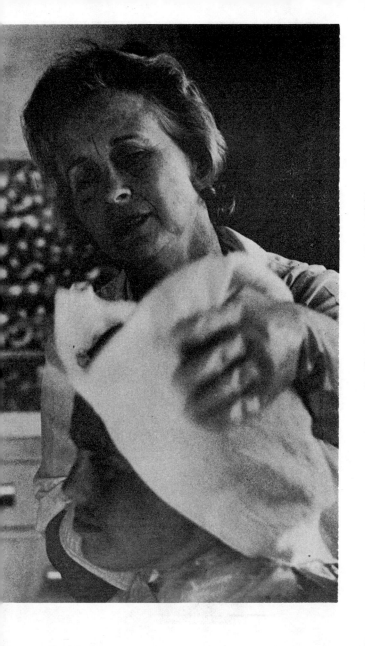

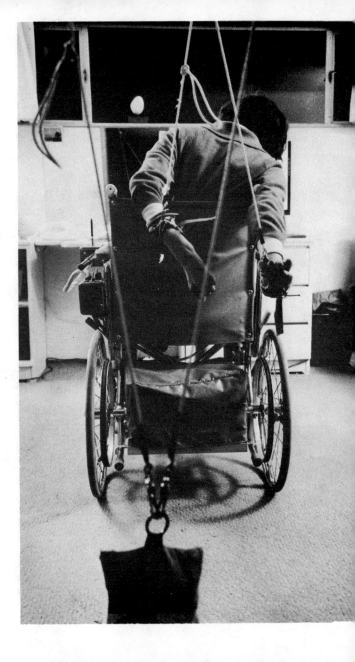

Left: Jill works out with sandbags to maintain the muscles of her arms and shoulders. Above: Jill lunches at home.

A family clam
dig. Right: Jill
tilts with Bob
while Jerry
and his wife
watch.

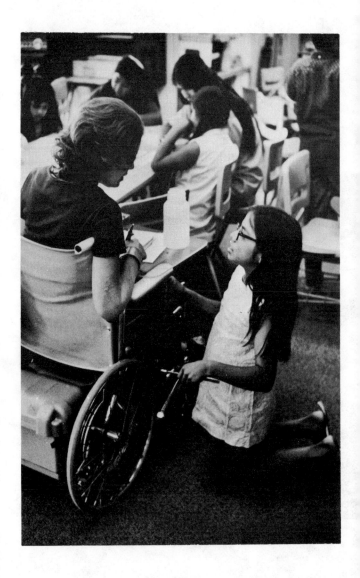

Jill teaches at the Owens Valley Indian Education Center on the Paiute reservation in Bishop.

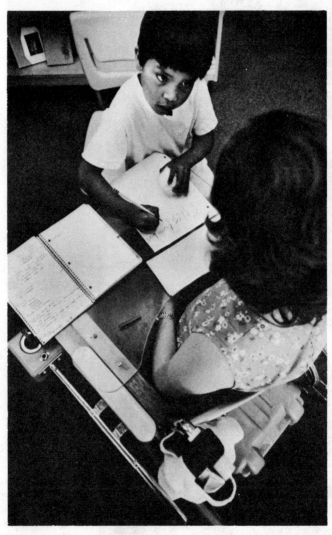

Top: David Moose writes a story. Right: Jill likes an original answer.

Jerry and Jill.

Jill's injuries and reasonable expectations. So Bill telephoned a friend of his, Ted Lynn, in Los Angeles.

Dr. Lynn flew up the next day. He said he was grateful for the chance to be of some help and he talked with Jill about the Rocking K. He wanted to know why it was that his trout had never been more than a couple of pounds while Bill Kinmont could stand beside him and pull seven-pounders out of the same hole . . . even when the two of them swapped rods.

He examined Jill, checked her records and X rays, and summarized the situation to Bill and June matter-of-factly. She had sustained a fracture-dislocation of the spine at the level of the fourth and fifth and sixth cervical vertebrae, resulting in transection of the cord. In other words, the spinal cord was completely severed low in the neck, which caused permanent paralysis, both motor and sensory, below the shoulders. No movement, no feeling. Breathing remained unimpaired, however, and the arms might retain some function.

It was difficult to account for all the vague optimism that had been wafted about the hospital throughout the week, for these facts were already on record, having been directly observed during the operation. At that time the spinal cord was seen to be mashed to a pulp and there was no continuity of the structure. Nor could anything possibly be done to restore it. Jill had been paralyzed from the shoulders down since the moment of impact.

Dr. Lynn said there was little hope for any improvement, although a few arm muscles might come back.

June said, "But her hands . . . ?"

"Physiologically, her hands are knocked out, too."

June absorbed this information slowly, soberly. She was confident that her daughter would live, and she thanked God for that; but she had not until now known about or faced the full extent and finality of the injury. She walked down the drab corridor and sat in the one worn leather chair with the shiny metal arms. She waited there, holding a handkerchief across her eyes, until she could muster enough cheer to return to Jill's room.

145

Bill went out with Dr. Lynn. "I guess this is the point where rehabilitation really begins," he said. "I mean for the whole family. And I guess that's what you've been trying to say to us, isn't it? The place to start from has got to be rock bottom." Bill was beginning to see how deeply the accident would involve the personal emotions and the practical affairs of each member of the family.

The practical questions of where and how the family would live and how the hospital expenses could be financed were tied up with all the other considerations, but these were Bill's responsibility specifically. He approached the problem as he had approached rough problems before, focusing his entire attention on it for several days until he had a solution and a detailed plan of action. He worried and figured constantly but consulted with no one. He sat alone, thinking, sometimes scribbling on a pad, crumpling the page thoughtfully in his big gnarly hand as soon as he had found the answer to whatever his immediate question had been.

Bill tried to appraise the Rocking K purely as an investment and as a business. But he remembered it first of all as the place he had always wanted and worked for, where he could bring up his kids to take care of themselves in the wilds and find their way in the mountains and learn the difference between a char and a trout, between a moose and an elk. He had wanted to live in the valley ever since the summer of 1930 when he and June Haines had run away to get married during a family camping trip at Mammoth. His mind's eye was most reluctant to see the ranch as so many improvements and so much livestock on so many acres with such and such a yearly gross. What really mattered about the Rocking K were the quail and jackrabbits the family found on summer evening walks. Or the willows that framed the White Mountains at sunset.

Bill tried to justify hanging onto the place. The most important argument was that Jerry was just at the age when the ranch would mean most to him; he deserved the same chance Bob and Jill had had to play and ride and swim and climb trees and fish and hunt and learn about

146

the mountains. On purely practical grounds, the ranch was an excellent investment with a predictable income during the season and great potential as a year-round operation as soon as skiing facilities up at Mammoth were expanded.

So it was not unrealistic to consider swinging a very substantial mortgage or a big loan and continuing to own and operate it. *Correct?* Impossible, unless he and June both were on the job full time. June's place now was with Jill. And what good would the ranch, or Bishop, ever be to Jill? She was going to need things like extensive therapy and college-level classes and a chance to develop new interests and search for a job.

The big, inescapable economic reality remained precisely what it had been: the sale of the ranch was the family's only possible source of cash to meet Jill's hospital and rehabilitation expenses. Bill Kinmont's conclusion was: sell immediately, keeping one selfish acre just in case it should ever become possible to return, and settle in some big city with a new home and a new job. "So we do what has to be done," he told June, "and we build around that, or at least we try to."

"I guess that's fair enough," she answered. "The accident happened to all of us, after all. I just hope we can still live as normal a life as possible. You know, family trips and everything."

Bill told Jill that the ranch would probably have to be sold to meet hospital expenses, and Jill tried in vain to think of some alternative. Bill then left for Bishop to see about prospects for a sale and to work out some way of operating the ranch for the season if he couldn't find a buyer.

Jill was stung by the news that the ranch would have to go, but she knew it was even more of a disappointment to her father, who had spent nearly a decade nursing his dream into reality. She remembered how he used to pile them all into the jeep and go looking for arrowheads and grinding stones in the desert or, after the first light snow, drive up into Buttermilk Country to see the hundreds of deer coming down from the mountains to feed. She remembered all the lakes and streams up behind Bishop Creek where they had fished together and she remembered tagging along when Bill took the boys duck hunting up on Hot Creek. He had loved to skate with them on the upper pond, too, and could sometimes be coaxed into a wild sled ride in the south pasture. He'd always seemed so much younger than the fathers of their school friends.

14

ON TUESDAY MORNING, JILL'S NINTH DAY IN SALT LAKE City, she glanced up into her mirror and saw a wheelchair coming in the door. She shouted, *"Josie!* What are *you* doing here?"

Audra Jo wheeled herself into the room and over to the head of the bed. "Hi, Jill." She sounded as casual as ever, although it required considerable control for her to appear offhand about what immediately caught her attention: the Crutchfield tongs hooked onto her friend's head and the oxygen tank at one side. She wasn't aware that she had been staring until Jill said, "Yeah, I've got holes in my head."

"Well, at least you didn't have to have a tracheotomy."

"How'd you get here Jose?"

"Don and Gloria drove me all the way from L.A. They'll be in in a little bit." Don Redman had been one of the original crew at Mammoth and his wife had put in as many hours in the ticket booth as Roma had.

"Oh, you crazy guys . . ." Jill tried to blink a tear from her eye. "That's a long way just to say hello. How was the trip?"

"We had a nice trip except for a little john trouble. You'd have *died*, Jill. At our last rest stop my chair wouldn't fit through the door into the john and Don had to just pick me up and carry me in and set me on the pot."

"Poor Don," Jill said, and they both laughed.

"Have you seen much of Bud?" Audra Jo asked. "What did he say?"

Jill smiled. "He only stayed a couple of minutes. But Skeeter—I just got a letter from her yesterday—she said

Buddy didn't say a single word all the way back to Aspen. How did you hear about the crash, Josie?"

"I was in Victorville, and at first we were all so relieved that you didn't have a broken leg. But then my uncle came in at noon with the paper and that terrible picture of you in the snow saying *I can't feel a thing.* And then on Tuesday, getting that letter you wrote before the crash . . . you saying the course looked great and you just hoped you could stand up, and all."

Later, when Audra Jo wheeled herself out into the corridor, three strangers nodded to her and one of them said to her, "You're looking a lot better, Miss Kinmont. It's good to see you up out of bed so soon." She said, "Thank you."

Audra Jo stayed for two days and spent most of the time reading Jill's mail to her. She also talked with June Kinmont and tried to reassure her about Jill's future. "Oh, she'll be able to get along fine, June," she said. "Just as long as she's got her hands."

Jill, for her own part, had not yet had time to worry about the future. It was enough to worry about now and an hour from now. Also, she had been busy with visitors and letters. She was aware that she might never race again, but the greatest disappointment was that she was already missing the Olympic tryouts. No one had yet suggested to her that she might not be walking again at some vaguely future time, and she had never compared herself with Audra Jo, whose horrible fate it was to be a victim of polio. Her greatest concern was Bud Werner—when would he be coming to see her again?

One morning Dr. Powell stopped in for more than his usual *You don't look sick* greeting. He said her condition was improving and she asked when she might be back on her feet again.

"Well," he said slowly, looking straight at her, "your journey back is going to take a long time. Just like your girl friend."

"What did you say?" The voice had been loud enough,

150

but for some reason Jill could not remember, five seconds later, what words it had said.

"I said it will be a long time, like your girl friend."

"Audra Jo?"

"The one in the chair."

Jill was glad, for once, that she could just stare at cracks in the ceiling. Dr. Powell apparently had left, for the room was quiet. Jill counted the years. Audra Jo had been in a wheelchair for nearly three years and there was no reason to think she would ever be out of it.

Jill did not think about skiing, or even about walking or dancing. She thought about her hands. In some mysterious way she knew what Dr. Lynn had said about her hands. He had not told her and neither had her parents, but somehow she knew. She said to herself, Just like your girl friend; except that your girl friend has hands and I guess you don't have hands; you can be practically in control if only you have your hands.

No one else was in the room, which was fortunate because it was important now to be alone.

If the break had been a fraction of an inch lower, she would have had full use of her hands. And of course, *if* she had slowed down, then she wouldn't have crashed and burned at all. And if she'd thought Andy would slow down there, then she would have taken the time to slow down also. But she had decided to win.

If, if, if, if . . . is a good game and any number can play and anything whatever can be pretended. If the break had been a fraction of an inch *higher* she could not have breathed without an iron lung. If just this or that tiny thing had been different, she would be dead. Life is a million *ifs* a day. But if *only* you had your hands you could be practically independent.

A picture appeared in Jill's mind. Rather, a memory of a movie she had seen somewhere, sometime. A pair of bear cubs broke into someone's pantry and managed to open a honey jar and a can of flour. The cubs were ingenious and full of hell and it was remarkable the number of tricks they mastered using just their paws.

Alone on her back under the cracked green ceiling,

151

thinking and trying to puzzle out the whole thing, Jill discovered a question . . . a simple question although she didn't know what the answer might be: *What can you do without hands; what can you do with what you've got?*

Jill received a short, informative letter from Dick Buek. He was still badgering the Red Cross, trying to get himself sent to Salt Lake City, but the U.S. Army wouldn't go for it. He would get to see her, one way or another, as soon as possible. He thought he might, anyway, make it back to the States in time to compete in the tryouts in New Hampshire.

Two days later, on February sixteenth, Bud Werner walked into the room. Jill saw him in the mirror and watched him tiptoe toward the head of the Stryker frame, unaware that she was watching him. He dropped a small package on her stomach and bent over her face and said, "Happy birthday!" Her eyes were already watering and she leaned her cheek hard against his hand. All she said was, "Buddy . . ."

He opened her present for her. It was a small St. Christopher medal on a fine silver chain. On the back was an inscription, TO JILL FROM BUD. "I etched it myself," he said.

"It's so pretty," she said after a long moment. "Really —I've always wanted a St. Christopher. How long can you stay?"

He said he was in town for two days. He was about to leave for the tryouts in the East and he told Jill all about the final week of training in Aspen with Andy and Skeeter and Nancy Banks.

"Gads, but you guys'll have fun."

The conversation was interrupted by Clark and Bud, the orderlies, and it concluded with Jill facing the floor. Buddy Werner said softly, "Jill, you'll be riding with me on the tails of my skis on every run down the mountain."

Buddy left and Jill asked a nurse to put the Christopher medal around her neck. It was not actively painful, but it felt as if it were about to saw its way into her healing scar. She asked the nurse to hang it on her mirror.

After lunch, a four-foot-high birthday cake was wheeled into Jill's room, followed by friends and reporters and officials and the mayor himself. She was given a $1,000 check from the Shrine's Golden Boot Patrol in Los Angeles and a ski trophy on which were engraved the words TO JILL—UTAH'S ADOPTED DAUGHTER. The cake was cut. There was enough for all 250 patients in the hospital.

The Mammoth gang was up at Badger Pass in Yosemite the following weekend for the Far West Junior Championships, which were now so well known that over 2,000 spectators turned out. Jill received a long telegram from Dave Sunday evening:

DEAR JILL WE REALLY TIGERED IT. DOWN-HILL SLALOM AND COMBINED BOBBY FIRST. . . .

The message also listed race results for Linda Meyers, who had won the girls' slalom, for Peanut, Poncho and Gary McCoy, and for jumpy Jerry Kinmont. The telegram went on:

JER THE HARE FIRST HIS FIRST RUN IN SLALOM BUT TOO MUCH HOPPITY HOP AND GOT OFF IN THE BUSH. THE GANG WAS SURE GLAD TO GET THE TELEGRAM IT ARRIVED AS BOBBY WAS IN THE GATE TO START AND IT GAVE EVERYBODY A BIG SHOVE. SEE YOU SOON. DAVE.

Jill saved a headline from Monday's paper especially for Bob, from whom it was certain to draw at least a groan:

BROTHER OF JILL SCORES AT BADGER

Jill Kinmont had picked up a few facts of life and death from her talks and visits with Audra Jo. Her medical education really began in the Salt Lake General Hospital, however, and it was built upon a foundation of profound naïveté. She knew she was paralyzed but she had no idea

153

why; she only knew it was vaguely like a lamp going out if you cut the cord.

The first thing that intrigued her was her own medical history. There is a game that hospitals play whereby everybody in the building, except the patient and his relatives, is free to study the patient's sacred chart; the patient is supposed to guess, on the basis of deliberately misleading clues, what is really going on inside his own body. But a pretty girl has certain advantages, and Jill's short cut to the truth was embodied in the persons of Bud and Clark, who found her chart and read it aloud to her. Thus it was that she heard for the first time fascinating phrases like *Crutchfield tongs, apparent total quadriplegia,* and *minimal brachial radialis function.*

"Boy, were you ever in lousy shape," Bud said. "You know you damn near kicked off about five times?"

"Gee, *really?*"

"Kid, that first week was really touch and go, it says here. On top of everything else you had a blood clot, and if *that* had moved . . . *splat!*"

Meanwhile, Jill was proving to be the best audio-visual aid the hospital teaching staff had ever had. The orthopedic students came in and they all had pins and pens. Big hatpins and little ballpoint pens. They pricked her with the pins and said, "Can you feel that? Holler when you start to feel something." When she said "yeh" or "ouch," they marked little crosses on her skin with the pens. Then a bunch of interns came in and *they* had pins and pens. Three residents came in with very serious faces but the same old pins. Jill soon had a forest of X's running across her body from shoulder to shoulder just above her breasts . . . and another forest across her back, slightly lower. Different medical students made somewhat different marks, a sort of code, perhaps, and Jill bore proudly her great array of conflicting brands.

A physical therapist named Mr. Green started coming every evening at 8:30 or 9. He was slim and blond and slightly bald and he wore a plaid hat and a heavy brown plaid overcoat. He brought a mysterious little machine in a big suitcase, but all it could do was to make some of

154

her muscles jump. He attached little pads to various spots on her arms or shoulders and pressed a switch so the machine would make insistent little *dz dz dz dz dz dz* sounds. Sometimes a muscle would make a small flicker of response and sometimes it wouldn't. She said, "Why can I feel with the front of my arm and not with the back of it?"

Every time Mr. Green found a muscle that jumped in response to his electrotherapy machine, he made Jill try to flex it. One evening he said in a low, earnest voice, "I've got quite a crowd of boys down on the corner hoping to get a look at you, Jill, in that low-necked sheet. I've been selling tickets."

Jill laughed and forgot about her muscles and Mr. Green said, *"Work, Jill Kinmont, work!"*

Jill made a number of discoveries. She began to speak of *flexors*, the muscles which bend an arm or finger, and of *extensors*, which extend and straighten. She located muscles she had never heard of—her deltoids and trapezius, which were in good shape, and her wrist flexors, pectorals and various finger muscles, which had been knocked out. She had worried about how her heart and stomach could keep working when she was paralyzed, and she now learned that digestion and circulation and glandular responses can operate independently of the spinal cord.

Mr. Green usually tilted Jill's mirror so she could watch the muscles he wanted her to work on. She could both see and feel a flutter of movement in two muscles she had been unable to move a few weeks earlier—the biceps in her right arm and one of the wrist extensors. Her sensory nerves had improved slightly and she could feel pinpricks as low as her shoulder bones at the back and almost down to the nipple line in front.

Once she saw the sheet twitch suddenly just above her knee, and this quivering of a leg muscle became a shy quiver of hope. She said, "Mr. Green, I think my right leg just jumped a little bit."

"Clonus," he said, attaching a small pad to her forearm. "It's just an involuntary spasm."

"Oh."

"It doesn't mean anything."

"Sort of like how a fish flops around on the dock after he's dead, huh?"

"Uh . . . I hadn't exactly thought of it that way. Anyhow, you're lucky to have so little of it."

"What do you mean?"

"Some people who are paralyzed have a lot of it. Their stomach muscles may suddenly contract in the middle of the night and there they are sitting up in bed. Or their knees slam onto their chests."

Early one morning Jill felt a sudden pain at the top of her head and heard something heavy hit the floor. A nurse was in the room and Jill said, *"Ick!* I think something's happened!"

She knew the tongs had pulled out of her head, and the *thought* of this little accident was even worse than the feeling of it. Her scalp was bleeding, and without the traction on her neck she felt like a turtle whose head had just shot back into its shell. The nurse could do nothing but warn her to lie perfectly still until a surgeon came on duty, and at nine o'clock she was wheeled back into the operating room. Again, a local anesthetic while two new holes were drilled in the top of her skull. This time she knew exactly what was going on, despite the sheet over her face, and her main thought was, I hope they know how far to drill because my brain's right there inside. The drill made a creaking noise and then it sounded as if it were going through a piece of wood.

The new skull drilling was followed by a completely new set of X rays on the hard, cold table. A few days later a nurse supported Jill's head while the Stryker frame was being flipped—but held on tight instead of turning her head along with the frame. All the X rays had to be repeated again. Jill apparently had suffered no further injury. The nurse was fired.

Letters from Bud Werner came several times a week and Jill frowned her way through every mail delivery looking for the familiar handwriting.

156

In March, *Sports Illustrated* ran an editorial about Jill and her "courage and uncomplaining stoicism." *The Skier* devoted its cover and three pages inside to Jill and her skiing record. Newspaper reporters still visited her four or five times a week and, for all their exaggerations and preconceived ideas, Jill had to admit she enjoyed reading about *Jill Kinmont, Girl Wonder*.

Most of the interviews were the same questions over and over again, but Jill did her best to return a serious answer.

"Will you ski again? Is skiing *worth* it?"

"Well, gads, you can get hurt or killed in a million ways. Is *life* worth it? Is *any*thing worth it? It *is* worth it. *I* think."

"Do you think it was God's will, the accident?"

"Well . . . gee, no. If there were a God he'd be doing his darned best to see that things go okay. But . . . no, I really don't think it's God's will. He's taking pretty good care of me now, isn't he?"

Responses to Jill's condition often revealed more about the person responding than about the nature of her difficulties. A skin specialist dropped by a number of times to look at a sore which had developed on her foot and he always asked—seriously—"Does it hurt?" Two little old ladies peeked into the room one afternoon and one of them said of Jill with a condescending coo, "Oh, look. She's eating her lunch. Isn't she the cutest little thing you ever did see?"

A more comprehending attitude was evidenced by Peanut McCoy, who had just contracted rheumatic fever and wrote:

Dear Jill,
    Dad just gave me an enema. I hate those things. How about you?

The Kinmont family was now more or less scattered around the country with Bob racing in New England and Bill running back and forth between Bishop and Los Angeles, trying to dispose of the ranch and keep it in working order at the same time. June stayed in Salt Lake City because Jill was still in *poor* condition and needed her more than anyone else did. Jerry was staying with Uncle Bob Lamkin and his family in Yosemite National Park, going to school there with the two. Lamkin boys. He wrote Jill an informative letter which ended, "I made a paddlewheel in the stream like I made in goodol Bishop where I wisht I was."

Bud Werner's picture appeared on the cover of the new *Sports Illustrated* and June pasted it high on the wall, facing the photograph of Jill on the cover of the January 31 issue.

On March 20 the girls racing in the North American Championships, which was one of the Olympic tryouts, telephoned from Stowe, Vermont. A nurse undid all Jill's tubes and wheeled her bed out the door and down the hall to the telephone.

Stowe, where Jill had never been, was suddenly alive in her mind, but after saying "hello" and "Skeeter?" and "yes, yes," she was unable to speak. She could smell the sharp winter air and see the fine dry powder on Mt. Mansfield and almost hear the *on deck . . . in the hole . . . ready . . . five . . . four . . . three . . . two . . . one . . .* GO. More than anything else in the world she wished that she were there and skiing. She cried for the first time since the accident. She cried because she was not going to the Olympics. She cried because she was not going to be skiing up on Mammoth Mountain next month in the toasting sun and corn snow. She cried because she was not going to be skiing again. Ever.

After the girls hung up, Jill was left alone in her Stryker frame and was grateful. She did not *think* about skiing; she simply allowed certain feelings and certain very alive sensations to sink slowly into the past, and she tried not to grab for them as they grew small and dim.

She let the tears run again, briefly. Then she thought of her mother, who was having a rough enough time without a daughter's weeping to contend with. She thought of thousands of strangers who had been led to believe she was an exceptional human being, loaded with *spunk* or *pluck* or something. She thought of Dave. She thought of Andy and of Dick, either of whom would have given her about one more minute before saying *Okay, you've had your cry, now pick yourself up and get with it.* Before the crash—she already spoke of this as B.C.— she'd had no use for people who felt sorry for themselves, and *now* was hardly the time to start making exceptions.

15

THE NEXT MORNING THEY TOOK OFF THE TONGS. THEY moved her onto a regular hospital bed and fitted her with a neck brace to hold her chin and head steady. The doctor checked everything carefully and lifted her into a sitting position, letting her legs dangle over the edge of the bed. He walked away and Jill was immediately dizzy. She felt nauseated and ground her teeth in fear of toppling over. She called to the nurse, *"Get me down!"*

She was cranked up in bed with more care thereafter, for a minute at a time at first and soon for as long as half an hour.

The best thing about sitting up was that she had some control of her arms. On her back, she could move them in only one direction. Seated upright, however, she could raise them and then let gravity pull them back down again.

Bob Kinmont stopped in on his way back to Bishop to finish high school. He was noticeably subdued in the hospital room, perhaps uncomfortable, but he warmed up once Jill asked how things had gone in New England. The tryouts were over and the squad had been selected. Bud obviously was top dog, Bob said. Kenny Lloyd had made the team as an alternate.

"And how'd *you* do?"

"Just great!" He let out a snorting laugh. "On Canon Mountain I fell on the downhill, fell in slalom and missed a gate in giant slalom. At Stowe I was the eighth American in the giant slalom and I broke a toeplate in slalom. Then I busted my Kneissl Kanonens, and it was so foggy practicing for the downhill that I had a spooky feeling about it. Buek said 'Don't race,' so I didn't." He did not mention that he had considered the possibility of a serious

accident and had concluded that this was one risk the
Kinmonts could perhaps do without at the moment. "Buek
fell, you know," he said. "Near the top of the Nose Dive,
a ways below the Seven Turns. In the fog. I guess he broke
his back."

"He broke his back?"

"Well, yeah, but not bad. He's in the Walter Reed
Hospital and he's just fine. There were a lot of crack-ups."

Jill was ominously silent and Bob said quickly, "Buek
was furious that the Army wouldn't let him come see you,
but he says they're losing money on him and they'll dump
him the first chance they get."

"I hope so."

"Buek helped me all the time in the East. He'd show
me a line, and I'd say 'I don't know' and he'd say 'Do it.'
His knee still doesn't bend but he'd be in the air ten feet
and he'd come down on the snow as easy as picking your
nose."

"He's really too much, isn't he?"

"Funny thing—I had one ski waxed before the giant
slalom on Canon and I went and kicked over my waxpot.
Man, I didn't know *what* to do. Buek just said 'What the
hell' and goes and steals somebody's waxpot for me and
said 'You can't lose, you'll have one fast ski no matter
what the snow's like.' "

Jill bit her lower lip, thinking of Dick and of Stowe.

"Buek is *cool*, Jill. Most guys talk cool and look cool
and that's the kind of coolness that Mom and Dad see in
a guy. But the guy that's *really* cool *isn't* cool. I mean at
least it doesn't show."

"But Dick is . . ."

"That's what's so great! Buek is a step beyond that,
even. He's like a saint. He's real, down to his *gut*, but he
doesn't come on square; he goes all the way back to being
superficially cool, too, at the same time."

Jill barely understood what Bob was saying and her
frown tipped him to the fact.

"I'll give you an example," he said. "I sidestepped down
to where he was there below the Seven Turns on a
stretcher with a broken back and bleeding from the nose

161

and ears, and a mess of skiers came up and crowded around and said, 'Jesus, Dick, what happened?' And he said, 'Don't sweat it. Just playing the role.'"

Bud Werner also was back from the East and stopped in Salt Lake City the next day on his way from Colorado to Sun Valley. "How long are you going to be here?" he said. "Are they really *doing* anything for you?"

"Oh, it's going to be a big deal here next week, Buddy. My neck's healed and I'm well enough to travel, so I'm going to Los Angeles, where we've got a lot of friends. I've still got four months to go in a hospital, and then maybe I'll go to the Rusk Rehabilitation Center in New York. I guess when you get out of there you really *are* something, ready for a job and all the rest. But, Buddy, you've got to decide ahead of time. What am I going to tell them? I don't know what I want to be."

"Jill," he said emphatically with a serious scowl, "you tell them you want to come out of there *walking*. That's what you want. Don't settle for anything less."

Jill said softly, wistfully, "Wouldn't that be something?"

"What'd you say?" He touched her arm.

"I said that's a good idea," she said. "Bud, I'm sorry, but it hurts my arm to be touched. The skin's hypersensitive for some reason."

"Oh, sorry." He straightened up and noticed the medal hanging from her mirror. "You're not wearing the St. Christopher."

"I have to wait, Buddy. I tried, but it gives me the creeps at the back of my neck."

Suddenly Bud's visit was about to end and Jill realized that they hadn't had a chance to really talk about anything. He hadn't said *I love you.* He hadn't asked how she felt about him . . . nor had she mentioned it. But she wanted him to know. She wanted to commit herself. Just before he left for Sun Valley she said to him what she had never said before, "Buddy, I love you."

Two days before she was due to leave Salt Lake City, Jill had her first brief excursion in a wheelchair—accompanied by reporters and photographers. The chair was a creaky old wicker affair, but it meant that she could see faces and walls and furniture when she was wheeled down the hall. All she had ever seen of the corridor before was the long bare green pathway of the ceiling during her few trips to X ray or surgery or the telephone.

A little boy was playing on the stairs at the far end of the hall, apparently waiting for his mother, and he watched Jill's chair approach with widening eyes. When Jill reached him, he said, "Well, what happened to *you?*"

Jill smiled. "I hurt myself skiing. I was going too fast."

"Oh!" the boy said with an explosive sigh, shaking his head. "That's terrible. Didn't your mommy tell you not to ski?"

Andy and Dave Lawrence arrived with Skeeter Werner to wish her bon voyage, and the four of them talked at length about Stowe and Canon Mountain and about the girls who had made the U.S. team and about those who had not. Jill was lying on her back and had moved her arms out to the side so her hands were close to her head. She said, "Andy, could you put my arms down to my side?"

Andy returned her glance bluntly and answered after a moment, "What's the matter with you? Have you tried to do it yourself?" Jill had not tried to do it herself and was ashamed because she had begged for help without first having made an effort. Andy moved her arms for her.

When the visitors had gone, Jill drew her arms out to the side and then tried to move them back. It seemed impossible, but after many attempts she discovered that she could move them if she gave them a slight swinging start by thrusting violently with her shoulders.

So Andy had shamed her into doing what she couldn't do. Dick Buek would have done the same thing, perhaps even more so. He would have said, "That's *your* problem."

Jill told her mother about the incident. June said, "Jill you're lucky. Most people don't get this kind of support

163

from their friends. From friends who expect them to shape up. Leave it to Andy to know just what to say."

After an early supper Jill and June and a special nurse, Hilda Gulbrandsen, were given a police escort from the hospital to the Union Pacific station. Mr. Green and his wife and four children were there to say good-by. The *City of Los Angeles* arrived on time and was delayed half an hour while a window was removed from the side of a Pullman car. Jill was on a stretcher, her neck held rigid by a big padded brace. She was lifted up through the window into a drawing room.

"Here comes the first train ride in my life," she said. "What a way to go!"

They were met at Union Station in Los Angeles at nine the next morning by Bill Kinmont and a crowd of fifty or sixty well-wishers. Jill was bright-eyed, with ribbons in her hair, and she was amazed when she saw all the people. She spotted Barni Davenport's father as they were lowering her out the window and she yelled, "Bud, where'd you get that crazy hat?"

"How do you feel, sweetie?" he called back.

"Swell." She was chewing on a stick of gum and grinning.

She was immediately surrounded by reporters. The questions were like a recording of what she had been through many times already, but this was a new group and she had a ball with them. Someone showed her a welcoming telegram from Mayor Poulson. Her arm slid off the side of the stretcher and she asked an attendant to lift it back for her.

Jill and her parents went by ambulance to St. John's Hospital in Santa Monica, where she was quickly and comfortably settled in room 141 as case 32089. She was scarcely alone for the first time when someone brought in the afternoon Los Angeles *Mirror* with I'LL SKI AGAIN and PLUCKY GIRL ARRIVES IN L.A. The bulldog edition of next morning's *Examiner* came in that evening, and Oscar winners Marlon Brando and Grace Kelly split top billing with COURAGEOUS JILL SAYS I'LL SKI AGAIN. Jill had a three-column photograph on page one right next to BOARD

SEES ANNUAL FEE FOR SEWERS. Another newspaper announced ATTENDANTS AWED BY SPUNK. It was also reported that she had been seen off in Salt Lake by Bud Werner, *handsome member of the men's Olympic team, who has been at Jill's side almost constantly since the accident.*

Dr. Schlumberger, Jill's new urologist, looked at the newspaper clippings and later stopped June Kinmont in the hall. "Mrs. Kinmont," he said, "when your daughter says she'll ski again . . . uh . . . does she mean it?"

June gave him her prettiest smile. "I really think she's smarter than that," she said. "Don't you?"

St. John's had a number of things to recommend it over old Salt Lake General, notably the fact that a lot of aunts and uncles and old friends were living nearby. The hospital had a sun deck, color television, and a beauty parlor —at which Jill immediately made an appointment to have her hair washed and set for the first time since January. Another advantage, in view of the pyramiding medical costs, was that June was allowed to take over the daytime nursing shift.

On her second day at St. John's, Jill was wheeled into X ray. The radiologist confirmed a *complete compression type comminuted fracture of the body of C-5.* The fifth cervical vertebra is commonly designated as C-5; the word *comminuted* means *reduced to fine powders.*

In addition, a posterior dislocation of C-5 and C-6 was reported as having become progressively worse since an examination seven weeks earlier. The verdict was: back in bed and no wheelchair for at least a month. *Patient may sit up in bed but brace is to be in place* AT ALL TIMES *unless flat on back.* She was allowed to be set up in a chair occasionally if her legs were first wrapped from the toes to mid-thigh with four-inch Ace bandages.

The X rays were followed by a physical examination, the results of which Ted Lynn summarized briefly:

Eyes-Ears-Nose-Throat okay. Heart & lungs clear. Neck

165

is still immobile. She can move shoulders & flex forearms—that is all. Remainder of peripheral apparatus is
gone. Bowel & bladder control lost. Tong holes in skull
are healed.

Otherwise, Jill was in very good health . . . which
conclusion was not just a sick joke. She had none of the
common complaints of paraplegics: body sores, kidney
stones, calcium deposits and other problems associated with
circulation or elimination. Her health should remain good
if she kept on the lookout for bed sores, drank ten glasses
of water every day and had the tidal drain for her bladder
set up every evening. No problem with diet, but a lot of
protein would be a good thing. And a final caution: *don't
catch cold!* She could barely cough at all, and when she
did the effort was totally exhausting. There was almost
no way of clearing her lungs or bronchial tubes if they
should become congested. Furthermore, she had little resistance to infection and there was a fair chance that a
cold might develop into pneumonia.

After Dr. Lynn had gone, a neurologist came in to see
how she was getting along neurologically. He entered as
if he were leading a choir, walking with long slow steps,
his head tilted far back and his arm extended stiffly. At
the end of his arm, stuck between his thumb and fist like
a piece of sheet music, was an 11-by-14-inch X ray.

"Well, let's see," he said, without even a glance at his
patient. "Fracture at the C-5 level. That means . . ."

"Diaphragm okay," Jill said. "Biceps but no triceps.
Supinators but no pronators."

The X ray and its thin aluminum frame fell to the doctor's side. He eased back three steps so he could look at
his patient face to face.

"Deltoids but no pecs," Jill went on. "Well, just a *little*
bit of pecs on the left side, but not much."

"You're certain about that? Pectoral function on the left
only?"

"It's a transverse fracture," she said, "so the left side's
a little stronger."

The doctor shook his head. "It scarcely seems I'm needed around here. How you feeling?"

"Just fine. How are you?"

16

APRIL BEGAN WITH A STEADY PROCESSION OF VISITORS. Skiers came from the Avalanche Ski Club and the Sporthaus ski shop and relatives came from everywhere. The McCoys arrived with a Lanz dress for Jill and the news that work was about to begin on Mammoth's first chairlift. Kandi was with her parents, and she asked immediately, "What you got on under the sheet?"

"Nothing."

"Not even your *under*pants? Lemme see!"

Warren Miller, a fine skier and producer of ski movies, made a tray with a transparent bottom so Jill could lie with her head beneath it and read letters placed on top. Jill's twenty-one-year-old cousin Jimmy Lewis made a large sign which he hung on the tidal drain:

JILL'S STILL

On the 10th of April, the Sporthaus gang gave Jill a special gift by financing a trip to Los Angeles for Bud Werner. Jill had been wearing his St. Christopher medal constantly since her neck had healed and she was flushed and bright-eyed when he arrived with Sally Neidlinger and several other friends. He came to the bed and touched her arm. "You look terrific," he said, closing his eyes and slowly shaking his head.

Bud stayed nearly a week, was regally wined and dined by local skiers, and spent some time every day at the hospital. Jill was cranked up in a sitting position for one of the visits but she had to wear her neck brace, a padded plate that fitted high on her chest and supported a big

168

leathery cup on which her entire lower jaw rested. Most of the brace was hidden under her blouse.

"At least it keeps your chin up," Bud said . . . and that seemed to be about as intimate as the conversation was going to get. Jill wondered why, since he apparently had come west especially to see her. On the surface he was just as warm and funny as ever. They talked about the spring races and about Sun Valley, where Bud had gone to coach the Colorado juniors, but not about themselves or about the future.

Jill knew that her paralysis was going to change a lot of things in her life, but she kept telling herself this wasn't the reason for Bud's backing off. It was probably another girl, or girls, or he was too serious about skiing and didn't want to get into an emotional tangle. She assumed he was like herself. She had been able to get attention and dates just by showing a little interest, but the moment the boy started getting serious she always backed off. All of which now seemed rather strange and rather sad. But she hadn't been ready to get involved; skiing was the big thing. So perhaps she was on the receiving end this time.

During Bud's last visit Audra Jo came in to show Jill her remarkable progress. She arrived on her feet, supported by crutches and by an extensive and complicated set of braces that corseted her from the chest down. Laboriously and proudly she made her way down the corridor and into the room alone. Each step required heavy, contorted movements and she was breathing hard.

"Josie, how did you *do* it? You haven't even got trunk muscles."

Audra Jo leaned against the wall, resting. "But I've got good shoulders and good balance and I've sure got arms. I've been working on the parallel bars for months."

Bud had been watching her intently. He remembered meeting her three years before at Winter Park.

Audra Jo didn't stay, and Bud said after she had gone, "She's really great, Jill." He stared out the doorway into the bare hall. "But you know . . . it's easier to accept her sitting in a wheelchair than like that." Jill knew what he meant but she couldn't help thinking how differently Dick

169

would have reacted. Dick would have been full of questions and totally impressed by the great feat.

When Bud was about to leave he kissed her and said, "My God, you look just great!" He kissed her again and promised to write and he said, "Jill, I love you."

Bill found a buyer for the ranch and got himself hired as manager for the first season. He planned to be open by May 1. There was a summer job there for Bob, and Jerry could join them as soon as school was out.

When Bill left Los Angeles, June moved into a $45-a-month room three blocks from the hospital in a house that looked like a pagoda. She was worried about Jill's reaction to the experience of her own helplessness and wanted Jill's awareness of it to come on as gradually as possible. She took pains to be on hand all the time to do things like straightening a sheet or pulling down a blouse or turning the pages of a letter. She tried to anticipate Jill's needs because she knew Jill was reluctant to ask for anything.

The strain of the past ten weeks was beginning to show, although June usually did not give way to tears until she was alone at night in her rented room. Praying probably helped, and so did the fact that she was very tired and therefore fell asleep as soon as she went to bed.

The most painful time of all was waking up in the morning. At night, when she was dead tired or half asleep, the accident and everything that had followed it seemed like a very bad dream, but the sharp light of the morning sun always dragged her back to reality and the realization that it was all inescapably and forever true. In addition, there was the reality of the chromed and polished wheelchair in the window of the surgical supply store she always passed on her short walk to the hospital.

One morning June arrived at room 141 looking tired and heavy-lidded. Jill said, "Mom, don't you feel very well?"

"I guess not," she answered, rubbing her eye and the left side of her head. "But I took a couple of aspirins so I should feel better in a little while."

"Headache?"

June shrugged. She tried for an hour to disguise the hard, knotty little pains at her temples, but a desperately tired look began to gather around her eyes and she said, "Jill, I think I'll go over to the house and lie down."

Jill said, "Good. I'll ask the floor nurse to call Aunt Beverly and see if she can't come over for a couple of days. You go and *rest!*"

Aunt Beverly Lewis came to St. John's immediately and took over as special day nurse for three days. June Kinmont spent the entire time in her room enduring the most violent migraine headache she had ever known. On the fourth day she appeared at the hospital, rested and refreshed.

Jill had her own bad days and tried without much success to hide them from her mother. She had never become despondent, as many friends and physicians had predicted, but at times she was certainly depressed. These very low points usually came when she was alone and unoccupied, staring out the window or perhaps counting the dots on the speckled ceiling—she claimed there were 8,192. She tried not to let anyone know how she felt, but the moment her mother came around—or anyone else who was close— she was irritable. Nothing was right. Her hair was frazzled. Her blouse was crooked. And she would ask for a dozen things at once: fix this, get me that paper, hand me a towel, straighten my lipstick, address that letter. She hated to have to depend upon someone else to write her letters and to make up her face.

One of her lowest points occurred late in April when her mother and one of the nurses dressed her in levis for the first time. She remembered Audra Jo's thin little legs and was prepared to watch her own legs atrophy, but she had not yet taken a long critical look at her physical self since the accident. Now her new jeans bluntly revealed her true shape, and she saw with horror that her abdomen had grown distended and flabby and that her bottom was almost as bad. Physical trimness and muscular tone had always meant so much to her . . . and she felt robbed. Someone had run off with her own waist and replaced it with a formless retread. She sighed and her eyes filled with tears.

Actually the nurses and doctors thought she was in far better shape than she'd had any right to expect, for her legs looked perfectly normal, her arms were tan and her cheeks were rosy and she was less than five pounds underweight after almost three months in a hospital bed. Jill was bleak nevertheless. She said, "I wish my hips and thighs *would* atrophy a little bit."

In May Jill was allowed to sit up most of the day, which was wonderful because she could at last scratch her own nose whenever she wished. She spent two hours a day with a physical therapist, Mr. Rossi, who put every joint in her body through its full range of motion to prevent it from stiffening. Even her toes. He said the most important thing was to develop every muscle that showed the slightest sign of life. He made her push against his hand with her shoulders as hard as she possibly could. He set up pulleys and weights for exercising her biceps and wrist extensors.

"You apparently have no triceps," Rossi said, "but let's give them a try, just in case." He held her arm closed, with her wrist against her shoulder, and she tried in every way to open it. The only response she could get was a vague burning sensation somewhere deep inside the back of her upper arm.

"Well, what we haven't got we can forget," he said. "But what we do have we can improve." He traced the position of three muscles in his own forearm which served to raise his hand when he held it out in front of him. "You have only one of these wrist extensors, but with some work it can do the job of all three. Even the one on your right arm, which barely jumps now."

Ted Lynn asked Jill what progress she was making and she said she was hopeful. He asked how Audra Jo was getting along and Jill said, "Great. She's doing fine in school and I think she's going to get a car. You know, with hand controls."

"I wish some of my patients could watch that girl

operate," he said. "By the way, do you have your heart set on New York for your rehabilitation?"

"Not if I can possibly stay around here."

"That's fine. CRC can do as much for you as Rusk, and it's closer to your family and friends." CRC was the Kabot Kaiser Institute, where Audra Jo was still living, but the name had recently been changed to California Rehabilitation Center. "I'll see that you are measured for a corset. You'll need a strong one if you want to sit up for any length of time."

"Good. I'll get my girlish figure back."

Dr. Lynn also arranged for John Campbell to come and see what he could do in the way of spoons and forks and pens. Campbell was an occupational therapist at CRC and was a most inventive designer of braces and devices. He measured Jill's hands and arms and explained the general nature of the problem. Jill was more or less helpless when she was on her back, but she had a lot working for her when she sat up. She could lift her entire arm, or her forearm alone, and rely on gravity to lower it. She could lift her left hand at the wrist when her palm was facing down. She had no control of the thumb or fingers, but almost any small object wedged between her thumb and hand would stay there until she shook it free. Her fingers were permanently curled but her hands looked relatively natural. Her right hand had no feeling. She could feel with the thumb side of her left hand and all the way up the inside of both arms.

"So there's no reason why you can't eat and write and brush your teeth and make up your face," John Campbell said. "If we can just figure how to manage it."

He had some ideas, but meanwhile he put her to work weaving a white-and-orange pot holder. Jill thought this might be fun, but every time she shoved the shuttle between the threads she had to make dozens of futile attempts before she could grab hold of it again. The task was so frustrating and her arms became so painfully tired that tears started flowing down her cheeks. She began sobbing and couldn't stop. Then she got hotly angry at

173

herself for acting so childishly and this made her cry even harder. She let her arms fall limp in her lap.

Days and days later she did finish the pot holder. It came out scraggly and shaped like an hourglass.

John Campbell, on his second visit, brought with him an odd splintlike contraption made of wire and tape and wooden tongue depressors. He fitted this onto Jill's left hand and attached a spoon to it. Jill raised her arm and after several attempts managed to get the spoon to her lips. The spoon had tilted 45 degrees by this time, but the experiment was promising. John replaced the spoon with a toothbrush and then with a comb. Everything almost worked.

"Too complicated," he said. "But don't worry." He left Jill with a new project: a box of numbered paints, a brush which he fastened to the brace on her hand, and a picture full of little numbered areas which were to be filled with color. Jill said *ugh*.

Finally John Campbell perfected a runcible spoon which he called a *spork*. Three rings had been soldered to it so they would fit neatly over the thumb, forefinger and middle finger of her left hand. Since she could lift her arm and straighten her wrist, she had enough control to get food to her mouth on her first attempt. On her second attempt she missed her mouth and on the third attempt she poked her cheek, but she averaged reasonably well. She had no way of bending her wrist inward, however, and the spork sometimes fell out and away from her. Still, it was nicer to spill her own food than to have a nurse dribble it for her, and it was a real thrill to be able to choose what she wanted a bite of when. If she wanted three bites of salad in a row, she could *take* three bites of salad in a row instead of being at the mercy of a feeder who went democratically from meat to potatoes to peas to salad to meat.

Jill's right hand was weaker than her left, but John made a right-hand brace to hold a ballpoint pen. She tried to write a sentence in the usual way, by moving her wrist. She had no success until she used her entire arm. She wrote the word *Jill;* it was legible but five inches high and rather shaky.

Her first letter was to Dave and Roma and was written on stationery measuring two feet by three feet. When she finished the page and raised her hand, the weight of the upper part of the pen tilted her wrist outward. She was left with her palm and the pen both pointing at the ceiling. She was more curious than annoyed and wondered if she could turn her wrist back without help. She had no control of the muscle that twists the wrist inward and she thought, Well then, what can I do?

She tried lifting her right hand with her left hand, but this was an awkward solution. She thought of swinging her whole arm out and up and around from the shoulder . . . and when she tried it, it worked; her hand turned palm down and she could again control it. She soon learned to swing her arm so subtly that she seemed to be doing no more than shrugging her shoulder.

Hospital routine was rather easygoing: sponge bath and breakfast around 7:30, an hour and a half for letter writing or painting, an hour of physical therapy with Mr. Rossi, thirty minutes on a tiltboard, lunch, a long nap, and then most of the afternoon free. Early supper and another PT session with much leg bending and massage.

Life meanwhile became a lot more pleasant when Jill was fitted with a stiff elastic corset to support her trunk. She discarded her neck brace forever. It was like being released from a vise.

Room 141 was coming to look less and less like the inside of a hospital. Visitors were there at all times of day and Jill could be cranked up in bed whenever she wished. She had thirty-eight stuffed animals, a gigantic bulletin board covered with ski photographs, a radio, a television set, a record player and records, a music box, and a closet full of attractive blouses—"all tops, you'll notice," she told Audra Jo. Jimmy Lewis' big sign still hung above the bottles and tubes of the tidal drain, but someone had added a word so that it now read:

JILL'S STILL HERE

Jill's handwriting was improving and by the first week

175

in June she was writing and printing letters half an inch high and less. She composed a 36-word birthday poem for her mother, who had gone to Bishop for Bob's graduation, and she painted six flowers on the front of it. The actual writing took about half an hour, with a rest period after each line. She found this new ability just as satisfying as feeding herself—to be able to write her own letters and not have to relay her feelings by way of a third party. Jill's handling of the spork improved also, but too often she would get a mouthful of food all the way up to her lips and her hand would roll over, dumping everything.

She next learned to pick up a glass of water by clamping her fists on either side of it. Her hands were steady enough, but she had some trouble with the balance of her whole body. Sometimes she was too far back in bed to reach the glass with both hands. At other times she was too upright, and the weight of a full glass of water would have been quite enough to topple her forward onto her face.

The spork and the writing brace made many things possible, but Jill's most exciting accomplishment was learning to pick up something with one hand without a brace. She discovered that there was a space between her thumb and forefinger when she let her hand hang, palm down. If she raised her hand by extending the wrist, the thumb and finger came firmly together. Her first success came with potato chips. After breaking several, she managed to catch the edge of one just inside her thumb. She lowered and straightened her wrist and carefully raised her arm. She had the potato chip neatly in her grasp. She then had no difficulty getting it to her mouth. She did not have an audience, but she was proud of herself and said, "Bravo, Jill Kinmont." She found she could pick up a letter in the same way if it was folded so that part of the page stood up from the table. Her "grip" was even better when she turned her hand outward so that the palm was up.

Jill was finally allowed in a wheelchair again the second week in June. It was an ancient wicker chair like the one in Salt Lake, but she was in no mood to be critical. She could at last begin to move around once more and see what was happening beyond the confines of her clean, small cell.

One mid-June afternoon she was sitting up in bed with a number painting, filling little areas with the prescribed colors, when Dick Buek strode into the room. He was wiry and full of life, wound up like a spring. He glanced at the nurse seated by the window and then at the bulletin board covered with photographs of Jill and Bud.

Jill put down her brush and said, "Well, hi. How are you?" She was very glad to see him but she didn't want it to show too much.

"I see Werner's been here playing the role," he said.

"Yes, he was here for a short visit. Why didn't you tell me you were coming? How was the Army . . . *ha ha!*"

"Don't stop your painting," he said. "Go ahead. Except, why the hell are you painting *that* kind of picture?"

Jill felt the same way about numbered pictures, but she said, "It teaches me control when I have to stay inside the lines."

"You're not doing very well." He held the paints for her, standing close beside the bed. The nurse thoughtfully left the room and the moment she was gone he shut the door. Jill thought *uh-oh* . . . and continued to paint.

Dick leaned over her and kissed her very gently on the lips. Then he started firing questions about her injuries and capabilities and about all the paraphernalia in the room. What muscles still worked, what sensation did she have in her body, could she feel pain, was she allowed out in the wheelchair, what were the tubes for, what about breathing and digestion and elimination? Each question demanded a complete, unhedging answer.

He accepted all the information nonchalantly until Jill explained the catheter. He asked if it was temporary, and she said, "It's an indwelling catheter and it's permanent, although actually they change it every few weeks."

Dick's brow pinched into a deep frown and his eyes turned from her toward the window. He said, *"Jesus Christ!"*

After a few more questions he said, "All this doesn't

square so well with what I've been reading in the papers. You're facing the future with a 'happy heart.' You're 'absolutely certain you'll fully recover and ski again.' By the way, I hear you have holes in your head."

"Take a look." Jill bent forward and he pawed around in her hair searching for the little round scars. "You finding anything *else?*" she said.

"They're not jumpin' today. By the way, how's your friend?"

"Buddy?"

"Is that a friend? I mean Audra Jo."

"Just *fine*. She comes over to do her homework a couple of times a week."

There was a knock on the door and Dick opened it to let in his friend Gardner Smith, whom Jill already knew. Dick said, "There's a new Porsche down on Wilshire that's just too much. Gard and I are going down to look at it and I think you ought to come along."

"Dick, they won't let me out."

"They won't, huh? Let's show 'em what you can do!"

"Gads, I don't have any clothes on."

"What's that?"

"That's a blouse, but that's all. All the rest is just blankets. And I've got a bottle . . ."

"Don't worry about a thing, old plucky Jill." He tucked the blankets around her and lifted her into the wicker wheelchair.

"Okay," she said, "but we've got to act like we know where we're going."

Dick and Gardner Smith together wheeled her sedately down the hall to the elevator, got her to the ground floor and through the lobby, and in a moment were out on Santa Monica Boulevard maintaining a pace that was anything but sedate. Dick took over the chair and wheeled north toward Wilshire Boulevard, pausing only for old ladies, baby carriages and sports cars. At the first intersection he slowed almost to a stop, tilted the chair back in a most graceful manner, and rushed across the street. The wicker squeaked and crackled.

Jill let him go for another half block before she said,

"Dick, *honestly* . . ." She realized at once that she shouldn't have given him the satisfaction of complaining. He began to weave back and forth. "Slalom," he said.

"Dick, *please,* I'm not supposed to be *jounced.* And don't forget the *bottle!* Dick, I'm starting to slide out of the chair!"

They were halfway across the street and the light was changing. Dick stopped. "I'm sorry," he said. He lifted her gently and sat her up straight again.

"Dick, the traffic's changing!"

"Nobody's going to run down a *wheelchair,*" he said. Cars were backed up on four sides and horns began to blare. Gardner stood behind the chair with one hand in the air, holding them off.

"Dick!"

"What, my dove?" He leaned forward over her so his face was almost upside down in front of her brow.

"Oh, you . . ." She glanced around and saw people everywhere, staring. "Let's go," she said. "You're a *nut!"*

He kissed her on the nose and the trio set off down Wilshire Boulevard at a conservative trot.

When Jill returned to the hospital the nurses were furious because she was in such a mess and the doctors were furious because the rough ride had left a sore on her bottom. Jill rather enjoyed the commotion. She was restricted to bed again until the sore healed, but that was a fair price for learning that she could still take off and have a ball and to hell with hospital rules and social niceties.

Her first *official* excursion was to St. Augustine's Church in Westwood where she was taken on a wheeled chaise lounge to attend Sally Neidlinger's wedding. She wore a white linen dress embroidered with lavender flowers. At the reception she caught the bridal bouquet.

Jill had been hospitalized for more than five months, and everything that could be done for her medically had been done. Her legs had lost some flesh recently but her weight had stabilized at 120 pounds, only ten pounds less than it had been in January. Although she had neither

179

feeling nor conscious control below the shoulders, she had developed a vague awareness of whether or not her body was functioning properly. At times she would begin to sweat suddenly or would notice a distant burning sensation, and this she now recognized as a sign of trouble . . . a cramped muscle or a full bladder or a cold draft on her legs or even a toe pinched between her wheelchair and a table leg. Despite her lack of abdominal feeling she had developed what her medical record called "an ability to time her bowel actions and to recognize the peristaltic indications thereof." She no longer required the constant presence of a nurse, but she would always need help dressing, going to the bathroom and moving herself bodily in and out of her chair.

Physically, then, her future was more or less predictable and there was no indecision about what had to be done. In every other way, however, it was like looking out over a trackless and gloomy moor. No horizons were visible and the view in every direction was equally murky.

Dave came to visit. He read her a line from an article he had brought with him. "Jill had been considered the one girl capable of giving Andy a run for her gold medals in the upcoming Olympic Games."

"Pa," she said, "what I did skiing was . . . well, I got there because of the push you gave me. You gave me the wish and the goal and one of the big reasons for wanting to get there." She was staring hard into his eyes, questioning. "But *now* . . . where am I to get another incentive for what comes now?"

Dave had no answer and no hint of an answer.

Jill dreamed that night that she was skiing and that she had everything in her life under control. She stopped and reached down to release her bindings. The moment she stepped off her skis she was in a wheelchair.

But she was tired of being known as *Jill Kinmont, the girl who might have been the greatest thing on a pair of boards*. She had once been interesting to people because she had really *been* something on skis. From now on people were not going to find her interesting for the old familiar reasons.

180

So, was there some other answer or some new direction? Probably. Maybe. Jill had no idea what it might be. She felt very sorry for herself. Then she became angry at herself for allowing herself to feel sorry for herself.

17

ON JULY 23 JILL KINMONT WAS CERTIFIED AS BEING in good health, allowing of course for permanent limitations imposed by her injury. After twenty-five weeks in hospitals, she was released from St. John's to begin a full-time program of rehabilitation.

It was only a three-mile journey to CRC, where she had visited Audra Jo eight months before, but it meant the end of being *sick* and the beginning of something resembling independence. Also she was given her own wheelchair, a lightweight powder-blue job that could be folded to fit in a car. Eight little rubber knobs had been screwed into the rim of each wheel and she learned how to press against them, one after the other, and shove the wheel around—slowly and with considerable difficulty.

CRC had changed in name only. Everything else about the place was just the same. It was still an oversized and dismal building with exposed pipes and torn draperies and dust. Several half-floors, supported on steel pillars, had been sandwiched between the original floors and the high ceilings. Dozens of plywood booths and flimsy partitions gave each floor the look of a toy city full of little unroofed buildings. Nevertheless, the location was marvelous—on the beach at the end of Pico Boulevard—and the routine was far more relaxed and interesting than what went on in ordinary hospitals.

CRC had about 60 inpatients and 40 outpatients and a staff of 70 which included 5 medical doctors, 5 occupational therapists, 15 physical therapists, and a number of nurses, orderlies and nurses' aides. The inpatient wards were operated like the wards in any hospital, but otherwise CRC was run more like a rest home or a school.

Patients were expected to report for their scheduled therapy classes, which might be either individual or with a group, but they could come and go pretty much as they wished as long as they first cleared with their doctors.

Jill went into Ward B on the fourth floor and her mother was able to rent one of the rooms on the top floor where there were both CRC "graduates" like Audra Jo and several mothers whose children were at CRC because of muscular dystrophy. Ward B had seven beds, although three were unoccupied. It was one of six wards into which a one-time ballroom had been sliced by means of thin plyboard walls. The ballroom had a high ceiling and tall arches above its narrow windows.

Ward routine began for Jill at 6:30 with washbasin and washcloth, thermometer, bedpan, breakfast tray and a lady who brought milk of magnesia and cascara marbled together in a shot glass. Jill was dressed by a practical nurse, and at eight o'clock she set out in her new wheelchair to begin the daily grind. She was learning to operate the chair herself, pushing against the little rubber knobs with the heels of her hands, but her weak arms and her inexperience kept her down to an average speed of 25 feet an hour. She worked on this continually, but for the time being she had to depend upon her mother or a nurse's aide to get her to classes on time.

Each patient had his own schedule, which was the same every day, five days a week. Jill's began with OT—occupational therapy—at 8:30, followed by two hours of PT—physical therapy—at ten. The first hour of PT was on the floor on a mat in a big area called Mats; the second hour was in a smaller room or on a table in an individual booth. After lunch she exercised with pulleys from two to three and then lay strapped on a tiltboard for thirty minutes. The last hour before "quitting time" at 4:30 she spent in the PT Muscle Check room or in the OT shop where she was being measured and fitted for wrist braces.

By her third day at CRC Jill knew pretty much what to expect at her various therapy sessions and how to get from one to another without a map.

The OT area on the third floor was crowded with 15

patients, 4 therapists, and 2 student nurses when she arrived at 8:30. One end was partitioned off to form a big U which was lined with work-benches. At the benches were patients in wheelchairs or patients standing, some with the aid of braces or canes. Slings of various shapes and sizes hung from the ceiling to help them support their arms or their tools. At the other end of the area were perhaps a dozen sturdy tables, widely separated. Large windows on the west side looked down on the beach. In front of one window stood an authentic ship's wheel which could be adjusted to turn easily or with any desired degree of resistance.

Jill was taken to a table on which was a set of small pulleys. Running through the pulleys was a cord with a tray for tiny weights at one end and a loop of muslin at the other. Jill's main task at these micro-pulleys was to develop her wrist extensors, which were extremely weak but extremely important to her. At present these muscles had a pulling power of only two ounces and she could not lift even the weight of her own hand when she held her arm horizontally. Eventually she would learn to type-write and paint and to use a saw with a canvas cuff on its handle, but she could do very little until she first strengthened the few "live" muscles she had left.

Mats—at 10 A.M.—occupied the back part of a huge room on floor 2½. The room had a concrete floor and a low concrete ceiling and looked like a boiler room without boilers but littered with big leather mats. The mats in turn were littered with patients and physical therapists. It was not a particularly pleasant sight because most of the patients were polio victims whose joints and paralyzed muscles were being "stretched" to keep them from stiff-ening. Stretching is done by a PT who forces his patient's limbs to move through their full range of motion even though they cannot be moved more than a fraction of this distance with comfort. The pain comes on full strength since poliomyelitis does not destroy sensory nerves along with the motor nerves. Jill, too, underwent stretching, but she did not feel the pain.

Jill's therapist was an unusually nice guy, she thought,

young and serious, with very blue eyes and dark-brown hair cut flat on top. His name was Lee Baumgarth and he was probably twenty-seven or twenty-eight. He put her flat on her stomach and flexed her legs and arms. He sat her up with her legs straight out and pushed her shoulders gently so she would have to keep her balance by moving her head. He pushed down hard on her shoulders while she tried to resist him.

"I read all those stories in the papers," he said.

"Really?" Jill was pleased.

"You *do* know what 'plucky' really means, don't you?" Jill frowned and he said, " 'Plucky' means 'fat.' "

At 11 o'clock Lee took Jill to a full-length mirror and sat her up in a chair in front of it. He made her practice balancing and sitting up straight. He and she were both surprised to find how strong and supple her neck was.

"Lee," she said, "would you cross my feet for me?"

He crossed her feet and she studied herself in the mirror. "Yeah, that looks kind of casual," she said. "Is there any way we could put one foot up higher than the other? Maybe in my chair, by raising one of the foot pedals? My friend Audra Jo did that and it looked real neat."

Lee placed Jill on a table and went to work on her feet, moving her ankles in every direction and bending each toe down and up. He was explaining how easily an unused Achilles tendon could shorten and stiffen when he stopped in the middle of a sentence and stepped backward. Jill turned her head and saw a long yellow stain on his pantleg from above the knee clear down to the cuff. Lee picked up the end of a rubber tube hanging down off the edge of the table and he said, "Well, that's nice, Jill." He took off his shoe and emptied it—or at least he pretended to empty it—in a basin. "Let's clamp the catheter next round, huh?"

Lunchtime was easily one of the best parts of the day. Patients were ready to let go after four hours of hard and often painful work, and so were the PTs and OTs, as the physical therapists and the occupational therapists were

185

called. Furthermore, the cafeteria hamburgers were excellent and the patio on the beach side of the concrete boardwalk was warm in the sun and fresh from the sea breeze. The Able Bodies, which meant anyone, including therapists, who was not in a wheelchair, played volleyball or walked in the sand or just horsed around in the patio. The rest kibitzed from the sidelines and griped about their personal problems and added what they could to the enrichment of local gossip.

Audra Jo was in Bishop for the summer and wouldn't be back until September, but Jill already knew half a dozen of these people. Polly, in her wheelchair in the Monday noon sun, sniffing back tears after a weekend at home but able, too, to laugh at herself. Sam, badly paralyzed and scrawny and down to 85 pounds, but very much alive and always talking. Arnelle, a bright and cheerful girl with deep-brown eyes, whose cheerfulness was often not apparent to strangers because part of her face was paralyzed. Benny, a paraplegic with one arm and the build of a weight lifter. Benny had been struck by an ore car in a mine but had a left arm strong enough to skyhook himself into an automobile by hanging from the roof with his great broad hand. The left wheel of his chair had an extra rim which drove the right wheel, and he could keep pace with any two-armed paraplegic in the building.

Sam was talking to Benny, making little *ung ung* sounds between words like a frog because he had to push air down his throat with his tongue. A young man came out from the cafeteria and picked Sam out of his wheelchair and began dancing around the patio with him. Sam's arms and legs flopped like an unstrung marionette's and he was frog-breathing madly trying to store up enough breath to yell. Everyone turned to watch the show and there was some laughter and a few encouraging cries: "Come on, Nick!"

Sam yelled, "Nick, put me down!" and somebody shouted, "Go on, show him how it's done, Sam!"

To Jill the scene was pitiful. She could not understand how anyone could laugh at poor Sam. But then she had to

186

admit it *was* funny, and she moved her chair back so she could see better.

When the mad dance was over, Sam regained his breath and surveyed the crowd from his chair with the disdain of an old trouper who finds his audience provincial and far too easily amused.

Jill's 2 P.M. session was Pulleys on the second floor. People of both sexes and all sizes were lined up along the walls, some seated and some standing and some on tables but all pulling endlessly on ropes which were attached to weights. Anything up to 50 pounds. Jill thought of galley slaves pulling on the oars of a trireme. Some patients were strapped to the walls, pulling pulleys by means of cuffs fitted around their hands or feet. Three of them wore skullcaps which were connected by ropes to pulleys on the wall behind them. Jill worked principally on her biceps and shoulder muscles, facing away from the wall and straining against a rope attached to her elbow or to her wrist. The heaviest weight she could lift with her biceps was 2½ pounds. Lee promised her she could triple that if she worked on it.

At three o'clock she was strapped to a pivoted horizontal table which was then tilted up to an almost vertical position for half an hour to improve circulation in her legs. Next she went to the Muscle Check room where a doctor tested her muscles one by one, rating each one "good," "fair," "poor" or "zero." Eventually every muscle in her body would be checked and specific exercises prescribed for those rated higher than zero.

Finally Jill went to John Campbell's workshop, which was located out behind the occupational therapy workbenches. He was making a brace for her left hand which would hold a small dowel projecting down from the palm. She planned to learn how to typewrite by striking the keys with either this dowel or the ballpoint pen that was held in a brace on her right hand. More than half the time, when she tried out a new brace or a new attachment, she would have to say, "I'm sorry, John, but it just doesn't work." He would take it back and try again.

187

At 4:30 the day's work was over and the patients dispersed, usually in small groups. Anybody who could so much as sit up in a wheelchair had the run of the boardwalk clear down the beach to Ocean Park or up to the Santa Monica pier, and Jill sometimes wheeled down to Muscle Beach with two or three other patients to watch the amateur acrobats and weight lifters. Some afternoons she joined a group at the Cheerio, a little bistro two blocks up Pico Boulevard. And sometimes she just went up to the ward to rest until supper at six.

On dull evenings Jill read or wrote letters or let June do her hair or went back to the cafeteria, which was open for snacks and gossip. But she was far from being a typical CRC patient, for she usually had visitors. Many of them. The Davenports, aunts and uncles and cousins, old ski friends by the carload, newspaper reporters once or twice a week, and the Avalanche Ski Club on Tuesdays. She was even turning down dates, which caused some sharp chatter in the ward.

Bedtime was officially 8:30, and nine o'clock was lights-out, but it was permissible to come in later. Jill liked to be in bed by nine unless she was out on a date for dinner and a show, which was the case about once a week. On weekends she found a positive pleasure in just staying away from the ward; when she was not visiting or out on the boardwalk she spent most of her time in her mother's room.

June Kinmont lived upstairs near Audra Jo's old room, but she was down in the wards most of the day. She combed Jill's hair, ate in the ward with her and cut her meat, pushed her out to the patio or along the boardwalk, and usually opened her mail, which averaged twenty letters a day. She spent many hours helping other patients and she ran out to shop for them four or five times a week.

June was continually conscious of the fact that the family was scattered and unrooted. She was particularly concerned about Jerry, who had been farmed out one place or another ever since Jill's accident and was now dividing his summer between aunts and uncles in Los

188

Angeles and his father and Bob in Bishop. June would have lived at home if only the Kinmonts had had a home in the city. Instead, she dreamed of being with her husband at the ranch but stayed at CRC, where she felt she was most needed. She never forgot her earlier fears that Jill might become seriously depressed. Even now the staff psychologists and psychiatrists kept dropping little hints and cautions to her and to one another. "The girl's fine so far, but wait until the attention slacks off and she finds herself alone . . ."

June hoped that what had not happened in six months would not happen at all. She once suggested to Ted Lynn that perhaps Jill had already weathered a period of despondency but just hadn't let it show. "I know *I* don't see any point in burdening other people with something that's troubling you," she said. "If Jill were despondent, she wouldn't share it with anyone. She'd be afraid of what it would do to us."

"Do you suppose it's a conscious effort? Not to show it?"

"Probably. I know she gets cross, but it's a little bit hard for me to tell if it's because she's despondent and that's just her way of getting it out of her system."

Many friends told June that paralysis was a lot harder on dancers and skiers than it was on the average person, and that the more skilled the person was the rougher it would be. This sounded just a little bit like assuring yourself that it pays to be untalented because then you haven't got so much to lose.

As far as Jill was concerned, the fact that she had been a fine skier had little to do with how she felt about the accident. It *was* satisfying to be able to say *crashed and burned in a big race* rather than something like *slipped in the tub* . . . but beyond that trifling advantage there were a thousand ways of getting it in the neck, and why should one make you any happier than another? Only one other CRC patient, a ski patrolman named Don Goldman, had been paralyzed in a ski accident. Gym highbars and pool diving boards had accounted for five broken spines and automobile accidents for perhaps a dozen. Al Nonemaker had been hurt diving into the surf, and his spotty paralysis

189

undoubtedly would have been less serious if his buddies had not given him energetic artificial respiration and then sat him upright in a car for the trip to the hospital. A girl in Jill's ward had been backed into by an automobile while she was sitting on the curb. She had retained enough sensation to feel pain constantly and now complained over and over again, always using the same words, "If this ass of mine doesn't stop burning . . ." She never got around to making her threat specific.

Jill kept trying to do things for herself, and even on her own she had a few successes. She discovered she could undo her blouse by hooking her left thumb into the front and lifting the buttons up to her teeth. She could even work a zipper in this way, but the metal electrified her whenever it touched a filling. Neither of these little acts was very practical—they took a long time and thoroughly wrinkled the blouses—but she was learning to put on her own lipstick by wedging the holder between the thumb and forefinger of her left hand at an angle which kept it from falling out when she pressed it against her lips. Also, her wheelchair technique was improving and this gave her a small freedom she had not known for half a year. It was not easy without chest or trunk or finger muscles and without feeling in her right hand, but it was possible . . . inch by inch, because she could only turn the wheel a short distance each time she pressed the side of her palm against one of the little rubber knobs. The building was equipped with ramps and elevators, so she could navigate freely except for the relatively steep ramp from the ground-floor elevators down to the lobby and dining room. Here Jill had to ask for help. She also needed an assist over the threshold separating the lobby from the boardwalk and the patio. She was surprised to find that PT's and OT's and patients always stopped to help her, or even came running over from the cafeteria, while nurses and doctors usually walked right by, engrossed in their own thoughts or conversations. It seemed to be a general truth that the therapists and some of the nurses' aides knew more about the patients' medical and psychological problems than did either the physicians or the nurses. And so did the patients themselves.

The same might be said for the patients' emotional and marital problems. Jill learned a great deal about the nature of life and love through the cigarette smoke at the Cheerio and through the thin partitions separating Ward B from Wards A and C. She was intrigued by tales of affairs between patients and student nurses and she was somewhat shocked to discover that there had been admitted alliances among married patients which broke off only for as long as the family of one or the other came to visit. She asked Lee if this kind of thing happened very often and Lee said he imagined that CRC was a good institution at which to pick up a liberal education.

The more Jill learned about her fellow patients, however, the less their behavior shocked her. They had been able to swallow their dreams and accept their unhappy fates, most of them, but more often than not their healthy spouses couldn't take it. Often there had been family problems of long standing, and these became suddenly explosive when severe disability was added to them. For the victims, the blow of physical accident or disease was soon followed by the collapse of love and emotional support from home, from family or from friends or from lovers. Arnelle's engagement had been broken. Sam's wife had left him and his son didn't come visiting very often. Marvin's world was restricted to places where his Monohan respirator could be plugged in, and his wife couldn't take that, so she ran off.

Jill began to feel like one of the more fortunate residents of Number 1 Pico Boulevard. Sam told her one day, "A lot of people around here seem to think I've got a lot of guts and a great sense of humor and I don't know what else. If it wasn't that I can't let these people down, I'd go wheel myself off a cliff."

Polly was having a rough time, too. She was in her late twenties and had two children whom she could care for only on weekends. She had been a surfer and a real queen. Her husband was fond of girls who could still surf. Polly went home every Friday night and returned weeping two

191

Sundays out of three. Polio had left her almost totaled out . . . she had good fingers on both hands and something left in one leg, but to move her hand or her arm she had to *crawl* it across a table or the arm of her chair with her fingers.

Jill wondered how it was possible for five dozen dilapidated human frames to be dumped together into such a dilapidated old building and yet come up smiling as often as they did. The only real trouble with CRC was that it was like a downtown intersection. You could never escape the traffic of people and the sounds of people talking about other people. Jill felt as if the accident had robbed her of her privacy along with everything else. Sometimes in the early evening she found the ramp out onto the beach deserted and wheeled herself outside just for the quiet pleasure of being, at last, alone.

Lee Baumgarth dated Jill several times in late August, usually for dinner and a show but once for a concert at the Hollywood Bowl. The bothersome mechanical problem of the catheter was on Jill's mind, but she found as much humor as embarrassment in the situation. Instead of dragging a bottle around with her, she could have the catheter clamped; but then she had to be drained every two hours. Lee took along a milk carton for this purpose, although once when they were outside she was certain he hadn't bothered with it.

At dinner one evening Lee said, "What are you going to do when you get out of here?"

"I don't know. Once, all I wanted was a gold medal and six kids. Now, I don't know. I don't want to be just an ex-skier. Have you got any suggestions?"

"No. Except don't eat lunch with only the wheelchair people."

"What do you mean?"

"Look at Barbara. She hasn't got a friend who isn't in a wheelchair. That's her whole world. Every one of them tries to stay here in this safe little castle as long as he possibly can."

"Don't worry. I'd like to *be* something."

"All they ever talk is shop. This muscle and that muscle

192

and how many steps I walked today and have you seen that new gadget Gus made to give you added leverage. That's all they know."

Later Jill said, "You know, Lee, I'm awfully glad I'm me and not Sam or somebody."

"You don't exactly have the choice."

"But I'm so lucky about my physical appearance. What if I were Arnelle? I'd die." Lee gave her a strange look and smiled. "What's so funny?" she said.

"Not funny, but sort of interesting. Arnelle told me she'd rather be the way she is, with her face the way it is and her trouble talking, than to be dependent like you and unable to take care of herself."

"There are some pretty great people around here," Jill said. "And I mean *really* great people, and who aren't skiers. I guess I always thought nobody was really anything at all unless he was something in the ski world."

"Stick around."

Out on the sidewalk after dinner he picked her up to put her in the car. "Hey!" he said, leaning back to study her face in the light of a street lamp, *"I* know who *you* are!" She looked puzzled. He said, "Didn't I see your picture on the cover of *Popular Mechanics?"*

18

JILL WANTED MORE THAN ANYTHING ELSE TO VISIT
Bishop. Bob Symons, the owner of the Bishop Flying
Service, volunteered to supply the transportation, and on
the Thursday before Labor Day he flew his four-place
Piper Tripacer into a small field in Santa Monica. He
stayed only long enough to load Jill and her mother and
the wheelchair into his plane. They took off, headed northeast across the Mojave Desert, and turned north into the
lower end of the Owens Valley. Jill was coming home
for Homecoming and she felt as if she had been away,
exiled, for many years. She loved everything she could
see, from the shriveled and crusty border of Owens Lake
below to the bare, unfriendly summit of Mt. Whitney 15
miles west and a mile higher than they were now flying.

Bob Symons circled Bishop, dropped low over the east
end of town and settled neatly onto the runway. About
twenty people were there: the three Kinmont men, Audra
Jo, Linda, Dave, Kenny, other good friends from school
and some of Jill's swimming pupils with their parents.
Someone pulled open the door and everyone shouted at
once. "Hi, Jill, you old son of a gun!" "Jill, you're looking
wonderful!"

Jill's eyes filled with tears but she sniffed quickly and
blinked them away. Bob Kinmont lifted her out of the
plane and put her in her chair, which someone had already
unloaded. Jill wanted desperately for everyone to feel at
ease with "Jill-in-a-wheelchair," so she kept up a stream
of questions. Who was in town for the rodeos? Who was
running for queen? How was the new lift coming along
at Mammoth? She told them all about the flight up from

194

Santa Monica. She made a very conscious effort to appear totally unselfconscious.

Jill was in Bishop for a week, and she stayed at the Rocking K, where Bill was still working as manager and guide. She had to rest two or three hours during the middle of the day, but there was little she wanted to do that she wasn't able to make time for. She went to the Homecoming dance Friday night. She watched Bob packing for Denver University, where he was going on a ski scholarship. And she "did" Main Street, with Linda pushing her and Audra Jo wheeling along at her side. Linda was just eighteen, slim and pretty in a tight-waisted gingham dress. People came out from all the shops just as they had when Audra Jo had made her first wheelchair appearance two years before. And, as before, there were hearty greetings and there were nervous hesitations. Audra Jo and Jill were both very good at calming the people who wept or choked and didn't know what to say.

At the rodeo Jill and Audra Jo were in their own favorite corner again, in the dirt between the chutes and the bandstand. Linda stood by to wheel them back under the bandstand in case a steer or a Brahma should come at them. After the rodeo Audra Jo took Jill and Linda for a drive in her new hand-controlled Chevrolet Bel Aire hard-top—white with aquamarine trim. The girls made a handsome trio and they were hailed by boys, both friends and strangers, all the way up Main Street and all the way back down again.

The Rocking K looked the same to Jill but it did not feel the same. Someone else was running the show now, and it was not pleasant to be there and yet feel restricted. The new owner tried to make the Kinmonts feel at home and his wife was very sweet—but the effort seemed overdone. The woman was trying to carry on as ranch hostess in the Kinmont tradition, but she wore very high heels and dressy silk dresses and it didn't come off the same at all.

There were still quiet times in the morning when the ranch was again warm and friendly and beautiful and smelling of damp pastures and dry bitterbrush. What Jill

195

missed most was *feeling*. She loudly missed the feel of warm mud under bare feet and the feel of tall grass against her legs. She had some sensation in her left hand, but she could not feel the satin touch of a horse's nose or the coarse texture of burlap or the tough resilience of saddle leather. What she missed most of all, to her surprise, was the feel of a toilet seat, its comfortable coolness and then its comfortable warmth.

Bob Symons flew Jill and her mother back to Los Angeles and Audra Jo drove her car south at the same time. It was good to return to CRC, where a surprisingly large number of people dropped in to the ward or stopped in the halls to say "Welcome back." *The Weekly Stretch,* the patients' mimeographed news sheet, acknowledged the girls' return with a small poem.

> What gems more precious could there be
> That one small town could dish up
> Than pretty Jill and Audry Jo
> Two princesses from Bishop.

Audra Jo moved in with Arnelle on the top floor and began commuting every weekday to the UCLA campus in Westwood, ten miles east of CRC. On Saturday she took Jill for a drive up the beach to Malibu. Jill had to have someone lift her in and out of the car, but Audra Jo had learned to hoist herself into the front seat with her arms, reach out and fold her wheelchair, and then pull the folded chair up behind her into the back of the car.

"I haven't seen your crutches," Jill said.

"I gave them up, Jill. They're a hideous amount of work and they made me look awful, and no amount of practice is going to make it any better. It was a good try, but I just enjoy life a lot more in my chair." She drove in silence for a dozen blocks and then she said, "Jill, Everett wants to marry me."

"He's sure a sweet guy."

"And he's been so good to me. For so many years. But

196

I just don't know whether, deep down, I want him for keeps for ever and ever. What do you think?"

"Gosh, I don't know, Josie. But I guess if you have to ask, you can't be really in love."

"I suppose," she said. "And how is it with you and Bud?"

"Haven't heard from him much lately." Actually she'd had about one letter a month, strictly informative. Bud was pitching for the local baseball team and Skeeter was working in a drugstore.

"Gee, I'm sorry," Audra Jo said. "Didn't he come all the way down to L.A. just to see you?"

"They gave him the trip, you know."

"Oh."

"Josie, I was thinking. If saying yes to Everett would be mainly because he's been so good and so devoted and all . . . if that's the main reason, Josie, then don't do it."

Dick Buek, who also had been writing about once a month, appeared at CRC one afternoon with his mother and two friends for a short visit. Jill went out with them that evening to see a Warren Miller ski movie.

The following morning June Kinmont said, "Jill, remember all those get-well cards you've been getting from someone named George Hardy? Well, he phoned up last night and he's coming to see you on Monday."

"Who *is* he?"

"I only know that he lives in a small residence hotel downtown and that he read about you in the paper."

On Monday afternoon Jill left PT early so her mother would have time to dress her. She didn't want to greet her visitor in a sweatshirt and jeans. She was very glad she had changed when she saw the stately gentleman who arrived in the corridor outside Ward B precisely on schedule. He carried a brown shopping bag and was wearing a brown suit, a rust-brown tie, a gray shirt, a brown felt hat and very shiny brown shoes. Jill met him in the hall, introduced herself and her mother, and asked him into the ward to sit down. He said, "No, thank you, this is fine."

"So you're Mr. Hardy," she said. "It's nice of you to come."

"I'll bet you've wondered who George Hardy was," he answered. "Probably thought I'd be some handsome young man."

"Have you always lived in Los Angeles?"

"No, only since I was nineteen. Of course, that was over fifty years ago." He emptied his shopping bag onto the tray of Jill's wheelchair. There was a sheet of the latest commemorative three-cent stamps, a bag of gumdrops, a box of chocolates and a box of writing paper, gift-wrapped.

Jill was charmed and overwhelmed. She opened the chocolates and offered him some. He said, "Those are for *you*. Wouldn't it be something if I brought those to you and then ate them up! Now if you prefer certain kinds of candy, you just let me know. The candy shop will put it up any way you want. What are your favorites?"

"Gee, how *nice*," Jill said. "Let's see. I kind of like chocolate-covered caramels and nougats and marshmallows. Oh, and Dad likes vanilla creams." Audra Jo came by and the talk shifted to UCLA's football prospects.

After a pleasant half-hour visit, Mr. Hardy said, "Mrs. Kinmont, I want to talk to you for a minute." He walked her off to a corner and asked what he might get Jill for Christmas . . . perhaps a typewriter? June thought a cashmere sweater would make a fine present.

Mr. Hardy consulted his gold pocket watch and said good-by to Jill. "I shall be back next month, if I may," he said. "Is there anything I can do for you uptown?" Jill shook her head and Mr. Hardy tipped his hat, turned, and went off down the corridor.

Lee Baumgarth had known Audra Jo slightly in the spring before Jill came to CRC, and after Labor Day he began to quiz Jill about her. What kind of music did she like? Was she very religious? Was she engaged or anything like that? What would she like to do on a date, do you suppose? The only things that came immediately to Lee's mind were tennis and swimming and hiking and golf.

Audra Jo meanwhile began to talk to Jill about Lee,

usually opening the subject with some variant of "You *sure* know how to pick your therapists."

Eventually, about the 1st of October, Lee asked Audra Jo for a date, and they went together regularly from then on. Lee introduced Jill to a friend of his named Bob Gotavac, and the four of them double dated. They covered most of the UCLA home games and several concerts at the Hollywood Bowl. Jill was sorry she could not move her legs with her hands the way Audra Jo did, crossing them or shifting them or folding them Indian-style when she was in a comfortable chair. She was self-conscious about the mechanics of her catheter, too, but this situation had been greatly improved by the availability of a new product called Disposa-Bag, a disposable, flat plastic bag which replaced the horrid old bottle.

Jill worked constantly on her wheelchair technique. At first she had been pathetically slow and—she had watched herself in a mirror—clumsy. She checked her progress by timing herself from the door of Ward B down the long corridor to the elevator. Already she had brought the time down from ten minutes to eight.

One day when she thought she was wheeling along quite normally she realized that she had allowed her head and shoulders to get too far forward. She began to fall. There was nothing she could do beyond turning her face to one side. She felt herself going, she watched herself going and she could only wait. She jackknifed, falling so her chest struck her thighs and her face came to rest between her knees. She was not hurt. She was soon rescued by a Lithuanian nurse's aide whom everyone called Ballsey. Ballsey cried, "Oo, mein Liebling, was ist denn geschehen?" and set her upright.

When Jill told her friends what had happened, they laughed. To fall on one's face was, apparently, a common experience. One of the boys had fallen face down in the mashed potatoes at dinner last year. Outpatients were always falling off the boardwalk into the sand on their way home, and they sometimes put in a few hours of good sleep while waiting to be found. Al Nonemaker had reached into his closet for a jacket one morning and tumbled out of his chair onto the closet floor; it was late afternoon before his roommate returned and rescued him.

Jill's second experience with falling occurred at lunch when she reached for mustard for her hamburger. She jackknifed again, and Audra Jo casually reached over and pulled her back up by the shoulder.

One of CRC's staff psychologists cornered Jill one day and said, "What are your plans? For the fall, for next year?"

"That's the awful thing," she admitted. "I don't have any."

"What about going to school?"

"College? When?"

"Spring term, I would think."

"So *soon?*" she said.

"Well, you'll be twenty by that time. Have you any ideas about what you might be able to do and might want to do?"

"No, nothing. Just nothing at all. But certainly not making pot holders."

"So why not sign up for a few courses at UCLA? Maybe you can look for some answers over there."

That night Jill had her old dream again—she was on skis, in control and full of grace and capable of anything, but the moment she stepped out of her skis she was in the wheelchair. She decided that UCLA was probably a good idea. Audra Jo was taking a two-year business course there and seemed to enjoy it. There was a good chance of getting a scholarship.

Mr. Hardy returned in October, as he had promised. He said, "How nice to see you again," and began to unload his shopping bag. He had news clippings about football and about plans for the Winter Olympics. He had a package of ornately flowered note paper, a strip of twenty new three-cent stamps, a pound of jelly beans, a pound of assorted gumdrops and a pound of candy corn for Hallowe'en. Plus a beautiful big two-pound box of MacFarlane's chocolate-covered caramels, marshmallows, nougats and vanilla creams. In addition, he was sending a subscription to *Sports Illustrated.*

Jill asked if he had seen the fights on television, and they talked about the fights. She asked him about his family and about his childhood. She learned that he was originally from Bangor, Maine, and that his favorite food had been Boston baked beans and day-old bread. His grandfather had been a doctor, he said, and used to sharpen his scalpel on a boot.

The visit ended with a glance at the gold pocket watch and a parting question. "Is there anything I can do for you uptown?"

The next morning Jill was wheeling down the corridor trying to make it to the elevator in seven minutes . . . and she nearly ran down Dave and Roma McCoy, who were just arriving. Roma clapped her hands and said in a high voice, "Golly, Jill! You're not only wheeling yourself, you're going like *mad.*" Then she stared at Jill for a moment and shook her head. "Levis and a sweatshirt! You might know!" Dave stood by the elevators with his hands in his pockets, grinning.

The McCoys spent the entire day with Jill, following her around through all of her various routines and therapies. They took her out for dinner, and when they brought her back Dave said, "I need you at Mammoth on Thanksgiving to dedicate the chairlift."

"Really? Ceremony and everything?"

"And Champagne!" Roma said.

Bob Symons flew Jill and June to Bishop for the long Thanksgiving weekend. They were met by Bill and Jerry and drove to Mammoth, where Jill christened the new lift. The bottle of champagne hung from a stout cord which she held in her teeth. She released it to crash against the steel tower at the lift terminal, and the brand-new double chairs began to move.

Jill spent most of her time with friends on the big sun deck of the warming hut, which people were now calling *the building* because it had grown to be twenty times the size of any normal warming hut. She also spent several hours on the snow, for Dave attached a pair of powder-blue skis to her powder-blue wheelchair.

201

Back in Los Angeles on Monday the sky was cold gray and Jill longed for the feel of the hot sun again. She discovered that she was extremely sensitive to low temperatures. When it was cold she was not only sharply aware of it in her neck and shoulders and arms . . . she felt as if her whole body were cold. It made her feel oddly alone and made her want to curl up inside herself.

The Rocking K's first season under new management was not a profitable one and the new owners found they had assumed more obligations than they could handle. The Kinmonts got the ranch back and had to advertise it for sale again. Bill stayed in Bishop through December, working on the ranch buildings and fences. Jerry had been with him in Bishop all fall and the two of them planned to move south in January; friends had offered them a cottage at Hermosa Beach, 12 miles south of Santa Monica.

The uncertain status of the Rocking K was financially unfortunate, but it did mean that the ranch belonged to the Kinmonts for the holidays. Bob came home from Denver and the whole family moved to the ranch for Christmas week. There was an inch of snow on the ground and they set up living quarters in the dining room so they wouldn't have to go back and forth to their bedrooms in the cold. Bill brought in a giant piñon pine and set it up in one corner of the dining room. Two sets of aunts and uncles and four cousins came up from Los Angeles, and the Kinmonts filled the dining room with rollaway beds. There was not much privacy, but it was a warm and happy Christmas.

Jill's finest present had been made a week before Christmas—an anonymous offer to send her—and her mother and a nurse as well—to the 1956 Winter Olympic games in Cortina d'Ampezzo. The psychiatrist at CRC was dubious about the trip for a number of reasons, including the fact that it would make Jill five days late for the beginning of UCLA's spring term. Jill decided to go anyway. She telephoned Colorado to tell Bud about it. He said, "You're going to Cortina? How *great!*" but he sounded somewhat hesitant. He said, "Are you sure your health is good enough?"

Late in January Jill left California for New York and her first trip abroad, headed for the Games she had worked so hard to get to as a competitor. On January 23 she arrived with her mother and Hilda Gulbrandsen at the Munich airport, which was about as near to Cortina as they could get in a commercial aircraft. They were to be met by a chauffeur who would drive them south through Innsbruck to Italy. Jill was excited about the trip and anxious to watch the skiing, but what she most looked forward to was seeing Bud Werner. It had been ten months.

The first old friend she met, however, was not Bud. She had not been on the ground five minutes when she shouted, "No! I don't *believe* it!" Walking toward her with perfect nonchalance was Dick Buek.

"So the gimp finally made it," he said, grinning. "Welcome."

"Well, gee, *hi,*" Jill said. "What are *you* doing here?" Before he had time to answer, she added, "Will you drive to Cortina with us?"

"Do you want me there?"

The bluntness of the question stopped her. It was Bud she wanted to see in Cortina, and Dick obviously figured as much. She said, "Dick, I don't care whether you come or not, but you're welcome to come with us if you care to."

"I have a better idea anyway," he said, pushing her toward the parking lot. "You heard what happened in Kitzbühel last week at the Hahnenkammrennen, didn't you?"

"Yeah. Buddy took second place behind Toni Sailer."

Dick stopped Jill's chair and spun it around so that she faced him. He said, "Man, you sure have a monorail for a mind. Katy Rodolph hit a tree in the Hahnenkamm and broke her back."

"Yes, I read that," Jill answered very quietly. "And she's in traction but she isn't paralyzed, thank God."

"So," Dick said, "we all just jump in your car and let

203

your driver drive us to Salzburg and we'll drop in at the hospital and say hello to Katy."

"Sure, why not? We can see Munich this afternoon and go to Salzburg in the morning."

Katy was surprised and delighted to see the visitors, but when she complained about her cast and the traction and the cold efficiency of the hospital, Dick gave her a very hard time. "What've you got to bitch about?" he said.

"All right, I won't complain. It's the Lord's will."

"It's nobody's *will,* for God's sake, it's just the breaks. There's nothing wrong with you that a couple of months can't fix."

The four Americans left Katy and drove south to Saalfelden, where Dick planned to stay on a farm with a friend. Jill and her mother and the nurse went on west to Innsbruck.

One of the things that struck Jill about Europe was the fact that everyone wanted to shake hands with everyone else all the time. It was thus quite impossible for her to ignore the fact that she was not very good at handshaking. Whenever she said "hello" someone said "Es freut mich" and thrust out a hand. When Jill offered her right hand, which was obviously frozen in its one and only position, the person didn't know what to do. The outcome was usually a tentative grasp, but sometimes total retreat.

After several days of this kind of awkwardness, Jill found a solution. When anyone was introduced to her, she offered her left hand. This told the other person immediately that she could not shake hands in the ordinary manner. Usually the new acquaintance hesitated, stared at her left hand for a moment, and then took hold of it and shook it warmly.

In Cortina Jill found half a dozen packets of mail waiting for her—fan letters in five languages and newspaper clippings in four. PLUCKY JILL WON'T MISS OLYMPICS. JILL TROTZT DEM SCHICKSAL; BEIM TRAINING STURTZTE SIE. She was getting more attention in the European press than if she had been competing. Her favorite letter was from Twisk, Holland.

Just now I read in my newspaper that you are unhappy because you're falling and sit still in an chair.
Perhaps if you use my invention "bacilcidi" it is possible
that your body return in the old situation as before.
Bacilcidi is very soft, made of vegetables and makes
people and beasts in a short time allright, it works fan-
tastis. If you will come to an hotel in Amsterdam for an
day, I will show you how to try it. I give it you with
great pleasure to help you hoping that you get again
an new sunny life for you and your parents. I set down
that I saw your foto sitting in the rolling chair and when
I now can help you we both mus do our utmost.

Yours truly
D. Scheringa

Cortina had almost no snow, and what there was was
icy. The morale of the American team was low to begin
with and on top of that the squad was billeted at various
spots around town and there was no place for all of them
to get together. Jill watched the slalom training for two
days before the Games began but she exchanged scarcely
more than a greeting with old friends. Bud was so tied up
with training and newspapermen that she had no opportunity to see him alone. During the opening ceremonies
she imagined herself marching with the Americans and
fought to hold back her tears.

The Europeans were good and you could tell that they
knew it, although Jill felt she herself would not have been
fazed by their cockiness. She would have been afraid of
the very hard snow on the downhill course, had she been
racing, but that would have been a good, invigorating
fear.

The U.S. team lacked both self-assurance and finesse.
It did poorly, despite Andy's fourth-place tie in giant
slalom. Bud put on a good show early in the men's slalom,
but he took a bad fall and didn't finish. Jill was surprised
to find that the European girls, for all the medals they
won, were not so great as she had been led to believe.
They could be beaten. She felt that she could have beaten

them if she were still on skis and had trained with reasonable diligence during the previous twelve months.

The U.S. team was given a big dinner at the Miramonte Hotel, where Jill was staying, and she was invited to come along as Bud's date. She was ready ahead of time, for once, but a French newspaperwoman cornered her shortly before Bud came in.

Bud arrived. The woman was very persistent. Bud was very impatient. The reporter ran through a string of questions like "How do you feel being here but not competing?" Four times Bud said, softly and with admirable restraint, "Madam, we have a dinner engagement."

The dinner was enjoyable and reasonably short, which meant there should be several hours to talk with Bud afterward. Bud wheeled Jill from the dining room into the lobby. He said, "You don't mind if I take off, do you? I've got to get back to that U.S.-Canadian hockey game. Would you like to stay here, or shall I see you up to your room?"

Jill thought perhaps he was joking, but he stood beside her chair, looking down seriously, waiting for her reply. She felt like a dog who had just been walked once around the block by a man who was glad the chore was done. "I'm all right here," she said with no inflection whatever.

"Gee, it's been great to see you again," he said. "So long."

He left, and Jill only saw him again for long enough to say "Hi." She wished very much that Dick had come to Cortina.

19

JILL RETURNED TO LOS ANGELES AND MOVED BACK INTO CRC, where both the sky and the beach now were cold and dismal. The next morning June drove her to the UCLA campus to check out her registration for an art class and the first semester of U.S. history.

Jill's faculty adviser had decided that Jill wasn't up to taking art. She told him, "That's the one course I'm really looking forward to!"

"But I don't think you can handle it."

"I think I can."

"I just want you to be realistic about the work required in the class."

"I think I know my own limitations," she said. "I've painted before my accident and I've painted at CRC since then. I have a special brace for my right hand and I can open the brace with my teeth to change brushes."

"Another thing, Miss Kinmont. The art class is on the second floor and the building has no elevator."

"It's no problem to line up some guys to carry me upstairs."

The adviser studied her silently for at least a minute. He said, "Well, you go talk to the head of the art department, then."

"I thought I was all set. I had approval to start the semester five days late and everything."

Jill went to the art department and talked with the department chairman and with the instructor, John Paul Jones. Jones told her, "This guy who's your adviser is full of beans. Sure, you can take art here. Did you know Renoir could paint with his teeth? If you can't get upstairs to the room, we'll move the room downstairs."

So Jill was set for art and U.S. history every Tuesday and Thursday morning. On her first day of school Audra Jo drove from CRC to the campus with Arnelle, and Jill and her mother followed in the Kinmonts' station wagon. The two cars parked along a curb, one behind the other.

Arnelle and Audra Jo lifted their folding wheelchairs out of their car and hoisted themselves into them while June Kinmont took Jill's chair out of the station wagon and opened it at the curb beside the front door. Then June tried to lift Jill from the front seat into the chair. Arnelle wheeled her own chair close to the door and tried to help, but Jill slid off the front seat and out of her mother's arms. When she stopped sliding and falling she was sprawled across the curb and in the gutter with her dress pulled up above her waist.

In anger and total dismay, Jill screamed at a group of boys passing on the sidewalk. They dropped their books and came to her rescue, each one tugging at a limb. She shouted, "Get under both knees! Reach under both knees! Not just one arm—both of them together! One of you behind and one in front!"

Soon she was in her wheelchair with her clothes straightened and her notebook in her lap, but the moment the boys left she bowed her head and began to sob. She imagined arriving at school like this every morning—in total disarray, stripped of all dignity. She must have looked like a poor run-over rabbit there in the gutter. She knew that her mother and Arnelle and Audra Jo were painfully aware of her humiliation, but each of them knew better than to try to cheer her up with some comforting little remark.

Jill sat up and dried her eyes and said, "Let's go to class." As her mother pushed her down the sidewalk she added with a dull sigh, "At least things can't get worse, starting from the gutter. You can't go much lower."

Arnelle took the same history course, and she sat with Jill at the back of the huge lecture room. Jill was unhappy to discover that three hundred students were taking the course, but she didn't feel much better when she learned that the class broke up into small quiz sections on Thursdays. The first day's lecture meant absolutely nothing to her.

Jill found a boy named Stu who was in both her history class and her art class and he offered to wheel her to the art building. Stu had no difficulty rounding up two or three boys to help him carry Jill and her chair up to the second floor.

Art with John Paul Jones was as much of a joy as U.S. history was a chore. The room was a real studio with a high ceiling slanting up to the top of the north wall, which was all window. Jones was a fine artist, one of the country's leading printmakers, and an exciting teacher. He was a small man, quite matter-of-fact about art and life, and his class of twenty students had an appealing Bohemian flavor. Jill worked on a drawing board on her lap. One or another of the students—usually Stu—clamped fresh paper on her board when she needed it and laid out sharpened pencils for her.

Jill still followed a rigorous program of physical and occupational therapy at CRC—all day Monday, Wednesday and Friday, plus Tuesday and Thursday afternoons. But going to college two mornings a week turned out to be the brightest thing that had happened in a year. She was testing a new, unfamiliar way of life, and it was a good feeling. She had qualified for a Will Rogers Scholarship for handicapped students, which gave her some sense of earning her own way. Stu wheeled her to and from classes most of the time, and she was becoming less and less timid about asking for a push from strangers when she needed it. UCLA had been carefully designed for the convenience of students in wheelchairs, and all classrooms could be reached by ramps or elevators—with the exception of those on the second floor of the art building, where the elevator space was occupied by a kiln. Rest-room doors were extra wide, and there were a number of low telephones in fat booths built to accommodate wheelchairs.

United States history turned out to be a revelation and a shocker as far as Jill Kinmont was concerned. Not because the course was unusual but because it forced her

209

to notice, and then to examine, the fact that she was unbelievably ignorant about the workings of the government and about current events. She had never known anything about politics and had never cared. She didn't even know whether Harry S. Truman was a Democrat or a Republican. The first two lectures left her completely confused. It was all news to her. She told Audra Jo and her mother at lunch, "I don't know *any*thing. And I never even knew I didn't know anything. I'm just starting to see how dumb I am, and the more I learn the more I see how dumb I am. Dumber and dumber."

A skier named Gene Asher telephoned Jill one evening and said, "Can I help you in U.S. history?" He was studying for his doctorate in history and offered to attend her class and take notes for her, which he did. More important than that, he showed her how to take notes in outline form and gave her some idea of how she might distinguish between essential points and mere trivia in a lecture. The pressure of note taking in class also forced her to greatly improve her handwriting. Of purest necessity she taught herself to write faster and more legibly and to reduce the size of her script.

Arnelle, too, was a great help in history. She was an excellent student with an almost intuitive appreciation for the underlying characteristics of an era. She was always offering pertinent comments at the quiz sessions, despite the fact that she could only talk out of the corner of her mouth. If her words were not understood, she calmly repeated them until they came clear. She was a realistic young woman and could not afford the luxury of being sensitive about her own shortcomings. What did make her angry—very angry, in fact—was anyone who pretended to understand her when he in fact did not. "It's like saying I'm an imbecile," she told Jill. "And *that* is something I am not."

Bill Kinmont sold the Rocking K for the second time and the family at last had an opportunity to live together again. He kept 20 acres, which he hoped later to subdivide, but he and June gave up the idea of ever returning permanently to Bishop. They decided to settle in Los

Angles so Jill could live at home and still continue her therapy at CRC as an outpatient. They went house hunting every day, looking for a place that could accommodate a wheelchair and was located within a reasonable distance of both UCLA in Westwood and CRC in Santa Monica. Homes in these two suburbs were far too expensive, however. Eventually they found a house they could afford in Westchester, which was nine miles south of UCLA by freeway and seven miles southeast of CRC. They made a down payment with half the money they had received as down payment on the ranch. There were similar houses close on three sides and across the street and there was an identical house five doors away. But it was all on one level and it was comfortable—three bedrooms, a den and a large living room separated by sliding glass doors from a tropical fern garden where Jill would be able to study and sunbathe.

Jill and her mother moved down from CRC late in February as soon as the house was furnished, and her father and Jerry moved up from Hermosa Beach. All of them missed the treasured privacy and spaciousness of the Rocking K, and Jill had a closed-in feeling about their new home. June, who had never before lived where neighbors were within shouting distance, worried about whether or not she was expected to make a special effort to be neighborly.

Jill had to report back to CRC every afternoon for therapy, and her mother drove her and picked her up. She also had to be driven to UCLA, but once on campus she could get around by herself, calling for a lift when she needed it.

The most important thing about the Westchester house, as far as Jill was concerned, was that she had a home again and no longer had to share big chunks of her private life with strange orderlies and nursing assistants. Home also meant dozens of happy little changes like the end of insistent pill ladies and the end of cascara and milk of magnesia every morning just as a matter of principle. Jill had come to hate pills and medicines because they dulled her senses. She would rather ache than be comfortable.

211

but lose part of what sensitivity she did retain; she much preferred mastering discomfort to merely escaping it.

Jill had lost weight during the trip to Cortina and her arms were noticeably thinner. But she had no unusual medical problems and did not anticipate any as long as the tidal drain was continued and as long as her feet were propped up at night so sores would not develop from the pressure of her heels against the sheets. She slept on her side with pillows at her back, under her head, between her knees and between her ankles. Whenever she woke up with a cold sweat at the base of her neck or with the feeling of her hair standing on end, she called her mother. This usually occurred twice during the night, and each time June would come in and roll her onto her other side and prop her up with pillows again.

Leaving CRC meant a big reduction in medical expenses, and it was the logical occasion for a review of the Kinmonts' financial status. Jill heard for the first time what it costs to be hospitalized for a year with a serious injury. On the credit side was more than $21,000 contributed across the nation to the Far West Ski Association's Jill Kinmont Fund, some $3,500 donated by the Shriners while Jill was still in Salt Lake City, and well over $1,000 from a special campaign at Mammoth Mountain. Plus $750 in accident insurance, a reluctant $2,100 from the Blue Cross, and the Rocking K money. The ranch had sold for $100,000, a quarter of which was due the bank for the mortgage; the Kinmonts had received $20,000 down with the rest coming in $550 monthly installments, and about $10,000 of this had gone into the Westchester house.

On the red-ink side were bills from eleven physicians; six months of special nurses, three shifts a day; hospital room at over $30 a day, and hundreds of smaller items such as X rays and ambulances. June had saved about $2,000 by taking the day nursing shift at St. John's and several physicians had charged nothing at all for their services, but the year's expenses still came to over $60,000. About $50,000 had been paid and the balance could be met by forthcoming payments on the ranch. There would still be predictable bills for things like Jill's continuing physical therapy sessions, but the Kinmonts could probably catch up with their debts and keep ahead of them as long as there were no further major expenses.

Bill Kinmont was looking for a permanent job in the city. Meanwhile he began working for the Sportsman's Show, setting up displays and selling exhibition space. He was slowly and reluctantly adjusting to the idea of being an employee; until the previous summer he had never worked for anyone other than himself or his father.

When Jill thought about all the things that had altered because of the accident she was surprised at how gradual most of the changes had been. The one overt physical change had been drastic, of course—from exuberant good health to permanent paralysis in a moment. Nevertheless, her entire life had certainly not changed in one big jolt. Thousands of small changes had followed one another throughout the past thirteen months and the ones that mattered most were probably the least obvious. Jill remembered what Audra Jo had said about her own misfortune: "It forced me to grow up." Jill was grateful that she had been forced to look beyond her small, bright little world of competitive skiing, to notice and begin to care about a broader universe.

She was pleased to find that the accident had not changed her parents' general outlook and philosophy. Bill and June were as flexible as they had ever been. They believed just as fully in independence for their growing children. Their sense of humor had not been noticeably dulled. On the other hand, every member of the family had become more sensitive to other people's problems and more aware of their own feelings and vulnerabilities and prejudices. All of them were less impressed than they once had been by immediate appearances, by manners and wealth and social status.

One of the benefits of living in a house again was that Jill could invite Mr. Hardy for supper, which she did the second week in March. He arrived at six o'clock, dressed as usual except for the tie and tie clasp which Jill had

213

given him. He put down his brown hat and his bulging brown shopping bag, said "How's Jill?" and asked if he might wash his hands. He returned to the living room, where Jill introduced him for the first time to her father. He then pulled his chair close to Jill's wheelchair and chatted amiably about politics. His pet hates, he admitted, were Republicans and, with the exception of Senator Kennedy, Catholics.

He opened his bag with large, unsteady hands. He had a ballpoint pen which was a gift from the man at the Arcade post office where he bought the new stamp issues for Jill each month. He had free postcards from the Continental Shop where the same saleslady always sold him Jill's candy. She had read that Jill liked Swiss chocolates, so Mr. Hardy had six small boxes of Tobler's chocolates in addition to a two-pound box of MacFarlane's chocolate-covered caramels, marshmallows, nougats and creams. He also had a bottle of loganberry wine for June Kinmont and a clipping about Linda Meyers which confirmed the best piece of news Jill had heard in months. Linda had placed fifth in both downhill and slalom at Sun Valley's Harriman Cup races and had captured second place in the combined. Jill explained to Mr. Hardy that Linda had had absolutely nothing going for her when she started skiing, but for four years she had been lifting herself by her own bootstraps. Jill had once sweated for what appeared to come naturally to Bob, and it seemed that Linda was having to sweat even for what had come naturally to Jill.

Dinner included baked beans—but no day-old bread—and it ended with blueberry pie. When conversation lagged, Mr. Hardy took out a little memo book in which he apparently had written things he didn't want to forget. "Oh, yes," he said. "I thought you would be amused by the terrible thing that happened to me in the late 1870's. I had to wear *curls* until I was seven years old!"

Finally he looked at his watch, said, "Anything I can do for you uptown?" and took his leave. He refused Bill's offer to drive him to the bus stop.

214

At school Jill was slaving to keep a C-minus in history, and her art work ranged from pure pleasure to pure frustration. Watercolor paper would dry out while she was trying to get water in the brush, and then she would get too much water and couldn't squeeze it out. She couldn't get a dark line with a pencil, and when she used a stick of charcoal the weight of her hand was quite enough to snap it in two. Hundreds of times she tried in vain for effects she had managed easily in high school.

Jill wanted very much to look casual on campus and to feel at ease, all of which required considerable effort. Without the corset which braced her trunk, she would have appeared casual to the point of total slump. With it, however, her posture was just a little too good to be true. She practiced holding her shoulders and her head in positions that made her look more comfortable. She envied people who could really *slouch*. At the same time she was upset if anything else about her appearance was ragged or wrong or ungraceful. If her hair didn't look right, if her lipstick was crooked, if her skirt was too high or her corset had slipped, or if her stomach seemed to stick out —any one of these was enough to ruin her disposition. She did not mind using a wheelchair but she did not intend to look as if she belonged in one.

Two copies of the latest *Pageant* magazine came for Jill in the mail. On the cover, beside a picture of a very well-stacked woman in a white dress, were the words

JILL
THE STORY OF A GIRL YOU'LL NEVER FORGET
PLUS
SEX ON THE JOB
INDUSTRY'S MOST EMBARRASSING PROBLEM

Inside was a long article about Jill Kinmont. "Boy, if you want to read something hammy . . ." she said to her mother. "Did you know your daughter was a tawny, lovely sprite with the glory-wind of racing howling in her face?"

On Good Friday Bob Symons flew down to Los Angeles in his Tripacer to take Jill to Mammoth for the weekend. He piled her in front and tossed her chair in back and took off into a clear blue sky.

They flew up the Owens Valley, passing over Bishop, and landed on a narrow strip between McGee Mountain and the Mammoth turnoff. Dave was waiting for them.

Easter weekend was warm and bright, and Jill spent most of the time out on the big sun deck at the front of the building. She wore dark glasses but was hatless so she would get as much sun as possible on her pale face. The new double chairlift was big and beautiful and fast and there were three times as many skiers on the hill as she had ever seen before.

As Jill was squeezing Sea and Ski from a plastic bottle onto the back of her left hand, she noticed a woman staring at her from the far end of the porch. The woman walked over and said, "Can you feel?"

The bluntness of the question from a stranger startled Jill. She rubbed the sun lotion on her face and on both hands. "Well, sort of," she said.

"To where?"

"Down to my shoulders."

"Is that all? How about your stomach?"

"No."

The woman said, "Boy, you're sure going to miss something in life," and she turned and walked off.

"Well, thanks a heap for letting me know," Jill said, but the woman probably didn't hear it.

Jill saw a great deal of Linda, who was now possibly the best skier in California and had her heart set on making the 1958 FIS team. In a sense, she had taken Jill's place, and she was aware of this. She had been staying with the McCoys at McGee Mountain, and Dave had been working her summer and winter for the past year. She was eighteen and had just finished her first season of senior competition—all the big western races with the exception of the Snow Cup at Alta, where she said she would never race. Her big event had been the Harriman Cup. She had come directly back to McGee Mountain from Sun Valley and had surprised Dave with her silver trophy.

"What'd Pa say about *that?*" Jill asked her.

"Oh, he was pleased. He told me I'd really done something, especially because of . . . uh . . ."

"What?"

"Because of your accident and all. Except that *I* didn't feel this way. But I guess Pa thought your accident bothered my skiing or something."

Jill noticed that Linda seemed to have Dave McCoy very much on her mind. She was always talking about him or doing something for him or following him around. Jill felt critical and just a little jealous.

"Hey," Linda said brightly, "you know what skis I raced on in the Nationals?"

"No idea."

"Your downhills. The Kneissl Kanonens Dave got you at the end of 1954."

"I was going to use them in the East last year."

"I know. I sort of said . . . at Squaw, I mean . . . I sort of said, This one's for Jill. Sorry I didn't do good things."

20

SHORTLY AFTER VACATION BEGAN IN JUNE, BOB KIN-
mont arrived in Westchester with his guitar, two man-
dolins and a suitcase and dusty blond hair hanging down
to his collar. He had decided to transfer from Denver to
UCLA for his sophomore year so he could be with the
family and help lift Jill and drive her to school and to
CRC. His year in Denver had convinced him that painting
was to be his lifework, and he planned to major in fine
arts at UCLA.

Bob went to work for North American Aviation in West
Los Angeles for the summer and Bill Kinmont took a
temporary job with a manufacturer of aircraft com-
ponents.

Dick Buek wrote Jill that he and Gardner Smith were
planning to fly to Chile to join Bud Werner and Ralph
Miller in a speed race down a straight steep ski track
somewhere in the Andes. Jill had a letter from Ralph a
few weeks later saying he had hit 109 miles an hour on
skis, which was apparently a world record. He said Dick
and Gardner hadn't showed up, and he promised Jill that
Bud was going to write her.

Jill went to Mammoth for three weeks in July and stayed
with the McCoys at the McGee Mountain house. She
looked gaunt but handsome; her dark-lashed blue eyes
seemed larger and deeper. Roma took care of her morning
and evening and drove her to Horseshoe Lake several
times. Most days Jill went with Dave to Mammoth
Mountain where he was busy building a second chairlift.
As always, he wore jeans and a t-shirt. He drove her
around the mountain in a jeep and took her up in the #1

lift. Linda was working at the upper terminal and Jill often spent part of the day there.

Late one afternoon when Jill was alone by the railing of the sun deck Dave came out and said to her, "Whenever you need something, I want you to let me know."

"Things are just fine, Pa."

"I know. But trips and things won't always be dropping out of the sky. When help stops coming, I'll be here. If you ever need *any*thing, don't hesitate to ask. Transportation or a job or money or even a home."

A few days later he said, "Jill, have you any plans?"

"Not really."

"Would you like to run the Mammoth Ski Shop?"

Jill was surprised by the idea and thought about it for some time. "I think I would like that," she said.

"Whenever you're ready, it'll be here for you."

In September Jill and Bob and Audra Jo all registered at UCLA. Audra Jo had just returned to CRC after a summer at Tehachapi. Bob drove Jill to the campus and back every day and took her to all the art galleries he knew in Los Angeles. They talked about pigments and design, about Picasso, about abstractionism. Bob made a special point of getting to exhibits of Morris Graves and Hans Hofmann and John Paul Jones. He himself was painting realistic watercolors but was starting to look for new directions.

Bob was incidentally the best lifter Jill had ever had, which was saying a lot because Dick and Dave and Lee were all excellent. Bob carried her easily, swung her neatly into her chair or onto the seat of the car. He never handled her, as some of her male friends did, like a sack of wheat. Jerry was jealous; he was in junior high school, already showing some skill as a tumbler, and he didn't see why he wasn't old enough and strong enough to carry his sister.

Jill no longer had to go to CRC for physical therapy because Lee Baumgarth volunteered to come to the house every weekday evening. At UCLA she was taking German, art and accounting. Art was less exciting than it had been in the spring, but painting became easier as she learned to handle the brushes and to use a slightly tilted easel on her lap. At home she had a supply of paints and muffin tins and a big jar stuffed with brushes and pencils.

Jill had been battling a light cold for the first three or four weeks of school, and one late October evening she began to choke on mucus that had caught low in her throat. It was difficult to cough and yet she had to. She coughed steadily for ten minutes with her mother pushing down on her stomach each time. She still could not get the phlegm up out of her throat. She was having a very hard time breathing and was exhausted from coughing. Bill Kinmont telephoned her doctor, who in turn called the fire department because he had no suction apparatus.

In a very few minutes a siren sounded and grew steadily louder until its scream lowered and died in front of the house. It was not just a resuscitation unit. It was a huge hook and ladder with a man steering the rear wheels. Half a dozen men in firehats and slickers swarmed into the house, went directly to Jill, who was lying on her bed coughing, and slapped an oxygen mask over her face. Finally they realized what her trouble was and put away the oxygen and brought out their suction machine. They uncoiled a little tube and rammed it down her throat about as neatly as if they were hooking up a hose to a hydrant. The job didn't require the services of the whole crew so three of them wandered into the kitchen and helped Jerry finish the supper dishes. The rescue operation was a total success: Jill recovered her breath and her composure and the story was in the papers the next day.

Dick Buek showed up in his Porsche and stayed for a very relaxed week. Jill was still in bed with her cold the first three days and they had almost unlimited hours to talk. Jill read him a scene from Goethe's *Faust* in German and he was impressed. He had been in Germany and Austria for the better part of a year and still could not read German. He told her at length about his midsummer attempt to join Bud Werner and Ralph Miller in Chile. He and Gardner had flown south but made a forced landing on a beach in Nicaragua. They had landed in the middle of a revolution and were helped back into the air at gunpoint. They never got to Chile.

Dick was curious about Lee's physical therapy treatments and made Jill explain everything to him. One evening he reached both hands toward her and began wiggling his fingers. He said, "I'll bet you wish *you* could do that, don't you?"

She didn't like this kind of teasing and he knew it. She thought of saying that she had graduated from high school and didn't he wish *he* could do that. Instead, she said, "What's this, a big personality test or something? I dare you to come over here and say that!"

He stood up, stepped close to her chair, and bent down in front of her face, grinning. She leaned back, pulling her left arm against her chest, and then turned her shoulders and swung her arm at him, catching him hard in the face with her knuckles.

"Hey!" he shouted.

"Well, don't be such a wise guy, then."

Dick stepped back and rubbed his face and shook his head. "Are you about ready to get married?" he said. "I think we ought to make the big move real soon."

He drove her to class the following morning and spoke sarcastically about *the college life* and about all the uncool jerks he saw dragging armfuls of books.

"Don't be bitter," she said.

Dick heard there was a John Wayne movie about war planes in the neighborhood and wanted to see it, so they made it a double date with Lee and Audra Jo. Dick and Lee wheeled the girls down the aisle, lifted them into their seats, and took the wheelchairs back up to the lobby. The plot was based on a true story, and there was a pertinent bit where John Wayne broke his back falling downstairs and was paralyzed—for a while, anyway. He wasn't going to be able to regain the use of his legs unless he first forced himself to move his big toe. There was a little guy with a ukulele who hung around all the time saying, *"Move that toe! You gotta move that toe!"* And John Wayne kept telling himself, *"I'm gonna move that toe!"*

After most of the audience had filed out, Dick and Lee went back to the lobby for the chairs. Jill soon heard a slight commotion at the rear of the theater and a soft yodel. "Oh, *brother*," she said and rubbed her thumb slowly across her brow.

Audra Jo said, "What's the matter?"

"They're whooping it up, Josie. Pretend you don't know them."

Dick and Lee were each seated in a wheelchair and were drag racing down the center aisle, shouting appropriate cheers and challenges. Neither of them could stop before they reached the front of the theater.

When Dick finally came to lift her, Jill hardened her face and turned the other way. Dick grinned. He started chanting, "Come on, Baby, move that toe! We'll never get cracking till you *move that toe!*"

Audra Jo and Lee visited the Kinmonts in Westchester on Christmas Eve. Audra Jo sat for a long while rubbing her fingers and Jill thought she was cold—until she noticed the engagement ring. She screamed, "Josie!"

"I thought you were *never* going to see it," Audra Jo said. "I was practically waving it under your nose."

"Oh, you guys . . ." Jill shook her head. "That's just *so great!* When's the date?"

"June. And I'm taking him up to Bishop this week to show him around. Are we going to see you there?"

"You just make sure you do. *I'll* be there."

Jill went to Mammoth the day after Christmas, and as soon as she arrived, Dave said, "How about a ride down the mountain?"

"I'd love it, but *how?*"

Dave carried her over to the lift, which stopped long enough for him to put her in a chair and sit down beside her.

"Why don't you cross my legs for me?" she said.

Dave crossed her right knee over her left and she looked positively blasé. At the top, he tied her on a first-aid toboggan, feet toward the back, and propped her head up so she could see. Then he put on his skis, grabbed the

222

handles at the front of the toboggan, and skied it all the way down to the building with Linda and Dennis and the McCoy kids hot on his tail, showing off for Jill's special benefit.

Audra Jo brought Lee to Mammoth and she and Jill decided to make a real skier out of him. They sat on the porch and told him what to do, sent him up on the old rope tow, watched him come down and then told him what was wrong. "You've got to lean into the mogul; you've got to drive with your shoulder." He went back and tried again. He wasn't really bad, but he worked so hard at it and put so much *oomph* into every turn that the girls were always laughing wildly by the time he stopped at the porch for their comments and further instructions. Dave's daughter, Kandi, came out on the sun deck to watch, and after a while she turned and shouted, "Geezo peezo, look at him fall!"

Jill said, "What did you say?"

"I said geezo peezo, look at him fall."

"That's what I thought you said."

Back in Los Angeles after Christmas, Jill read about a fabulous new electric wheelchair on exhibit downtown and her mother went to look at it. "It's true," June said that evening. "It moves as fast as a person walks, forward or reverse, turns beautifully, and it's all controlled by one little lever. I had a ball riding in it. There's just one hitch."

"It *costs*."

"Five hundred and fifty dollars."

Jill said, *"Geezo peezo!"*

The *Mirror-News* printed a story about Jill in which the new chair was mentioned. The story was seen by someone at the Everest and Jennings Company, which had manufactured the chair, and the company decided to give Jill one for her twenty-first birthday. By coincidence, the Bob Crosby Show was planning to devote a half hour to Jill and Dave and Mammoth Mountain, and the chair was presented to Jill during the program. It was a magnificent machine powered by two automobile batteries and controlled by a stick the size of a fat pencil which stuck straight up on the left arm of the chair. Pushing the stick forward sent the chair charging ahead and pulling it back reversed it. Right for a right turn, left for a left turn. It took a lot of practice to learn how to navigate through a narrow doorway or turn neatly around the corner of a table. The chair's only failing was that it could not easily be folded. Jill used her old chair when she went anywhere by car or plane.

Linda Meyers finally hit her stride in 1957. She won the Women's National Downhill Championship at Aspen and placed third in the Harriman Cup downhill at Sun Valley. Dick Buek also did well; he couldn't stand up straight because of his back, but he refused to give up his dream of winning a world downhill championship. He raced in the Roch Cup downhill wearing a body brace and assured himself of a berth on the 1958 FIS team by finishing among the first three Americans.

Late in March Dick invited both Jill and Linda to stay with him in Soda Springs during the North American Championships at Squaw Valley, which was only 20 miles away. This was the final tryout race for the next year's FIS team and Linda was a favorite.

Dick flew down to Los Angeles on Thursday to pick Jill up at the Santa Monica airstrip. They flew to Reno, where Dick's father met them and drove them up to the Bueks' octagonal house at Soda Springs. Linda showed up an hour later and Dick seemed disappointed. He said, "Is she going to dress you and everything?"

"Sure. You asked her to come. What's the matter?"

"Nothing. Only I figured this was a good chance for my mother to get started taking care of you."

Linda told Jill that she owed her Harriman Cup medal to Dick. "It was cold and bitter," she said, "and the course wasn't in very good shape and I just didn't want to face the cold or the mountain or the race or anything else. But just before the race Dick told me, 'Look, if you think you're just going to ski down, just get to the bottom, you're crazy. If you think that's all you can do. You've got to want it and you've got to force yourself. If you don't put everything into it, nothing comes out of it.' "

On Friday morning Linda appeared on the lodge porch at Squaw wearing her bronze H from the Harriman Cup downhill. She pretended to be nonchalant but she was obviously very much aware of the H and of the people who noticed it. Dick watched her for a short time and decided to take Jill home to Soda Springs for lunch. Back at Squaw in the afternoon, he marched into the lodge wearing every medal he had ever won. Thirty-five medals of various shapes and denominations blanketed the front of his sweater from his shoulders to his waist. He walked around the lodge for an hour and a half, introducing himself to everyone in sight. He always said, "Good afternoon, I'm glad to make your acquaintance. My name is Linda Meyers."

On Friday night Linda told Jill that Bud Werner had said, "I hear Jill's here. I want to see her. I really want to talk to her. I don't want her to think I don't want to see her." Jill felt no reaction to this particular item of intelligence.

On Saturday and Sunday Jill sat on the lodge porch announcing the racers over the public-address system as they approached the finish gate. The competition was sharp and included the French FIS team, but Bud took the slalom easily. Dick was the first American to place in the downhill. At the banquet Sunday evening the trophies were awarded and the 1958 team was announced. Linda was named and Skeeter Werner was not.

After the banquet Dick saw that Bud wanted to talk with Jill, so he made himself scarce. Bud came up to Jill clutching his beautiful silver cup and said, "Jill, I want to talk to you." He sounded extremely melancholy.

"Yes, Buddy?"

"Jill, I'm sorry." He held out the silver cup. "Jill, I'd like for you to have this trophy."

"That's nice of you, Buddy, but thanks just the same."

"Take the trophy."

"Buddy, you don't owe me anything."

"Jill, take the trophy. You *deserve* it."

"Buddy, I don't *want* your trophy."

"Jill, Jill, I'm sorry," he said, still holding out the cup. "I'm sorry . . . I *really* am."

Dick, Linda and Jill drove back to the Bueks' at Soda Springs, and Dick flew Jill to Los Angeles Monday morning.

On Thursday, Jill was riding with her mother in Santa Monica when something caught in her throat. She tried to cough, and June reached across to help her by pressing on her stomach. It seemed that one last effort would do the trick and June pressed very hard—so hard that her foot slipped and hit the brake pedal. The car lurched to a stop and Jill felt herself going. She was in the middle of a cough and totally helpless and falling and she didn't even have time to figure which way to turn her head. She watched the dashboard coming up at her, blooming in size as it struck.

Her mother, with one deep sob, grabbed for her. "Oh, *honey*girl!"

"I'm okay, Mom," she said. She was sprawled sideways against the door and her mouth was bleeding. Gently, June pulled her upright in the seat again.

Jill's lip was cut and one front tooth was gone. It was a few minutes before she felt like speaking again. She said, "Now, Mom, it's okay. The dentist can fix it up just fine."

The Rocking K became a problem again because the latest owner had a heart attack and could no longer operate the ranch. The Kinmonts still had $51,000 tied up in the property and Bill figured that the only way to protect the investment was to buy it back. This he did, although he had to sell the Westchester house and also take on a partner who supplied the balance of the necessary cash. He still had another 20 acres of unimproved land in his own name.

Bill left his job with the Sportsman's Show early in May and went to Bishop to reopen the ranch. At the moment he could only guess what the next move might be, but there was some faint hope that the Kinmonts might be able to live and work at the ranch after all. It would even be convenient for Jill if she took over the Mammoth Ski Shop.

The family was able to stay in the Westchester house long enough for Jill, Bob and Jerry to finish school and for Jill to give a shower for Audra Jo. The wedding took place a week later at the Presbyterian church at the corner of Main and Line streets in Bishop. All the pews were filled and people along the back wall stood on tiptoe when Audra Jo and Jill were wheeled down the aisle. Jill wore yellow and the bridesmaids were in green.

Jill was fearful of losing the ring, so she pushed it snugly onto her little finger. When the moment came for Audra Jo and Lee to exchange rings she couldn't get it off. She worked on it, gritting her teeth, and finally managed to slip it to the bride long after the carefully rehearsed cues had been repeated and abandoned. Audra Jo changed into a pink suit at the church and Lee carried her out to the car. They drove away dragging the inevitable tin cans and old shoes.

The Rocking K was almost like old times, although Bob had stayed in the city for summer school. Many of the old guests were back because they knew the Kinmonts would be there again. Jerry tramped the desert looking for specimens for a new museum. Jill spent some time at the arena every day watching the cowboys or the dudes. Business was very good and Bill had hired a full staff: the wrangler, two women in the kitchen, a man for the office, a hostess with two daughters who waited on table, and Uncle Bob Lamkin as bartender. Guests occupied the old family quarters in the "house" as well as the seven cabins, and the Kinmonts themselves lived in a new two-bedroom trailer that Bill had put on blocks behind the swimming pool.

21

DICK BUEK FLEW IN TO THE ROCKING K OFTEN THAT summer, and his visits usually began with a long round of horseplay in Jill's old wheelchair. He always put her in an ordinary chair or in a deck chair at the pool so he could use the wheelchair. He became expert at balancing on two wheels, keeping the little front wheels in the air while moving and turning and backing in the dining room or the patio or on the tiles at the end of the pool. Once when Jill was in a bathing suit he put her in a large inner tube and shoved her toward the center of the pool. She could paddle with some slight effect, and when she thought she might be slipping through the tube she shouted, "Come and get me, or *you'll be sorry!*"

Dick seemed to know instinctively when Jill was cold. He always brought a jacket or a blanket at the right time, or carried her inside or turned up the heat. In the evening when he came up to the trailer to say good night he always kissed her slowly on the lips and touched her cheek with his hand.

One day Jill went to Yosemite with Dick and a couple Dick knew from Palm Springs. They borrowed Dave's station wagon and left at four in the morning. They drove up past the Badger Pass ski area to Glacier Point and all over Yosemite Valley. Dick's friend made the mistake of saying something about the Merced River being too shallow for swimming. Dick stopped the car, walked back to the middle of the bridge he had just driven across, and dove from it, fully dressed, into three feet of water. If he had scraped bottom, it didn't show.

The four sightseers started back early in the evening. It was still light when they crossed Tuolumne Meadows and started down the back side of Tioga Pass toward Lee Vining. Dick's friend challenged his driving ability and Dick deliberately kept his foot off the brake pedal for half a mile down the steep and snaky old mountain road. Jill asked him to slow down, but the tires kept squealing and she had to wedge herself against the back of the seat and the door to keep from toppling over. Jill thought of screaming. Instead, she simply stopped hanging on. It took only one sharp right turn to pitch her sideways onto the seat. Her head grazed the steering wheel and struck Dick's leg.

He stopped the car. He was scared. He lifted her gently, saw that she was not hurt, and drove on down the pass, slowly. His only words were, "Okay, you win!"

Dick's plane ran out of gas on his next visit and he landed on a farm five miles short of the Rocking K. He borrowed three gallons of gas from the farmer and flew on down to the ranch. His faded old levis had more rips and patches than they'd had on his last trip, and his general appearance was more scraggly than ever before. The first thing Jill said as he came loping and limping up across the south pasture was, "How come you haven't shaved?" His hair was down to his collar at the back and he had a beard a quarter of an inch long.

Nonchalantly he replied, "Why should it matter?"

"Dick, don't be difficult."

"I'm not difficult, I'm *easy*."

After supper they picked up the argument on a different level. Jill said it was terribly important to make a good impression on people and Dick said, "Play it straight and the hell with what the jerks out there think."

"Well, I sort of believe that, too," she said, hooking her right elbow behind the handle of her chair.

"You want it both ways," he said.

"Look who's talking! How come it's so important to you to impress everybody with the fact that you don't care whether you impress them or not?"

The remark apparently surprised Dick. He thought it over. He shrugged.

The next day he went off riding and returned with his pants ripped at the fly. When Jill saw him, the material was being held together in some miraculous way by a small stick. The levis were obviously busted and buttonless, and Jill assumed he was going to change immediately. But he did not, and after half an hour she took him aside and said, *"Dick Buek, why don't you clean up?"*

He tilted his head and stared at her quizzically. She added, "Here we are, trying to run a *guest* ranch, and you . . . oh, Dick, Mother's upset and, I don't know, so am I!"

Dick nodded sagely, and soon after that he disappeared. Three hours later he walked into the dining room, late for dinner. He was shiny and clean-shaven and combed and smelling of cologne and wearing a benign Mona Lisa smile. He was dressed in brand-new Bermuda shorts, heavy brown knee socks, a silky, striped shirt and a little stringy tie. He stayed at the Rocking K for three more days. He always wore these same new clothes. He never mentioned them or intimated that this was not his customary attire.

Late in August Dick flew in to invite Jill and Linda to spend a week at the cabin he and his father were building on the south shore of Lake Tahoe. Linda drove to Tahoe but Jill flew with Dick in his old Piper Cub with its old 65-horsepower engine. Dick had finally got a new engine, he said, a 90, but it would take some time to install it. They landed at Carson City, where Dick had left his pickup truck, and drove up to the half-finished cabin at the lake. Linda didn't show up as expected that evening so Dick shoved Jill into a sleeping bag, clothes and all. They slept on the cabin floor, but since it had neither roof nor walls, the starry sky was open above them.

Linda had misinterpreted Dick's meager directions and did not find the cabin until noon the next day. Jill had been counting on Linda to take care of her in the morning, and she was still in her sleeping bag when Linda arrived. Dick's parents had turned up in the meantime and Dick and his father built a six-foot-high dressing room of tarpaper for her.

The lake was cold but the weather was hot. Dick and Linda waterskied and Jill rode in the motorboat. They all went sailing . . . without a single life jacket, which prompted Jill to say, "Don't either of you *ever* tell my mother." One very hot afternoon Dick rolled her wheel-chair down the beach and into the water until she was knee-deep. The fearful and indignant cries from strangers on the shore pleased both of them.

Jill and Dick were alone together most of the next two days. He surprised her by saying suddenly, "You don't think I can take care of you, do you? Well, I've thought about that. I have an instructor's license and I'm going to get a commercial license. With that I can make great money cropdusting anywhere in the Central Valley."

"Dick, you've had me half convinced before, and then you go do something crazy. I'd need you sometime and you'd be off doing loops over Donner Lake."

He leaned back and studied her with obvious enjoy-ment. "You're pretty," he said.

"Look, there are things you'd have to do, and I'd have to say 'Dick, you have to do this and you can't do that.' And that's not right! I don't want to restrict you. I accept you as you are, but . . ."

"I know I can't just blow in across a field when I feel like it. Let me show you something." He went out to the pickup and brought back a stack of five books and per-haps a dozen pamphlets. "All I have to know for a com-mercial license is right here." He sat beside her and they studied the books and pamphlets together for several hours.

"I don't suppose you can have kids," Dick said, snapping a book shut.

"Technically I probably could, Dick. But the chances of my dying in the process would be very high, it seems."

"Does that make you pretty envious? I mean, of other girls?"

Jill shrugged and brushed her hair away from her cheek with the back of her hand. "I love kids. They're always so full of life and imagination. I wish I could have them. But only if it would be in my own situation. I don't wish

I was in some other woman's shoes, ever." She watched him quietly for a while. "You'd like kids of your own, I know."

"Well, sure, but after all . . ."

Dick took his commercial flying books back to the pickup truck and returned with a large brown paper bag which had been slit open and spread out. On it were plans and sketches in heavy pencil. He smoothed it out on Jill's lap.

"What is it?" she said. "Looks like plans for a house."

"That's right. No steps, see, and no halls. Just shallow ramps. And *wide* doorways. And it's a straight shot from one room into another. No little jogs and corners."

"It *would* be nice, wouldn't it!" She leaned forward with her left elbow on the arm of the chair and her chin resting on her fist.

"And look . . . no rugs, just asphalt tile. The sink is low. The basins are low. Real low counters."

"And what's this big room out here?"

"Combination garage and Cub-port. The Tripacer can taxi right in and stop by your ramp, here."

"Do you really think a plane and a wheelchair are going to get along together in the same house?"

Dick laughed and kissed her and folded up his big brown paper bag.

At the end of the summer the Kinmonts struggled through yet another change in their already confused and shifting plans. Jill needed more physical therapy and she wanted to go back to college, so the family decided to live in Los Angeles rather than Bishop. But they still could not get rid of the ranch; in fact, it seemed as if the Rocking K itself had made up its mind not to be disposed of or even shared. It had made money during the summer, but the partnership wasn't working out. So Bill sold off part of the 20 acres he had kept for subdividing, and with the proceeds he bought out his partner. He then went to Los Angeles to find a place to live—a rental, since there was no money to buy a house, and something near Westchester so Jerry could continue at his old school with his old friends. He soon found an apartment on the beach at Playa del Rey, three miles west of Westchester, and the family moved in just in time for the beginning of school. Bill returned to Bishop to carry the ranch through the hunting season and get it in shape to put on the market again in the spring.

Bob was majoring in art at UCLA and Jill signed up for merchandising courses that might help her with the Mammoth Ski Shop. They chose their classes so they would keep more or less the same hours on campus, and Bob drove Jill to school every day. But this tied up the family car, so they tried to find a better solution. A girl in Bob's art class knew of an older student named Lee Zadroga who lived in Playa del Rey, and Jill and Bob made arrangements to ride with him.

Lee Zadroga knocked on the Kinmonts' door the first morning at 7:15. He was on crutches—Kenny sticks—and walked with difficulty. He was five-feet-nine and husky, with a rugged crew cut and graying hair, and he was smoking a cigarette in a holder. Jill apologized at once for having made him come to the door. He said, "That's perfectly all right, Miss Kinmont. No trouble."

"You're very kind," she said, "but next time you just honk and we'll be waiting."

Jill and Bob and Lee Zadroga talked about their classes and professors during the first few rides, and soon Jill began asking him about himself. He lived a mile from the Kinmonts with his wife, Betty. He was an ex-Marine and had been a fireman until 1954 when he became mysteriously ill during a camping trip in the High Sierra. No one then or since had been able to diagnose the disease although he was still subject to periodic tests and spinal taps and bone marrow samplings. He had lost all use of his limbs at first, but then he had improved to the point where he could drive a car and walk with crutches when he had braces on his legs and a heavy steel brace on his back. He had decided to go to college and to finish in three years. He was now at the halfway point.

Jill soon gained the impression that Lee Zadroga knew everything, and she was embarrassed by her own ignor-

233

ance. He talked a lot about the hard realities of war in the Pacific. He quoted poetry as if it were a natural part of everyday conversation. He was hard to take when he described the event of death or the smell of dead Japanese soldiers. He was fascinating when he talked all the way home about Lessing and Schiller. But when he asked *her* a question, she could only say, "Lee, I don't know a blasted thing about eighteenth-century drama. I only wish I did."

"That's no problem," he said. "If you want to know, all you have to do is plunge in."

Jill spent many afternoons and evenings at the Zadrogas' arguing about life and love and politics or quizzing Lee or leafing through his very well-stocked library. Lee and Betty both loved to argue, and both were strong supporters of Adlai Stevenson. Betty was five-feet-two, blonde, and could not have weighed much more than 90 pounds. She knew precisely what Lee was up against; she was his caretaker and cook and lover and typist and file clerk, as well as a baker of delicious bread.

Lee took his dogs to the beach every day and forced himself to walk a grueling mile in deep sand without his leg braces, hoping to build up his legs again. He had to work with his body at each step, dragging one foot and then the other. His large bony face was always taut and wet with sweat when he was out in the sand and his leathery skin took on a greenish cast. He never complained, although Betty told Jill he was in pain every time he moved a muscle. He smoked heavily, two packs a day, even though it was a minor accomplishment for him to get a cigarette into his holder and light it. He had no use of his fingers or thumbs and had to rely on a special strap that gave him something of a grip between his thumb and forefinger.

Lee soon had Jill thinking of the university as something more than just a place to learn about operating a ski shop. He asked her why she wasn't going on with college and why she'd had no courses in philosophy or psychology. She began to wonder what she'd ever *thought* about back at the Bishop Union High School four and

234

five years ago; she and all her happy-go-lucky friends had seldom cared about anything farther away than the coming weekend. Lee was pleased to hear that Jill was now earning $1.50 an hour tutoring several neighborhood children who were having difficulty learning to read.

Jill used her electric wheelchair most of the time, but she always wheeled herself in the old chair for twenty minutes each day for exercise. She also worked out with a set of pulleys which were weighted with sandbags and hung from a doorframe. She had a telephone installed in her room, and she could either wheel under the edge of the table or lift it onto the tray of her chair. She dialed with the ballpoint pen in the brace on her right hand. She could pick up the receiver by jamming it between the thumb and fingers of her left hand and could then hold it with her hand or hug it between her shoulder and cheek.

Bill Kinmont returned from Bishop as soon as the hunting season closed. On Hallowe'en Jill received a note from Dick saying he might get down to Los Angeles in a few days. There were snow flurries every day at Soda Springs, he said, and the thermometer was well below freezing.

On the 4th of November Bob put Jill in the car to take her to school. He was backing out of the driveway when his father came striding out of the house with the morning paper in his hand.

Bob waited. Bill came to Jill's window and for a moment he didn't speak. Then he said, "Honeygirl, I have some sad news for you. Dick is dead."

Jill sat in silence, scarcely breathing. She couldn't cry. She couldn't think. She turned toward her father without looking at him. He said, "Do you want to stay home?"

"I'll go to school," she said.

Bob said, "How?" The word came out strangely, choked off. Bill only shrugged and walked back toward the apartment. Bob drove slowly down the street. Jill never did cry, although there were tears on her face all the way to school.

235

Jill was numb. The details, which she later read in the paper, meant nothing to her. The story said CRASH KILLS OLYMPIC SKIER. Dick had been instructing someone from Truckee and they were practicing power stalls 200 feet above Donner Lake. When the wreck was recovered someone noticed that the throttle cable had been pulled clear out of its casing. Both men had been killed. Dick's death was due, technically, to a broken neck.

There was nothing to be said, nothing to be done. Jill found Barni at lunch and told her. She wanted to talk about Dick, and found it was easy to talk about him, although she heard herself speaking as if she were someone else, some stranger. She thought about the funeral at Sun Valley and remembered everything old Mad Dog had said about it. The dead man was in good hands and *he* wasn't crying. Death is rough only on the living. Jill's emotions seemed to have been turned off. She said once under her breath, Oh, damn you, Dick Buek.

The next morning she received a letter from him on stationery that said *Buek Ski Shop . . . Rentals Sales Repairs . . . Telephone Soda Springs 2772.*

dear jill;
    at last we are getting caught up on our work around here, the shop i am speaking of. at the present time my dad is in the city geting some goods for the shop and i am on a vacation. i thought i would get down to la but just as i was planning to leave a bud came by for a few days, so i had to stay home and keep him company. dont sweat it tho, as i think i can get some time off again soon if i talk to my old man (dad that is) hows everything going with you. so they are sending some of the team to europe early, whats the reason for takeing some now and leaveing the rest of them home? i should think they would keep them a team and have them travel together, starting from here. what do you think? i know your in favor of seeing linda leap off early, so am i, but never the less i still dont think its fair. went flying today for about twenty min. sure was good to get up again, wish you were here to go along, not that i think you would have enjoyed it, but you did weigh, or dont weigh as much as

236

the passenger i took up. i sure cant wait to get the new 90 motor in my bird, i think i will be able to land it here in my back yard when i do. i had my hair cut real short the other day, but already it is growing out and by the time i get down to see you it will be long again. warren miller had his movie in reno tonight, or was it last night, i forget, anyway i didnt make it. are you going when it comes to la? i hear it wasnt to hot, not that i think much of any of his work, but then im a odd ball at times. after all, look at this letter. geting sleepy so think i will close for now please write if you think about it.

md

22

FOR WEEKS JILL STUDIED, WENT TO CLASSES, DID HER
exercises, spoke when spoken to, and betrayed no sign
of either gladness or sadness. She was somber, yet on edge.
She jumped whenever a light switch clicked. Despite her
aversion to drugs, she began taking phenobarbital. She was
never hungry. She was always cold. People talking made
her nervous, and when someone asked what was the
matter she answered sharply.

She wanted to be alone but there were always people
around. There were always people around *helping* her.
Always, someone was saying *Here comes Jill. Somebody
help Jill. Jerry, go help Jill. Bobby, see if Jill's all right.*
Her hair was always scraggly or itchy or out of place and
she could never keep her skirt down and her blouse
straight. Normally she would have fought against self-pity,
for she liked to impress people with the fact that she
didn't go for that kind of thing. But now . . . what was
there to prove? Who was there to impress?

She remembered things Dick had said at Sun Valley
about the funeral and things he had said at Scottie's about
Jim Griffith: *Death? Well, that's the way it is; that's the
way things go; that's life.*

Jill was aware of other people's plans and problems and
tragedies but she felt as if she were watching from a distance. The Baumgarths were in Venezuela, where Lee
had a temporary job. Barni Davenport was about to get
married. Bob Kinmont had left UCLA and was teaching
skiing at Mammoth for just long enough to pay for a
ticket to New York, where he planned to paint and see
all the galleries. Bill Kinmont still had the ranch and

was working on a scheme to run it for the summer and then subdivide some of the acreage and sell the lots.

These events were only half real to her, like pages in someone else's family photograph album. Bob Symons, her friend and "private pilot," had just died in a glider accident. Linda was in Europe as the first California girl ever to race internationally for the United States. Bud put on a beautiful show at the World Downhill Championships at Bad Gastein and then fell a few hundred yards short of the finish.

Jill was just beginning to feel, to know, how much Dick Buek had meant to her. She cried now because she had always, while he lived, taken his devotion for granted. And because she had always worried first about what other people would think, because she had never failed to bitch about his hair or his beard or his ragged clothes. His words now had more meaning for her than they'd had before. Don't sweat the little things. Stay loose.

Jill went to Mammoth for a visit and someone there asked her if she felt sorry for herself. She shrugged. She was later asked if she envied Linda, and she said "No." She was surprised to notice, as she sat in her chair on the big sunny porch of the building, that she was not particularly envious of the skiers she was watching. She loved the snow and she loved Mammoth, but she still looked forward to getting back to Los Angeles. She even missed the boys she was tutoring in Playa del Rey two or three afternoons a week. They had become curious about reading now, excited about it, and their grades in school were improving.

One afternoon the following week, when she was riding home from the university with Lee Zadroga, she realized that she envied Lee a lot more than she envied Linda. She would have given anything that morning to have been able to enter fully into the discussion in class, to have had something pertinent and profound to say. She mentioned this to Lee and he told her for a second time, "If you want to know, all you have to do is plunge in."

"Where?" she said. "You know so much that it makes

me feel incurably stupid. How is it possible I could have coasted all the way through high school—and with good grades, even—and not learned a thing?" She was overwhelmed by the thought of how much learning it would take her to become at all learned. It would be like going from toe straps to Olympic gold medals.

She was willing to try, however, and Lee was pleased to help her. He lent her his books and his old class notes and spent many hours talking about books and explaining the notes. When she worried about what courses to take or questioned her own half-formed plans for the future, she went to Lee. When she mentioned teaching as a possibility, they talked about that and he encouraged her. She said one day, "It was always important to me to *be* something, Lee, but as far as contributing anything to the world, or growing as an individual, I didn't know about those things. I didn't know you did them, I guess. I didn't know that other people were concerned with them."

Jill changed her major from merchandising to languages, Lee gave her a summer reading list that began with *The Great Gatsby, Wuthering Heights, The Sun Also Rises, Jane Eyre, Pride and Prejudice* and *Rebecca.*

The Kinmonts spent Memorial Day weekend at the Rocking K. The Bueks—Dick's father, mother and sister—were driving through Bishop and came to the ranch for Saturday lunch and part of the afternoon. It was a quiet visit, although Carl Buek teased Jill about her letters to Dick. "Pretty hot stuff," he said. "Dick had kept them tied together in a bundle, every letter you ever wrote him."

"But you didn't really *read* them!"

Later Jill said suddenly, angrily, "Darn him, anyway! Why did he have to keep doing all those crazy things!"

Carl said, *"You* should talk!"

Just before the Bueks left, Carl said to Jill, "Dick never cried but twice in his life, Jill, aside from when he was a kid. Once when Jim Griffith died. Once when you were hurt."

The Kinmonts sublet their apartment for the summer

and Jill and her mother and Jerry joined Bill at the ranch as soon as school was out. Jill was just in time to make the fifth reunion of the Bishop High School's class of '53.

The Baumgarths were in Bishop for a visit, and Jill and Audra Jo immediately retreated to a private corner of the Rocking K dining room. "So what's new since Venezuela?" Jill said.

"We're going to have a baby."

Jill was so startled that she choked. When she found her voice she said, *"What . . . what?"*

"We're going to have a baby."

"Oh, Josie, *really?*"

"Yes, really. I'm two months along."

"Gads, how *great!*" Jill said. "How do you feel? Does it feel any different?"

"No, it doesn't feel any different. Not yet, anyway."

The two girls talked at length about Venezuela and about Dick's death and about the fact that the Baumgarths were planning to live in Bishop while the Kinmonts were planning to leave Bishop. Lee had recently earned a teaching credential and now had a job in the junior high school at Tehachapi; after a year or two he expected to find an opening at Bishop.

Linda Meyers came to spend the summer at the ranch. She worked as a waitress and often took care of Jill so June might have some free time. Jill herself was in excellent health and was enjoying a full night's uninterrupted sleep for the first time in three years—she no longer had to be turned once or twice every night to avoid cramped muscles or bed sores.

Jill and Linda decided they wanted to go camping, so they planned a four-day trip to Red's Meadows and the Devil's Postpile National Monument, which were at the end of a ten-mile dirt road running down west from the base of Mammoth Mountain. Linda loaded a jeep with food, a Coleman stove and lamp, books, sleeping bags, fishing tackle and a large suitcase.

When the girls were ready to take off, Dave lashed Jill to the front seat of the open jeep with two straps across her chest and put the folded wheelchair on top of the sleeping bags. The road ran easily uphill for the first mile and then dropped 1,700 feet down into the watershed of the San Joaquin River. Jill wished she were at the wheel because she wanted to be in control going down the steep mountain road. Driving fast through trees on a narrow roadway was the one thing that brought back the feeling of quick terror she'd had at Alta, flying toward the trees, hopelessly out of control. She now said under her breath, "I could sure drive better than Linda, if I could drive."

When they reached camp, Linda lifted Jill from the jeep seat, lowered her onto the suitcase and eased her down onto a sleeping bag. Then she went off with her fishing rod and returned an hour later with more than enough trout for dinner. In the morning she dressed Jill and sat her up against a tree and made breakfast. She got Jill into the jeep by squatting in front of her, bracing Jill's knees against her own, and pulling Jill up by the arms until she was able to swing her over onto the seat.

The girls spent their time fishing or reading in the sun or exploring in the jeep. On their last day they banged their way southeast about five miles down the old abandoned Red's Meadows road, which had not seen wheeled traffic for years. Hikers were sometimes annoyed and sometimes amused by the jeep's invasion of their quiet forest trail. One boy studied the diagonal straps holding Jill against the back of the seat and said, "What's the matter, don't you trust her driving?"

Near the bottom of the old road, Linda drove down a steep stony hill and came to a stop in front of a big tree trunk that had fallen across the trail. It was impossible to back up the hill. Linda said, "I guess there's nothing to do but walk on down the trail until I find some *people.*"

She returned ninety minutes later with five hikers, and by this time Jill had perfected several theories about how to get the jeep out of the jam it was in. She told Linda and her good-hearted rescuers how to drag and roll the log. When this didn't work, she told them to clear the loose stones from the trail behind the jeep and push it backwards up the hill. This almost worked. She suggested letting some of the air out of the tires to get better traction. It took an hour to get the jeep up the hill and headed back toward Red's Meadows.

At Mammoth the day after the camping trip, Jill was sitting on the sun deck in front of the cafeteria when she heard someone inside talking to Bob Seaman at the hamburger counter. "You wouldn't believe it, back in the wilderness miles from a road," a man's voice was saying. "But here they were, these two stupid girls in a jeep who had no business being where they were. And of course they were stuck, and the darnedest thing I ever saw was that one girl was working like a horse trying to get the jeep out, and we were tugging at it, too, and all the time this *other* girl just sat there in the jeep giving orders. Boy, I guess it takes all kinds!"

Five minutes later the man came out onto the sun deck. He was with a woman and both were munching hamburgers. They were two of Jill and Linda's five rescuers, and they recognized Jill at once when they saw her watching them from her wheelchair. The woman choked on her sandwich and they both eased away from her, walking with a kind of sidestep, and disappeared around the corner of the building.

Jill had a slight cold when she returned to Los Angeles, and by October the congestion in her throat was so bad that she entered the UCLA hospital. It was the hospital's first acquaintance with her and the official diagnosis was:

1. virus bronchitis
2. cystitis
3. cervical cord injury with quadriplegia.

A generous dose of antibiotics cleared up all symptoms of lung and bladder infection except for her temperature, which was up to 102 every day. The doctors were worried and kept her for three weeks.

One of the doctors had been Lee Zadroga's physician at a Veterans Administration hospital in 1954, and Jill

243

asked if he knew what Lee's trouble was. "Never diagnosed," he said. "We thought it might have been some kind of bone cancer. He's a lot better now, I understand, but still we really don't have any hope for him." Jill thought of CRC where the patients were in pretty bad shape but at least were improving in *some* degree month by month and year by year. She had not considered what it would be like to know that things could only get worse, and *would* get worse . . . until at last there would be nothing left.

Jill felt fine except for the unbearable heat, and by the end of the third week someone tumbled to the fact that her high temperature coincided with the unseasonable hot spell which was still holding noon temperatures up to 100 in the hospital and 106 outside. The doctors concluded that Jill's body temperature probably fluctuated, like that of a cold-blooded animal, along with the temperature of her environment . . . which might also explain why she felt so miserable when she was cold. June talked the hospital into letting Jill go home to the beach where it was 20 degrees cooler, and there Jill's temperature returned to normal immediately. The only lasting damage was to Jill's grades—C's in history, geography and French, and a D in psychology.

The year ended with Jill about halfway through college and the Rocking K disposed of—everyone hoped—for the last time. Jill was unable to figure what class she was in at UCLA; she had been going to college for almost three years and planned to keep going until she had enough credits for a degree. She could probably have qualified as a junior.

As for the ranch, it had been bringing in just about enough income to meet daily expenses and monthly mortgage payments. Bill had an offer, and he sold it—at a sacrifice. He still kept some 12 acres which he was busy surveying for lots and roads and water lines.

Nineteen-fifty-nine was a tryout year for the Olympic Winter Games, and Bud Werner collected several gold medals in European races during January and February.

244

In March he and Linda went to Squaw for the North Americans, where both of them placed first in both downhill and in slalom. Kenny Lloyd placed second to Bud in downhill and later won the Silver Belt at the Sugar Bowl. Meanwhile, two other Mammoth skiers, Joan Hannah and Dick's friend Gardner Smith were winning medals in the big Eastern races. Gary McCoy became national junior slalom and combined champion and was named the outstanding junior racer in the country.

In the great world of skiing, apparently, Jill's best friends were doing the best things. She was deeply pleased for all of them, knowing how hard each had worked and for how long. But she herself could see no particular merit in clinging to the coattails of this world that had left her behind.

Jill was still tutoring and had two regular pupils. College was much easier for her now although she missed Bob, who was back from New York but had just entered the Army. She had enrolled in five tough courses, including Goethe, American literature and nineteenth-century German drama. She knew, finally, what was expected of her, and she now could take notes as efficiently and as legibly as anyone. Her term papers were also improving as she learned how to follow Lee Zadroga's extensive and pointed advice. *Write like a writer. Keep yourself out of the paper. Support your comments. Make every sentence say what you mean. If you have a big idea, use a big sentence; otherwise, don't.*

Lee had been elected to Phi Beta Kappa and had graduated in February after only three years of college, without summer school. He was now working on his master's degree in English literature, for which his thesis was to be on Coleridge and Wordsworth. The greatest compliment Jill had ever received came from Lee when she asked him for a letter in connection with the renewal of her scholarship. Lee wrote:

During the course of my friendship with Jill Kinmont, I have been most impressed by her growth as a scholar and as a person. As colleagues at the university, our

245

friendship is largely based on the community of interests and problems we share in this environment. She possesses a fine mind with a constantly developing ability to think clearly, precisely and thoroughly. Her interest, stimulated by a profound and genuine intellectual curiosity, is sustained by an impressive diligence and sense of responsibility. During a brief but remarkably successful athletic career Jill Kinmont had won a fine reputation as the best kind of competitor. Her conduct since an accident ended that career, the courage and persistence with which she has overcome tremendous obstacles, have made her one of the most admired figures in international sports. The qualities of character and ability which have gained for her this reputation are equally manifested in her career as an aspiring scholar.

During the summer of 1959 Jill spent many days at Mammoth. She knew everyone there. She loved the mountain. She loved the building. She liked the look of the ski shop and was impressed with the quality of its clothing and equipment.

One afternoon when she was riding with Dave in his station wagon she said, "Pa, I've been thinking. And I think . . . honestly . . . that the ski shop isn't what I want for the rest of my life. I mean, I don't think I should work in the shop. Because I don't see how it could *satisfy* me. Running the shop is really something *any*body can do."

"Maybe you have something there," Dave said.

"What I want, Pa, is something *I* get, not something handed to me."

"Do you know what that might be?"

"Maybe. I think I'd like to teach, Pa."

Dave nodded.

23

SENATOR JOHN F. KENNEDY CAME TO UCLA EARLY IN the fall to address undergraduates in the main auditorium. Jill's last class that day was upstairs in the same building, so she had a classmate push her directly to the balcony.

She had expected a political pitch, but the Senator was not just out scrounging for votes. He said that "politics" was not a dirty word. He said that anyone who thought politics to be an irresponsible profession should climb into the arena at once and *do* something about it. It was going to take a lot of work to get the country moving again. Furthermore, peace in this world was not going to be achieved unless the people who cared about it did something about it. A man must do what is important to him, but he has an obligation also to work for things that are broader than the borders of his own back yard.

Jill felt as if she were being told for the first time what it meant to do something *useful* in life. She also felt that the Senator's sentiments confirmed her decision to dump the Mammoth ski shop in favor of something like teaching. She said to Lee afterwards, "This all fits into the same thing Dr. Bone had to say in American Lit. He's the one who really made me sit up and take notice and take a look at what life is all about and opened my eyes. Well, I don't mean Bone said, 'Do something,' but he did say, 'Freedom and justice for all, ha ha, that's a bunch of hogwash.' And now Kennedy adds to it, 'But let's see if we can't do something about it!' " The Senator reminded her of Dave in the way he set his sights on what he wanted and then simply went after it and got it.

Jill read Kennedy's *Profiles in Courage* the following week. The entire book impressed her, but what she re-

247

membered most vividly was Hemingway's definition of courage as "grace under pressure." She repeated this to a friend, and he said, "I guess you're the living example of it."

"I'm not being courageous any more than somebody else is being courageous," she said.

"Well, you're graceful, anyhow."

"I hope so. I'm not under any pressure, so I guess at least I'd better be graceful."

In February Jill attended the 1960 Games at Squaw Valley as an official hostess and also as a special sports columnist for the Los Angeles *Examiner*. Dave Lawrence and Andy were there as manager and coach of the women's team. Bud Werner, who had been considered America's great hope, was there as a spectator, thanks to having broken a leg while training at Aspen; he was engaged to a Denver girl and planned to open a ski shop at Steamboat Springs. Linda was there, fresh from a win and a first-place tie in European races; she was in great form . . . until her second event, the giant slalom, in which she struck a metal slalom pole and broke her right collarbone. Dave McCoy was there on crutches, having slammed into a snow-covered rock coming down the Gravy Chute at Mammoth; he'd had a compression fracture but had skied on down and gone off to see a doctor without anyone at Mammoth having noticed.

Squaw was very different from what it had been when Jill had last been there with Dick, and with Linda and Bud. It was now big, busy and impersonal. The Games this year excited Jill in the way that a good show excited her, but there was nothing like the flush of feeling she had once known at all the big races.

The Olympics cost Jill a week of classes at UCLA. She had gone to Squaw immediately after the beginning of the spring term, and now she was trying to catch up on Schiller, the history of Greek philosophy, and three courses she would need if she ever decided to get a teaching credential. She had not committed herself to the idea of teaching, but she had been worrying about what she would do for a livelihood once she got out of college. To come out of school with nothing more than a college degree wasn't going to mean very much. And to be independent—as independent as possible in as many ways as possible—was of unique importance to Jill because she was so dependent physically.

Her rehabilitation was over and she anticipated no basic improvement in her physical abilities. Her handwriting was excellent and she had trained herself to handle her spork gracefully, although trying to balance something wobbly like jello was still good for a few moments of dramatic suspense. She always typed her own papers for school and her skilled hunt-and-peck technique gave her a speed of 26 words per minute.

As for her health, her only complaints were that she always felt cold and that her ankles swelled up when she was in her chair more than eight or nine hours a day. She still exercised with weights and pulleys several times a week and still had to drink eight glasses of water a day and have the tidal drain set up when she went to bed at night. She had learned to balance a glass of water on her fist, take a deep breath of air, and then drain the glass at one draught.

June Kinmont was still caring for Jill and had to be with her every morning and evening except on special occasions when Linda or Roma or Aunt Beverly might take over for a few days. June said to her husband, "Jill feels sorry for me sometimes and I don't like that."

The family was at last accepting the city as its permanent home. The Rocking K was gone except for a few lots Bill had not yet sold. There was no money in the bank, but there were no debts outstanding, either, for the lot sales had taken care of the last of Jill's hospital and rehabilitation bills. Bill sold another parcel of the ranch property for enough to make a small down payment on a house on the hill at Playa del Rey, and the family moved in immediately. Bill accepted a position as sales manager of a small firm, specializing in the manufacture of hydraulic pumps.

Jill began reading the news carefully, with particular attention to Eric Sevareid and James Reston and Walter Lippman, and she went through all the campaign literature she could get from both the Republicans and the Democrats.

The Democratic convention was held in Los Angeles in mid-July and a school friend of Jill's managed to reserve a pair of seats in the Golden Horseshoe at the Coliseum for Senator Kennedy's acceptance address. Jill and her date sat directly behind the podium and across the aisle from the Senator's brother Robert. Linda, who had been staying with the Kinmonts and going to summer school with Jill, was also at the Coliseum, but she was lost out among the 120,000 general admissions.

Kennedy was even more challenging and more to the point than he had been at UCLA nine months before. He said too many Americans today had lost their way and their will and their sense of historic purpose. He spoke of a New Frontier which was not a set of promises but a set of challenges.

The next day Jill telephoned the Democratic headquarters in Los Angeles and volunteered her services. She explained her limitations but said she would be happy to type or lick stamps or answer phone calls. They put her to work on her own telephone rounding up volunteers to register voters in Westchester and Playa del Rey.

Jill and Linda were both for Kennedy—Jill strongly so—although they didn't think much of Lyndon Johnson, who was running with him. Political discussions at the Kinmont house were relatively hot because Bill and June and Aunt Beverly all had been Republicans since birth. The autumn's two memorable events were the Kennedy-Nixon debates on television—the Zadrogas came over to watch—and election night, when Jill stayed up until two. She was surprised to hear that Linda voted for Nixon.

Only after the election was Jill able to buckle down to school work again. Meanwhile she had written Secretary of State Christian Herter describing her extensive knowledge of German and asking about a job with the

State Department. The answer was that the kind of position she had in mind entailed readiness for overseas duty at any time, and for this she did not have the necessary physical qualifications.

President Kennedy's inaugural address on the 20th of January was articulate and exciting, and parts of it struck Jill like a personal message. Lee asked her, while driving to school, what the speech had meant to her. She rubbed her thumb thoughtfully across her lips. "Well, Kennedy is saying that we all have to start caring about education and poverty and disease and getting rid of prejudice. You and I and all the rest of our generation. He's making us responsible for working for things that matter."

"Like teaching."

"That's right." She leaned back and studied Lee's face. She smiled. "How did you know?" Then she said with a frown, "Yes, like teaching kids to read. I've always liked that, especially when you can see the results. You know these kids in the neighborhood that I work with? Well, I find that things really happen for them. Their curiosity comes through and their grades jump from D's to B's. And it's fun to see this happening, Lee. But like we were saying, about Kennedy . . . this really gives me the feeling that I'm on the right track and that something like teaching *is* what I want."

She knew she had to have a teaching credential before she could teach, and she knew this would involve student teaching and a number of education courses. She didn't know where to begin, so she went at once to her faculty adviser. He glanced at her chair and at her hands and said, "I hope you're being realistic about what is required of a teacher, Miss Kinmont." She returned his stare and said nothing. He set up an appointment for her with a counselor at the School of Education.

The Education Building was the only building on campus with steps at the front door, and Jill had to find two boys to carry her up. Once inside, she wheeled herself about a tenth of a mile south to the end of a long brown corridor, took the elevator to the third floor, and wheeled herself a tenth of a mile north down a long brown cor-

251

ridor. The counselor was a middle-aged woman, squarely built, with a square, unsmiling face. "What are your plans?" she said, shuffling papers on her desk.

"I feel I can qualify to teach German, and I want to find out what classes I'll need to get certified." The counselor raised her bushy eyebrows but made no other response. "I have a pretty free choice of classes this next semester," Jill said. "I'd like to use the time to good advantage."

The woman asked a number of questions about Jill's injury and about her physical abilities and her academic standing. Then she said, "Have you been accepted by the School of Education?"

"No yet. That's what I'm . . ."

"You'll have to see one of the assistant deans, then."

Jill was sent to the Admissions Office, where no one was free to see her. She returned the following day for an interview with a young man who greeted her efficiently and said, "What are your plans?"

Jill stated her case again and was again asked the same questions about her injury, physical abilities and academic standing. At length the young man said, "I'm sorry, but it does not appear that you are going to be able to qualify."

"What do you mean? Why not?"

"Well, for reasons of health, obviously."

"Which reasons? I've probably been sick less than anyone in any of my classes. You can't say I'm not healthy!"

"Well, all right. Perhaps you should run over to the health office and see the doctor who's on the Board of Admissions."

A day later Jill was at the health office explaining her plans and qualifications and problems to a woman physician who nodded at every sentence but was otherwise unresponsive. Eventually the doctor said, "Now, let's be realistic about this. Teaching in a public school has many barriers. What about college teaching? Are you good enough to take an advanced degree?"

Jill's foot began to vibrate on the footrest of her chair. It was noisy and she let her left hand press down against her knee. "I am good enough," she said, hoping the spasm would pass quickly. "At least my grades are good enough. But that *isn't* what I want to do."

"Oh?"

"I want to teach German on a high school level. I'd really like to work with younger children, but I know I'm not up to blowing noses and handling fire drills."

"Miss Kinmont, the board meets in September to consider candidates for the School of Education. I could present your case at that time. How*ever* . . . in the past we have accepted cases such as yours and they did not work out. So now we require a physical examination. And one of the rules is that the student must be able to walk up steps and be able to stand on his feet all day."

"Look, I'm only asking to be allowed to teach school! It's obvious I can't satisfy *those* rules."

"In most of the schools where they have student teaching, Miss Kinmont, they have *steps*."

"But surely not *all*."

"In most schools in Los Angeles they have steps."

"I wouldn't apply in a school that had steps."

"I've told you what the rules are, Miss Kinmont."

In the end everyone at the School of Education turned her down. She told Lee Zadroga they were all complete fools and petty bureaucrats. "All they know how to do is go around patting me on the head like somebody's spaniel. They are jerks, Lee. They are real asses, if you want to know the truth." She thought of Dick's *Don't sweat the little things* . . . but it was precisely the littlest of little things that were gumming up all these educators' minds.

"Sounds somehow familiar," Lee said.

"They want me to be *realistic*—to dump teaching and go out on the corner and sell pencils or something."

Lee said, "You can sell pencils even if you're *not* handicapped, and you can teach even if you *are*. You might have to change the rules or look somewhere else, but if you know what you want and really *want* it, then you're going to get it and you're not going to let yourself sell pencils or weave baskets."

Jill wore a cap and gown for her graduation ceremony

253

and Jerry, who was about to graduate from high school, wheeled her up to receive her diploma, a B.A. with a major in German.

Mr. Hardy was there, along with June and Bill. Dave McCoy came down, too, which was a special surprise. Dave took movies and Betty Zadroga took snapshots. Lee was there on crutches to receive his M.A. in English.

Dave was tremendously proud of Jill, although he knew little about her reasons for wanting to teach. Jill felt slightly sad to find herself so far removed from the world of skiing, but she was tremendously proud of Dave because three quarters of the American Women's FIS squad for the coming season—Linda, Joan Hannah and Jean Saubert—had been trained by Dave McCoy at Mammoth Mountain. She was also proud of what he had made of the mountain, which now handled thousands of skiers a day on two T-bars and four big chairlifts . . . with a fifth lift under construction and an aerial tramway to come.

Lee asked Jill if teaching was her first choice for a career.

"The Peace Corps is the thing I'd most want to do," she said. "If I had the full choice. It means being involved in something that matters, and it's such a wonderful chance to be selfish and altruistic at the same time. But . . ." She shrugged. "Well, I do know there are many many people you can touch right where you are, and you can do something for them. And so you don't have to be in the Peace Corps to do that. But you don't talk about it, either, you just do it."

Jill received a scholarship to the University of Vienna's summer school on the Wolfgangsee near Salzburg. She was also granted a $1,000 loan, through the Institute of International Education, to help finance the trip to Austria with her mother. The summer was a delightful change and she returned to Los Angeles primed to renew her battle with the School of Education.

She was advised first to check out her professional qualifications and potentials with the local Office of Vocational Rehabilitation, and this she did. She had a series of conferences with a Mr. Arthur Poinc, who agreed that teaching was a fine idea—*if* she could get a job.

She said, "If I could get a credential, I could get a job."

Mr. Poinc thought she should consider other things in addition to teaching. He suggested a Federal Service Entrance Examination and a battery of vocational aptitude tests, and Jill went through the whole works. She failed the Civil Service exam. The vocational tests indicated that the ideal profession for her would be teaching.

Jill ran into a girl she had known at CRC who was now teaching in a parochial school without a state credential. She sat down the next morning and telephoned all the parochial and private schools in the area. No luck, except that one school implied it might be in the market for a teacher with a *provisional* certificate. This seemed to be the obvious answer for Jill, and she wrote at once to the state Department of Education.

The department said she would be awarded a provisional certificate if she could get a teaching job, keep it for at least two years, and take the necessary education courses in the meantime. Student teaching would *not* be required.

Jill went to the School of Education to sign up for the courses she would need. A counselor in the Admissions Office said, "To take these courses you have to be enrolled in the School of Education."

"Fine. Will you please enroll me, then."

"Miss Kinmont, you've got to be realistic. You cannot get into the school unless you can meet the physical requirements."

"Because of the student teaching."

"That is correct. The schools are all multilevel and they have steps."

"But I don't have to go near these schools because student teaching isn't required for provisional certification."

"But the *courses* are required, and you can't take them without being enrolled."

"And you won't let me enroll because I'm not qualified for the student teaching which I don't have to do!"

255

"Miss Kinmont, we have our rules. In the past, students such as yourself have studied to become teachers and then found they could not physically handle the job. So now we require a physical examination. And one of the qualifications concerns steps."

24

Jill registered for several postgraduate courses she felt would be helpful to her as a teacher and continued to ride to the campus and back with Lee, who was now a teaching assistant and doctoral candidate.

Lee became very sick late in the fall. He was shipped off to the hospital, but he appeared on campus again in a wheelchair just before Christmas. His eyes were sunken and his cheeks were hollow and he was losing four or five pounds a week, but he kept teaching and he kept working. Jill didn't ride with him any longer, but she went to his house regularly to talk with him and sometimes to ask for help with her English papers. He wanted to know what luck she was having with the School of Education and was upset when she said, "None." He asked her one evening, "What do you want out of life?"

Jill was sitting casually with her right elbow hooked behind the right handle of the chair. She said, "To have given something, I think." She frowned and pouted, blowing her cheeks out slightly and then letting the air escape. "I know that sounds corny, Lee, but I think you can give and gain at the same time. I like that idea. If I can help a kid to learn to use what he has, to . . ." She shrugged. "You know . . . to keep up a little better with the other kids or to stretch himself a little further."

"Yes, I know very well," he said.

In February Lee had a stroke, a blood clot that affected his speech and the right side of his body. He could not walk or talk, although he kept working on material for his Ph.D. thesis. He and Betty decided that the most important thing was to learn to speak again, and he embarked on a course of treatment and speech therapy. He did learn to make some sounds and to say "ya" or "na," but that was all. He could move one arm and was able to make many signs that Betty understood. He still loved to smoke, although Betty had to light each cigarette for him and put it in his mouth. Jill visited him whenever she could, and he always wanted to know about Bob. Jill told him what she knew, including the fact that Bob was out of the Army, was painting on the island of Ibiza off the east coast of Spain, and had just become engaged to an American girl he had met in Versailles.

One day on campus Jill heard about a young man named Bill Judd who was in a wheelchair and was teaching at a place called the Clinic School. She looked up Clinic School in the UCLA bulletin and found that it was run by the university's Psychology Department. It was for boys between the ages of nine and fourteen who were of average or above average intelligence but who nevertheless were unable to keep up with their elementary or high school classes. The school was staffed by several instructors and by students enrolled in a course concerned with learning disorders.

Jill telephoned the school and the call was referred to a Mr. Jenson. "This is Jill Kinmont," she said. "I'm a friend of Bill Judd, who I understand teaches at the Clinic School. I'm also in a wheelchair. I'm twenty-five and I have a B.A. from UCLA. The school bulletin says you offer a training course where the students work right in the classroom with the children. *Now* . . ." She took a long breath. "The School of Education won't accept me because of my handicap. I would like to know if you would accept me in your course for the summer session."

Mr. Jenson replied, "I don't know why not."

"I can write and I can move myself around in the classroom, so I really think I can do it. And I have tutored kids at home and I like that sort of thing."

"Fine. I'm certainly willing to give it a try if you are."

Jill visited Lee especially to tell him that she had been accepted at the Clinic School for the summer. She had no definite plans beyond September, she told him, because she wanted first to see if she could handle the work at the school. Also, she had always preferred flexible and rather vague plans so she could keep open for new possibilities.

Lee could not speak or express himself in any way except by gesturing with his left arm or by letting an emotion reflect in his face. He knew what teaching meant to Jill and he knew how important the Clinic School was to her. Tears filled his eyes and slid down his cheeks. He had so much to say and so many emotions to communicate. The tears were as close as this highly articulate man could now come to articulating what he deeply felt.

Jill liked the Clinic School from the first session. She was one of four psychology students working two hours a day with a class of fifteen boys. The instructor was a tall, easygoing young man named Don Mayhew.

The immediate and most important task assigned to Jill and her three fellow students was to get each boy to write a story every day. Jill was asked to work with any boys who needed help or couldn't get started on their stories. On the first day three boys said to her, "But what's there to write about?"

She began with a sixth-grader named Peter. "Didn't something interesting happen to you last weekend?" she asked him. "What did you do that was fun?"

"Nothin', really."

"What would you *like* to do if you had the chance?"

"I don't know."

"What do you do after school?"

"Nothin' much. Surf."

"Can you surf?" Jill was genuinely surprised.

"Well, sure."

"Gosh, I don't know anything about surfing, Peter. Why don't you write about how it feels to surf?"

"It doesn't feel like much."

Jill was stuck and had to ask Don for help. He said, "Be sure and leave him a way out. As a last resort you can always tell him he can sit and do nothing instead of writing a story. And I really mean *nothing*. No pencil, no paper, no book, no talking, just be perfectly still for half an hour."

Jill went back to Peter and said, "Why *don't* you write something about surfing?"

"That's a good idea," he said, and began to write.

Whenever one of the boys needed a word that he did not know or couldn't spell he raised his hand. Jill then wheeled over to his desk, wrote the word for him and pronounced it; then she had the boy trace it three times and write it himself. Each new word was kept in his file and reviewed periodically until he had mastered it. There was no restriction on subject matter and the titles ranged from "My Dog" to "The Crawling Eye" and "Murder in the Outhouse."

After the first week the boys began asking detailed questions about Jill's accident. "Why are you in that wheelchair?" "How can you sleep?" "Why are your hands like that?" "How do you get to school?" They all wanted to push her and she had to be very firm about *no pushing*. Many of them perfected a frustrating little trick of jamming a foot under one of the wheels and smiling innocently when Jill tried to move the chair. They reacted to her situation in a variety of ways. One boy said, "You poor thing." Another said, "Gee, wouldn't it be neat to have a chair like that! Man, would it ever make time down the hill behind our house!"

Jill at one time had been afraid she wouldn't know how to behave as a teacher was supposed to behave. Now the problem never occurred to her. She sometimes thought about Dave, however, and about how he had always managed to make skiing exciting even though everyone was working like a dog. The same kind of thing should be possible with schoolwork if you could just muster enough knowledge and imagination. But that wasn't going to be easy.

The School of Education still stood in the way of Jill's becoming a teacher, but she had no doubts about her own capability. Nor was she worried about practical, physical problems that were bound to turn up with some regularity. Most of them could be met with no great strain and some of them would even provide an intriguing challenge. She always felt on top of the world when she solved a problem

260

without having to ask for help. Even something as ordinary as moving a window shade. She was alone in a classroom one day and wanted to let in the sun, so she wheeled over to the window and batted at the shade cord with her fist. Finally she got the cord swinging violently enough to grasp it in her teeth. Then she jerked her head backward and let go. The shade went reeling up with a loud flutter.

After the end of summer session Jill went to Mammoth for two weeks. Audra Jo and Lee were now living in Bishop and Dave drove Jill down for several long visits. Lee was teaching science at the high school and had bought a new house west of town with a large back lawn and an open view of Mt. Tom. The Baumgarths had two children, Eric and Lisa, aged three and a half and one and a half.

Lee was interested in Jill's problems with the School of Education and in her philosophy of teaching. He asked her how far she felt a teacher's responsibilities should go. She said, "The least a teacher can do, *I* think, is to decide to reach every single child. I sometimes work half the night at Clinic School, Lee, just to dig up enough *ways* of saying what the lesson is about that each boy will be tuned in at *some* point. And I keep searching for what kind of thing will open each one's eyes and make him join in rather than playing with his pencils or kicking somebody under the table. *Why* do kids respond one day and then look at you like a dead fish the next, Lee?"

"There are dozens of answers and they keep changing, just as the individual kid's responses keep changing."

"I know, Lee, and it's so crazy sometimes. Lots of times I go in cold without anything thought out . . . and the day goes beautifully. The kids are with me and it doesn't feel like work at all."

In September Jill enrolled in the second session of the Clinic School and registered for classes in abnormal psychology and educational psychology. Her father bought her a big, old thirdhand motorized chair—Jill named it the Monster—with power enough to make all the grades on the UCLA campus. It was a long pull from the Clinic School across to the athletic building and on up the hill to the psychology building, but with the help of the Monster and the elevator in the Student Union, Jill could just make it during the ten-minute break between classes.

Lee Zadroga died late in September.

Everyone had expected it, including Lee. He had planned the funeral himself, a quiet, simple memorial service with some of his favorite poetry to be read by Professor Griggs, under whom he had been working toward his doctorate. The small chapel was crowded with about a hundred people, including most of the professors in UCLA's English and history departments. The coffin was covered with a flag.

Jill did not feel as shocked or as beaten by the event of death as she had in the past. During the service she thought about Lee's death and about Dick's death and remembered many things that one or the other had said about living and dying. *Now* is the only time there is. Gain all you can from each day, for death is not going to wait around for you to finish up. If you don't put everything into it, nothing comes out of it. If you want to know, all you have to do is plunge in. Don't forget what the word *mortal* means. However things work out or fail to work out—stay loose. And don't bitch. Don't sweat the little things.

Dr. Griggs spoke of Lee with words that Lee had loved. "Now cracks a noble heart. Good night, sweet prince, and flights of angels sing thee to thy rest!"

One sunny morning immediately after Jill's class in learning disorders, Mr. Jenson came in to say that there would be a job opening for a regular teacher at the Clinic School next semester. Jill went to see him the following day to say she wanted to apply. The Clinic School had been pleased with her work; she had plenty of drive and asked for no favors, and she had a sense of respect for children that made the difference between teaching and

262

merely instructing. Mr. Jenson said she would have to make an official application, but there would be no difficulty about her getting the job. No teaching certificate was required.

Jill wheeled out of the building and stopped her chair as soon as she found herself alone on a quiet path. She leaned her head far back in her chair, stretching with joy and relief, and closed her eyes. She felt as if spring sunlight were beaming on her after a gray winter.

25

In 1963 the Kinmont family moved to Renton, Washington, a few miles east of Seattle. Jill was accepted by the College of Education at the University of Washington, where every building has dozens of steps at the front and at the back, inside and outside. She was a student teacher at the Ingraham High School in Seattle and handled four classes a day.

One of the first things Jill learned from her high school pupils was that she was not very well informed and that she was going to have to read everything possible, from *Mad* to *Foreign Affairs,* just to keep up with them. The hardest thing was knowing whether or not she was getting through to the class and being sure that she really knew what she was talking about. To face a class and talk her way through it without bluffing, no matter what came up . . . this, she found, required courage. To carry this off was to maintain grace under pressure, and it had nothing to do with whether or not you were in a wheelchair.

Another student teacher asked Jill what she did about kids who just didn't care. Jill said, "They care; they just show it in different ways."

"Like telling you they couldn't care less?"

"Yeah, that's one way. It's supposed to be pretty square to *care*, you know, so you wouldn't want it to show. If you're a teacher, you just have to work like mad to figure ways to get to them in spite of it."

In February, 1964, Bud Werner concluded a decade of international racing at the Olympic Winter Games. He had spent more and more of his time coaching and encouraging his younger rivals, and Jill wrote him a long

264

letter while he was still competing in Innsbruck. She told him that what he had done for competitive skiing in the United States seemed more important to her than gold medals. She said also that she was sorry he had felt guilty for having gone away from her after her accident. She wrote, "Remember, Buddy, at Sun Valley, how it was for us? The most important thing was skiing. Skiing was my first love and your first love. We both have come so far since then, and we've had to grow and change. But I do hope that the Games can give you what you thought was so important then." Bud retired from racing in March. In April, he was killed by an avalanche while skiing in Switzerland.

Outfitted with a new electric wheelchair, Jill applied for a job with the Mercer Island School District, which is between Renton and Seattle. No one there knew who she was and no one knew she was in a wheelchair until she arrived for an interview. She was hired to teach remedial reading in a pair of elementary schools administered by the same principal. This would be much like her work at the Clinic School—the kind of work she most wanted to do and the age group she most wanted to work with.

Life as a student teacher was further complicated by the invasion of LIFE Magazine, in the persons of reporter Jan Mason and photographer Burk Uzzle; Jan was a few years older than Jill, Burk somewhat younger. Jill assumed a LIFE story would involve her in a long interview and photo session, and she had been through many interviews and photo sessions. She was in no way prepared for the fact that "long" could mean not several hours but fifteen long days of incessant questioning and picture-taking. She agreed, however, and Jan and Burk began their exhaustive investigation of Jill Kinmont. They met her each morning and were with her at breakfast, at school, at lunch, on the way home, at home in the afternoon, at supper, and often until bedtime and even later. They exhausted themselves and they exhausted Jill. At times they exhausted school personnel and they exhausted Jill's parents and brothers.

The two journalists were at first concerned with where the real story of Jill lay. The theme that occurred to them most strongly was that of a girl with severe difficulties now poised at a turning point in her life. How was she reacting under pressure, and how could her typically underplayed responses be caught in words and pictures? Burk never set up a picture but was always prowling, hoping to catch a telling flicker of emotion or the non-verbal *sense* of a relationship. At the same time, he and Jan were worrying about the technical requirements of a "good story." What picture should the story open with? What kind of a closing photograph was needed? What did they want to say about Jill in between?

Jan and Burk were also very much aware of their own initial awkwardness. Jan fumbled her first greeting because she couldn't decide whether or not to shake hands with Jill. She was afraid she might crush something, and the moment bumbled by without a handshake. When Jill apologized for remaining in the corner because her wheelchair batteries were being recharged, she said, "Sorry. I'm plugged in and I can't move." Jan looked up in alarm, imagining that Jill's kidneys must be, in some weird manner, attached by a catheter to something in the wall.

A further discomfort arose from the fact that both the reporter and the photographer stood back for the first few days, observing and recording the fine details of how Jill and her family managed to cope with everyday physical problems. They found it very difficult not to run to push Jill's chair or open a door or help lift her into the car or hold a glass of water for her, and the Kinmonts began to wonder what kind of removed, untouching creatures they had opened their lives to. But once Burk got the photographs he needed—things like Jill's difficulty picking up a pen or the way Bob slung her into the car like a sack of wheat—both he and Jan literally joined the family. Jan was soon cooking breakfast for all of them, and the distinction between "friend" and "professional" melted.

266

The first week's notes and photographs were shipped to New York, and editor Dick Meryman telephoned Renton at once to say the material was on the whole much too kind and much too distant. It captured the emotional impact all right, but there was nothing of the agony and effort that must have been involved every time Jill had to do something "simple" like brush her teeth or get up out of bed. Burk and Jan both felt it would be a gross invasion of Jill's privacy to move in that close on the most personal details of her private life, particularly items such as getting dressed and going to the bathroom.

Jill, it turned out, didn't feel this way at all. She said, "Jan, when you have been pawed over by as many doctors as I have, there's very little room left for false modesty."

In the end, the LIFE team retired with three complete steno pads of notes (both sides of every page), some ten hours of audio tape and more than 800 photographs (Jill said she thought it was 8,000). Jan personally learned two things from Jill that she will never forget. First, that her own heaviest personal problems appeared to be suddenly trivial when stacked against Jill's. And second, that this was not really true after all. "My own problems are to me as great as Jill's are to her, no more, no less. Maybe no one ever has it as easy as it appears."

The 14-page picture story appeared in LIFE in June just as Jill received her elementary and secondary teaching credential from the State of Washington, and the story led to the publication, in 1966, of this book about her life as champion skier and quadriplegic.

Jill began her teaching career at Mercer Island in September. Remedial reading at the Lakeridge and Island Park schools was concerned with students whose abilities were average or above but who needed to improve their reading skills in order to cope with their classwork. Also, many did not know how to study. Jill's task was to teach them how to retain written information and give this information back in class. She worked with small groups ranging in size from a social studies class of ten down to three or two or even one. She also conducted a reading enrichment program for unusually bright students.

The following summer Jill attended a workshop in elementary school reading skills at UCLA and in August visited Linda Meyers Tikalsky near Durango, Colorado. Linda was a veteran of both the 1960 and the 1964 Winter Olympic Games and in seven years of major competition had placed four times in the Harriman Cup at Sun Valley, had won the Silver Belt at the Sugar Bowl twice, and twice brought home from Aspen a Roch Cup gold medal. She was planning to coach junior racing teams and to teach skiing at Purgatory, Colorado. She was newly married to Frank Tikalsky, a psychology professor who did not—as yet—ski. They subsequently had two children, Peter and Jill, and in 1974 Frank was named director of the Mono County Mental Health Center at Mammoth Lakes.

After two years of teaching, Jill was awarded a grant to attend a six-week interdisciplinary study of reading at the University of Oregon. She spent August with her family. Her father, who was now a cost analyst at Boeing and senior supervisor in his department, slept a great deal during their two-week vacation on Orcas Island in Puget Sound. This was unusual for Bill Kinmont, and so were the repeated headaches that followed. He went to a doctor and was told that his trouble was psychosomatic. By mid-October the headpains were extreme, and a brain angiogram revealed a tumor that appeared to be malignant. He underwent surgery, was back home by Thanksgiving, and returned to work for three weeks. Again the severe headaches caught up with him; he was lucid but seemed to be daydreaming most of the time. On Christmas Eve he went back into the hospital, and three weeks later he died.

The Kinmonts had many friends and relatives in Los Angeles, and Jill and June decided to move south as soon as school was out in the spring. The move was not welcomed by Jill's pupils, as the following letters indicate.

Dear Miss Kinmont,

I have always been an admirer of yours. I would like to thank you for helping me with social studies and things i did not understand. Please stay!!!

But I know you must go to California and become that great movie star. Your name up in lights.

"Miss Kinmont The Spectacular."

Best wishes, Gayle Jack

Dear Miss Kinmont,

Why are you going to leave? The school will be lost without you.

You've been so kind to everyone and you're the nicest person I know.

You're our hero and you're the only one we've got.

Peter Donnell

In order to move to Los Angeles, Jill had to find a job there. She began the search in January while in L.A. for her father's funeral. She wanted to teach in Watts or some other low-income neighborhood—not so much just to teach, she said, but to understand that part of America. It seemed obvious to her that a physical handicap could be an advantage with black students who were socially and economically handicapped.

Jill was certified to teach in Washington but not in California, which meant one strike against her. Strike two was the fact that she had been stamped with the label, *cripple*. The L.A. school system, which includes Watts, was not about to take on such a liability. The first three Los Angeles school officials Jill talked with each started dodging her questions as soon as they discovered she was confined to a wheelchair. After this, Jill refrained from mentioning the disability in her initial inquiries. Interviews nevertheless kept ending with somewhat condescending lectures about how important it is for would-be teachers to be free of health problems. "How can you teach if you're unable to stand up in front of the class? Besides, all of our schools have steps. How can we hire you if you can't walk up and down steps?" The person to see, Jill was told, was the school district physician.

Back in Renton, she sent out a barrage of letters and applications. She discovered that L.A. county contains 90 school districts in addition to the city of Los Angeles, and she applied to 18 of them. Twelve districts invited her for interviews, and she went the rounds during Easter vacation. A friend loaned her a van and she was driven from school to school by an old skiing buddy, Buck Holland, and, on alternate days, by her cousin Warren Haines.

Los Angeles city school officials would not consider Jill's application until she had been cleared by their physician, and Jill was slightly encouraged by the fact that the physician was a woman and had grown up in Bishop. The 45-minute interview began with reasonable questions such as "What would you do in case of fire?" and "What if a child has a serious accident?" As the discussion progressed, it became clear that the doctor was in no way concerned with Jill's ability as a teacher. She was worried about such things as her table manners, whether other teachers might be uncomfortable in her presence, and about *steps*. "Now we must be realistic; a great many of our schools have steps." Jill sighed and said under her breath, *Here we go again!*

The doctor gave her a sweet smile and a pat on the head. "We would love to be able to hire you, Dear, but you must be realistic."

"I think it is you who is not being realistic, Doctor. You have no idea what I am capable of. After all, I have been teaching for nearly three years."

The only reply was an oddly wistful remark. "What a tragedy. A young girl cut down in the bloom of youth."

"You make it sound like a western or something," Jill replied. "The only tragedy is that you won't hire me because of this injury."

"The answer is still no."

"Well, I don't think you're the one to make the decision. You're only the doctor. Who is it that makes the final decision?"

"The School Board. You have to pass a medical ex-

270

amination first, however. Waivers would have to come through the Board."

Jill met with two members of the School Board and soon afterwards received a written reply. "We do not find it advisable at this time to. . . ."

Jill then visited the Los Angeles county school offices, and there she found precisely the kind of help she needed. The county superintendent, Dr. Toland, went through a list of all available schools, selecting those which had programs that matched Jill's interests and ability and discarding schools he knew would be "nice" without offering any real help. As a result of many phone calls from the county office and a series of interviews, Jill found three school districts that wanted to hire her—San Marino and two of the best-paying districts in the state, El Segundo and Beverly Hills.

Jill was asked if she had been able to attend faculty meetings at Mercer Island (yes, she said, all of them) and how many days of school she had missed (a total of two days a year). And she was questioned in detail concerning her professional background and her approach to various kinds of reading difficulties. As she went from person to person in this final stretch, she began to feel as if she were being wooed. She said, "I went to the head of personnel, two principals, and then the Beverly Hills reading consultant, and it was beginning to sound like they were trying to talk me into coming with them. It sure was a good feeling."

Two weeks later she was formally hired as a reading specialist by the Hawthorne Elementary School in Beverly Hills. The problem of steps at the school was handled very simply by building several wheelchair ramps.

When school was out in June, Jill and her mother sold their house in Renton and drove to West Los Angeles, where they found a ground-floor apartment. Jill needed eight more academic credits to qualify for a provisional California teaching credential, and these she earned by enrolling in summer school at UCLA and by taking a correspondence course on the side.

The year at Hawthorne went beautifully, and in June

271

and July Jill attended summer school at the University of Arizona. Then she went to Bishop to visit the Baumgarths. Audra Jo was president of the School Board, and Lee was still teaching high school science and working part-time as a physical therapist. Their two children were now almost teen-agers.

Lee and several other teachers had been trying to set up a summer camp for blacks from Los Angeles, and they had already enlisted Jill's help, putting her in charge of raising money for the project. By the time she reached Bishop in early August she had rounded up several thousand dollars to buy food, sleeping bags and other camping gear and to hire an enthusiastic black football player from Whittier College named Leon Geiggar. Leon had never been in the mountains before, but he proved to be a natural woodsman. Jill credits him with holding the project together that first summer and again every August for four more years. Audra Jo was responsible for logistics, which meant getting together all the food and equipment and arranging for it to be transported up to the trailhead leading to Long Lake, high on the steep eastern slope of the Sierra just west of Bishop.

Ten boys, aged 10 through 18, arrived for the two-week adventure in the wilds. They were city boys in every sense, and the Bishop High teachers underwent a learning experience of their own in the form of such items as switchblades and a few minor rip-offs at Parcher's Camp Store. The boys packed their gear in three miles to the lake and were met by rain, hail, thunder and lightning. They were sure they were going to die, but were soon busy landing trout for the first time in their lives. They had never been in the mountains and they were all terribly afraid of the dark. They nevertheless told very spooky stories around the campfire every night. They were followed by a second group of ten who stayed until Labor Day.

Meanwhile, Jill had been interested in American Indian culture and had thought of working with Indians in Arizona, helping them with reading skills in exchange for learning about their traditional ways. Then she remembered, of course, that there were 1500 Paiute and Shoshone Indians in the Owens Valley, most of them living on the reservation in Bishop. Furthermore, many of the local Paiutes were very independent, cut off from the non-Indian community in Bishop, and extremely poor. They enjoyed very little social status in the Valley, with the exception of a few high school athletic stars. The Indian children had the lowest grades in school and they commonly dropped out at an early age. Only a few of them ever went to college or even considered it. The very young had friends among the white population of Bishop, and primary grade Indian children were usually included in the birthday parties, but social gatherings in middle elementary school years excluded the Indians. The women usually worked as domestics or in the local laundry. The men were mostly seasonal road construction workers, and few of them could count on anything regular.

Jill had written to Gerald Kane, chairman of the tribal council of the Paiute-Shoshone Band, suggesting that she select a group of 20 Indian children who were having difficulty in school and teach them to read more fluently. Kane, who had played football with Bob Kinmont in high school, took the matter to the next tribal meeting. The council was delighted with the proposal. Jill was offered a room in the Valley Presbyterian Church, which had been an abandoned schoolhouse until it was rebuilt by the new minister, a Sioux by the name of Sydney Byrd.

The Reverend Mr. Byrd was elated, but he was concerned that Jill might not be able to understand the Indian way and would thus be unable to work effectively with the children. His comments were helpful, but Jill felt intimidated at first by his concern. Soon after this, the Reverend Mr. Byrd summarized his feeling about what was needed and about Jill's qualifications. "If you are going to teach an Indian child, it is not enough to have ordinary credentials. You must have some Indian background, some understanding of the Indian child. The Indian has a different value system. He does not try to compete. He doesn't want to be better than his friend, doesn't want to show up his friend. He may know the

273

answer but he doesn't want to embarrass his peers. And when the Indian child fails to achieve, he has a built-in excuse: 'I'm just an Indian.' Jill Kinmont is like the Indian. She really had nothing. All the things she had against her . . . she was able to rise above them. She is able to show others that, whatever the handicaps, they can achieve."

Jill began her classes within a week after arriving at the Baumgarths'. She had brought with her from Beverly Hills just about every movable item in her schoolroom, and she set out all the books she had been able to find about Indian culture and crafts and history.

Jill worked from nine until one, dividing her students into five groups of eight or less. Bishop public school teachers gave her lists of Indian children with particular difficulties and explained to her precisely what each child's problem seemed to be. Gerald notified the children's parents, and the church provided transportation. The Reverend Mr. Byrd's wife provided Kool-Aid and cookies.

More than one person in town told Jill not to expect much because the Indian kids "probably won't show up." Every one of the 20 pupils in fact showed up every day, never missing, always on time.

Jill was asked why she had chosen to spend half her summer vacation working, for nothing, with the Indians. Jill said, "If it's possible to help, I think it's a good idea for all of us to do that. And since I happen to have the tools to help a group of people who want the help—and it's really fun doing it—I'd just as soon do it. It is much more meaningful to me than working on my Master's. An M.A. is totally ego-oriented. This is personal in a different way."

The students were a stoic bunch, but after several unpromising days, Jill discovered that the key to these children was her own curiosity about their unique skills and culture. The moment she asked about things they really understood—such as how to catch rabbits or pitch a fastball or lure Owens River trout—they delivered a sudden flood of information, filling her easel with words related to the subject and using the words to write about

274

their own experiences. Many of them drew beautiful pictures to illustrate their own stories. Jill said at the time, "It's amazing the way they've come out. Just today. Yesterday I was ready to shoot myself, and today they've just . . . blossomed." Soon they were bringing handmade baskets and pots and toys from their homes and they began to collect legends they had learned from their grandparents. They also started bringing their brothers and sisters to class. Jill had built up a library of 150 easy-to-read paperback books, and her older pupils were soon reading a book a day. One girl who had never read a book in her life went through 30 paperbacks by the time the summer classes ended.

The children were interested in the wheelchair but, compared to her city students, asked very few questions about her physical condition. Jill said the city kids typically would hold a paper out at a point where she could not reach it, whereas the Indians came right up and put the paper exactly at the place where it was most easy to work on. "No one told them to do this," Jill said. "They just do it. In the city they almost always have the paper facing them when they lay it down. The Indian kids have it facing me."

Jill was accepted by the Indian community in a way that few non-Indians are. Indians put great stock on physical prowess, and she found that the adults treated her a bit condescendingly, in a way they dared not deal with other whites. "They treat me protectively, too. The wheelchair puts them six steps ahead of me and they know it. But with the kids, it's different. Their simplicity and honesty with me is so total."

When the month was over, the Indians gave an enormous surprise party for Jill. Whole families came, including babies and grandparents, about 70 people in all. They had moosemeat and frybread, cakes and home made ice cream. They brought gifts they had made themselves—deerskin moccasins, beaded hairclips, earrings. Each summer thereafter, Jill's Indian summer school ended with a big bash. In 1974 it was held at the Mill Pond, an old saw mill pond next to the Rocking K. Indians of all ages dug into a feast of hot dogs, punch, potato salad, potato chips and ice cream bars. The kids played King of the Mountain on a raft in the middle of the pond, swam in their clothes, throwing one another into the water, and sometimes jumping behind Jill's chair to shout, "OK, you guys, you can't get me now!" It was a lifeguard's nightmare to keep track of everyone. Jill is not a demonstrative person, and neither are the Indians, particularly in the presence of whites. But whenever the younger Indians see Jill going down Main Street or East Line, they always wave and honk and yell.

The tribal council had been thinking of building a study center on the reservation about the time Jill had first contacted Gerald Kane, and the success of the reading program became an added encouragement. By Jill's second "Indian summer", the Owens Valley Indian Education Center was a reality housed in a portable classroom. The first program at the new center was Jill's reading class. Adolescents and mothers from the reservation worked with her as tutors so they would be able to continue the reading program during the school year. Jill taught the tutors how to make out lesson plans for each student, but since she wanted the children to learn to work independently the students were later taught to make their own lesson plans. The education center also had a library, an athletic program and an increasing number of classes in subjects ranging from reading and mathematics to operating heavy duty equipment. It was so popular that it subsequently served as a model for similar Indian centers throughout the state.

During the second summer program, Jill had felt ill much of the time and suffered from colds and mild bladder infections. She felt like a shell, her eyes often went out of focus, and the glands in her head felt, she said, like pickles and sour lemons. In late September she was very sick for two weeks and had to take six weeks off from school. Her physician could find no specific ailment aside from a big stone in her bladder, so Jill went into the hospital for a thorough physical examination. She was met with a barrage of embarrassing questions. "Have you been doing your breathing exercises?" (Not for the past 17 years.) "Have you been drinking your four quarts of water each day?" (Two is more like it.) "Have you been clamping and releasing your catheter so the bladder will stay elastic?" (No.) "Have you been taking medication?" (Not for 15 years.) "Have you been doing your physical exercises?" (No.)

She began drinking a gallon of water a day and seeing a physical therapist three times a week. She also began regular visits to her urologist, who diagnosed a low-grade urinary tract infection which he treated with mandelamine and an antibiotic. Jill took up painting again in order to take her mind off the way she was feeling. Gradually, her health and her sense of well-being returned.

In 1971, Jill and June Kinmont purchased a house near the ocean in Pacific Palisades, eleven miles from the school in Beverly Hills. The Kinmonts held a Bring-your-own-paint party, and 25 relatives and friends covered the dark, drab house with two coats of white paint. The affair was incidentally a family reunion, and Bob and Jerry stayed on to build a large sun deck at the back of the house and ramps for Jill's wheelchair. Jill now had a VW bus with a ramp so that she could be wheeled into the car without leaving her chair, and her brothers built a "dock" in the side of the garage to make loading easier.

Bob Kinmont was now a sculptor with several shows to his credit and a number of works at the Nancy Hoffman gallery in New York. He had taught sculpture in Toronto and San Francisco and was presently—during the school year—teaching at Lone Mountain College in San Francisco. This particular summer he spent in Bishop, where he taught a water color course for college credit. Jill had developed an extraordinarily subtle, almost ethereal style in her own painting since learning to use a pen and brush again, and she was one of Bob's students. Bob encouraged her unique approach, but he is a hard teacher and he let her get away with nothing in his class.

Jerry Kinmont had studied marine biology and for five years was assistant curator of fish at *Seaworld* in San Diego, where he also collected sharks, porpoises and whales. He then formed his own company to design, construct, stock and maintain aquariums. The company was not a success, and Jerry found himself doing a lot more paperwork than fish work. After a year in Bishop working as a carpenter, he plans to move to Canada to work both as a marine biologist and as a carpenter.

June Kinmont had been spending much of her free time taking classes in philosophy, music, geography, wood-working, sewing and quilt-making. During a wonderful fall holiday in Scotland in 1973 she tracked down the history of Kinmont Willie—who appeared in Sir Walter Scott's poetry—and other Kinmonts involved in the English border wars. She also joined a pair of long-lost Australian Kinmont cousins who had located Jill after reading the LIFE article.

June and Jill were accustomed to spending part of their summers in Bishop and often stayed at Dave McCoy's home on the Rocking K Ranchos, which had once been part of the Kinmonts' old Rocking K. As for the McCoys, Dave was enamored of Moto-cross motorcycle racing and was placing high in most of the races he entered. He still owned and ran the Mammoth Mountain Chairlifts—fourteen lifts now, including a gondola to the top and chairs running up the west side from just above Red's Meadows. Dave himself was too busy to ski very much but still sponsored young racers. His earlier protegés had left an impressive record: three of the six women on the 1964 Olympic squad were from the Mammoth Ski Club and all six girls on the 1966 FIS team were Dave's trainees: Wendy and Cathy Allen, Susie Chaffee, Joan Hannah, Jean Saubert, and his daughter, Penny McCoy. His son, Poncho, skied on the men's team.

By 1974 five of the six McCoy children were married —Kandi to a former Olympic skier, Penny to a stuntman, and Randy to a local girl whose mother had once raced for Leevining against Jill and Audra Jo. Randy, Kandi, Penny and Gary were all living in Bishop and Poncho in

Denver. P-nut was working in the woods for a Mammoth pack outfit and had grown his hair long enough that the Mammoth Mountain employment office refused to hire him. His plans were to run a cattle ranch in Wyoming for Peter Mead, Andy Lawrence's brother. Gary was president of the Sierra Pacific Airlines, which Dave had purchased shortly before the tragic crash that killed 31 actors and film crewmen who had been shooting the television documentary, "Primal Man," on location at Mammoth. Gary does not want any of his four children to go into competitive skiing, although Roma now and then sets up gates for them on the mountain.

In 1973, Jill and June rented a house for the summer in Bishop from John Boothe, a diesel truck driver who hauled cattle and ore in Oregon, Utah, Nevada and California. John's family had pioneered the Owens Valley, and he visited often that summer, telling stories of the town's early settlers. His Grandma Lucy had made fried chicken and baked cakes for the men who had plotted to blow up the new 350-mile aquaduct when the City of Los Angeles began to draw the water out of the valley. John took Jill on many drives to his parents' 400-acre cattle and alfalfa ranch south of Bishop and to the old and beautiful log cabin on the South Fork of Bishop Creek where the family moved in the summer to run the Rainbow Pack Station. John and Jill enjoyed mountain picnics and big family gatherings at the ranch or the pack station or at the Kinmonts' house, and Jill's wheelchair is frequently seen in the back of John's pick-up. The relationship, she says, has brought a new richness to her life.

26

The latest chapter in Jill's life is *Jill's Life*. The film version.

LIFE Magazine published a follow-up story on Jill, which caught the eye of Ed Feldman, a producer at Filmways in Los Angeles. Jill agreed with Feldman's proposal for a film, tentatively called "The Other Side of the Mountain." She was hired as a technical advisor and will also receive a percentage of the profits.

Jill first met with screenwriter David Seltzer in September, 1972. Seltzer had spent summers in Bishop and was familiar with polio since his brother had contracted the disease at the age of nine. Seltzer had been moved by the LIFE article but was concerned about the fact that Jill had never undergone a true depression, and he wondered how he could dramatize her reaction to her accident. He talked a lot about what liberties he might legitimately take in rewriting her life for the movies.

The script was completed early in 1973 and sent to Jill for her approval. "When I read it, I cried four times," she said. "I thought, oh that poor girl, what a tragic life. But I never thought about her as me." As for the factual details, Jill described the situation as very frustrating at first. "I had to do a lot of rationalizing. In the film I'm very depressed, for example. And I was very concerned about my friends, the way they were depicted. It seems a lot of conflict had to be developed between people, and there was so little conflict in my actual life outside of competing on the slopes. Audra Jo comes off dominant and has to tell me a thing or two before I'll shape up. That feels so wrong. Still, I can understand how her lesson was one of an example stretched out across two and a half years, and how can you show an audience what I learned from her in just a few minutes on the screen."

Jill telephoned Seltzer and said, "I really liked a lot of the parts." After an awkward silence, she told him what she was not comfortable with. She then wrote four single-spaced pages of objections and suggestions concerning technical things as well as personal and emotional items. She went to Ed Feldman's home to go over possible changes with Feldman, Seltzer, director Larry Peerce, and Feldman's assistant, Judi. Jill felt the occasion was a bit spooky. "Larry on every count was agreeable," she said, "but I wasn't sure if he was listening patiently and then going his own way. But David took me very seriously, was hurt at some times and elated at others because I didn't want to change something. He did make many changes in the script, and I felt good about our meeting."

One of the suggestions not followed involved the scene in which Jill and A. J. fall out of their wheelchairs at UCLA and wind up giggling in the gutter. As Jill put it, "That's not exactly how it happened. At the same time, the project as a whole was a delightful adventure. I mean, how often do they make a picture about someone who's alive?"

Arrangements were completed with Universal to finance and distribute the film, and the search for the right "Jill" was begun. Out of a field of nearly 400 girls in New York and Los Angeles, the actress finally chosen was Marilyn Hassett, 26, whose film experience was limited to a part in "They Shoot Horses, Don't They?" and some commercials. During the filming of a commercial in 1969, an elephant had stepped on her, leaving her legs temporarily paralyzed and confining her to bed for five months and to a wheelchair for some months after that. She also suffered serious depression and later decided to give up acting—until the part of Jill Kinmont was suggested. Marilyn is precisely Jill's height (five, six and three-quarters) but, unlike Jill, has brown eyes. For the screen test she was given a scene between Dick Buek and Jill in which the two are talking about marriage and not being able to have children. Marilyn was the only one of the girls tested who did not think the scene called for tears and sobbing. She was chosen partly because of her natural quality of gentleness and what Peerce calls "a certain fragility." Also because she is attractive. "We wanted a pretty girl," Feldman said. "It is my belief that people relate to pretty things that are broken."

The part of Dick Buek is played by Beau Bridges, an experienced actor of 33. Audra Jo is played by Belinda Montgomery, who originally tried out for the part of Jill. Jerry Kinmont plays Jerry Kinmont in the film and Lee Baumgarth plays himself also. Kandi McCoy appears in the role of Andrea Mead Lawrence. (Andy herself now lives at Mammoth, where she sometimes tangles with Dave McCoy on conservation issues at town council meetings.)

Filming began in late April, 1974, with nine days on location at Mammoth. Jill spent three days up on the mountain, in a snowcat, her wheelchair strapped on the back, and the emotional impact of this experience was vivid—not because the filming brought back early skiing competition and training but because she now felt so very much at home with the mountain. "It was wonderful being up there again and not just down on the porch in my chair." It was also a pleasure just being back at Mammoth, although the size of the place was overpowering. Jill had raced there when a crowd of 250 was "enormous." In 1974, the employees alone numbered 800 and it would take 10,000 skiers on a weekend to merit the adjective "crowded."

Jill's technical work began with the first scenes to be shot, which included Jill's happy days at Sun Valley with Buddy Werner. Jill found that Marilyn's acting was not "physical" enough, and she coached the actress on how it felt and how it looked to be 18 years old, very athletic and very much on top of things. Jerry Kinmont was able to spot many mannerisms that could be made more technically accurate or more "Jill-like," and he often moved in briefly during rehearsals to clue Marilyn in.

For the key skiing scenes, Marilyn had several doubles, including four former members of the U.S. team, Penny

282

McCoy Barrett, Katie and Robin Morning and Janie Rollins. Jill had planned that Penny would ski as Jill, but Penny was four months pregnant. She doubled for Jill in a few scenes but couldn't risk any hard skiing.

All doubles were dressed like Marilyn, who was dressed to match the photo of Jill on the cover of Sports Illustrated the week of her accident. The three doubles saved a lot of camera time because of the time it took "Jill," after each take, to ride up the mountain on the lift and ski down to the pitch where the cameras were waiting. The big scene—Jill's crash—involved Katie and Janie skiing as Jill up to the point of the accident. Here, stuntman Loren Janes, also dressed as Jill, took over for the actual fall. He deliberately went off a cliff and was in the air a distance of 40 feet, accidentally breaking a ski when he landed. The camera was tilted so that his vertical fall appears to be almost horizontal in the film. In the final crash scene, Marilyn lay crumpled in the snow while the real Jill looked on calmly from a nearby snowcat and the real Audra Jo talked about how things had really been way back then. Jill was fascinated by the technical aspects of filming the nearly fatal fall but could not feel any connection between the filming and the original event. The director meanwhile aimed his bullhorn at the actors just below, shouting, "This is the scene where Jill crashes and breaks her neck. It's terrible, do you hear, terrible! Look up the hill. I want you to see blood. Do you see blood?"

The first ten days of May were devoted to shooting in Bishop. The air was still brisk in the early morning, the wild iris was blooming, and the entire town was caught up in the excitement of putting the Bishop of two decades ago on film. Local tradesmen and high school students and Indian children had been cast several weeks before, and enough cars of the vintage of 1939 to 1950 had been rounded up to stage a realistic reproduction of "draggin' Main" in 1952. The high school students did their own costuming—including a number of odd haircuts and several greasy ducktails—after researching the styles of a quarter of a century ago in their home town.

The high point of the week was the re-creation of Dick Buek's wild flying, with airplane stuntman Frank Tolman doing loops over the high school band which had assembled to welcome "Jill" home from the rehabilitation center. The most emotional scene, however, was the one in which Jill bid goodbye to Dick for the last time, ever. Crewmen and visitors alike were weeping, and Jill said, "What's the matter? It's only a movie!"

The balance of the shooting—the hospital, the rehabilitation center and scenes on campus—was done in Los Angeles. These were rough days for Marilyn, who was in all but about three scenes. She was up at 4:30 every morning, on the set at 7:30 and at work for 12 to 15 hours. Jill felt Marilyn did a tremendous job as skier, as quadriplegic, and as a silly teenager. She had to go through a great range of emotional scenes within a period of 32 shooting days. Jill said later, "Maybe the traumas of playing me were much more than those I had to deal with, spreading it out over the years."

One of the last scenes to be shot was the ordeal in the hospital where Jill had been sandwiched in a Stryker frame and stretched by the Crutchfield tongs notched into her scalp. Marilyn was lying in a frame with tongs on her head when Jerry Kinmont came on the set to report what had just happened to Jimmy Lewis, the cousin who had visited Jill in St. John's Hospital in Santa Monica 19 years before to hang a large sign—JILL'S STILL—on the tidal drain beside the bed. Jimmy, now living in San Jose and the father of six children, fell out of a tree he was trimming and landed on his back across two logs. His back was broken near the waist and his neck was broken at the sixth or seventh cervical vertebra. He was paralyzed from the shoulders down but retained the use of both arms and one hand.

The film was edited and scored in Los Angeles during the summer while Jill returned to Bishop to work with her Indian children and prepare for her seventh year as a reading specialist at the Hawthorne Elementary School. Producer Feldman planned to stage a benefit premier of the film with the proceeds going to the Jill Kinmont Indian Education Fund.

Jill is still asked occasionally to describe the nearly fatal accident recreated at Mammoth by Marilyn Hassett and the three doubles. Jill always begins, "It was a beautiful morning and the snow was like velvet. . . ." A friend asked her if she still thought about skiing. She was silent for a while and then she said. "When I'm alone with myself and it's absolutely quiet, I can feel what it's like, skiing. I can still remember the runs—every slalom course, every downhill—and in my mind I can still feel where I want to prejump and where I'll have to check. I know I could still ski . . . if I could ski."

THE BEST OF BESTSELLERS
FROM WARNER BOOKS!

THE BEST OF BESTSELLERS
FROM WARNER BOOKS!

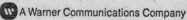